Graphic Communication as a Design Tool

Graphic Communication as a Design Tool

Omar Faruque

VNR VAN NOSTRAND REINHOLD COMPANY
NEW YORK CINCINNATI TORONTO LONDON MELBOURNE

Designed and illustrated by Omar Faruque

Library of Congress Catalog Card Number: 83-19845
ISBN: 0-442-22633-0
ISBN: 0-442-22634-9 pbk.

Manufactured in the United States of America

Published by Van Nostrand Reinhold Company Inc.
135 West 50th Street
New York, New York 10020

Van Nostrand Reinhold Company Limited
Molly Millars Lane
Wokingham, Berkshire RG11 2PY, England

Van Nostrand Reinhold
480 Latrobe Street
Melbourne, Victoria 3000, Australia

Macmillan of Canada
Division of Gage Publishing Limited
164 Commander Boulevard
Agincourt, Ontario M1S 3C7, Canada

15 14 13 12 11 10 9 8 7 6 5 4 3 2 1

Library of Congress Cataloging in Publication Data

Faruque, Omar.
Graphic communication as a design tool.

Includes index.
1. Communication in design. 2. Visual communication—Technique. 3. Graphic arts—Technique. I. Title.
NK1510.F34 1984 745.4 83-19845
ISBN 0-442-22633-0
ISBN 0-442-22634-9 pbk.

To my Parents

Contents

Acknowledgment

I extend special thanks to my graduate and undergraduate students who have been a source of inspiration for writing this book. Many of them, from time to time, suggested the idea of writing a book covering the special points I made in design and graphics studios. Their suggestions prompted the preparation of this work—they are the cause of this book.

I also extend my appreciation to the following individuals:

James Koch and Robert Fisher for encouraging the project;

Jeffrey Hall, Paul Laseau, Marvin Rosenmen, John Russell, Jack Wyman and other collegues in the College of Architecture and Planning for their comments and moral support;

Leonor Linares and Beth Shaffer for typing the manuscript;

Larry Hager of the Professional and Reference Division, Van Nostrand Reinhold Company for encouraging the project from the beginning and for his continued patience;

Alberta Gordon for her dedication in coordinating the production;

Finally, I am indebted to my wife Sabiha for her patience and continued moral support. Without her many sacrifices, I could not have completed this project.

Preface

This book is aimed at design professionals and students alike. It articulates some of the fundamental but profoundly important concepts of graphic communication in the design process. These concepts normally do not receive enough emphasis during the training of design professionals and, in many cases, are simply not made clear to them. Consequently, the majority never learn to use graphic communication as a design tool to its fullest potential.

Normally we think of graphic communication as a tool for presentation of our ideas. While its functions as such is only one facet, there are other aspects of graphic communication which profoundly influence the process of generating and evaluating design ideas and options. This book promotes greater understanding of all these aspects by probing into the areas of problem solving methodology, visual thinking, perception, and recent research on the human brain and creativity.

Sketching is more than just making pretty pictures. It is both generative and evaluative so far as the act of design is concerned. It is no less, if not more, intellectually stimulating than the numeric interpretations of a statistical approach. Those who have not yet caught up with graphic literacy may find this difficult to accept. For them, this book is a plea through a series of demonstrations in graphic decision making and problem solving.

The design field is a single continuum encompassing environmental planning, landscape architecture, architecture, urban design, interior design, fashion and industrial design and graphic art. Throughout the book I have aimed my discussion at professionals and students in all of these areas.

In preparing graphic examples, I have attempted to represent various design areas and, in order to make the illustrations more meaningful, each has been reproduced in its original size.

Omar Faruque

Part One

Prologue

Design: A Problem-Solving Process

Design, both as a noun and as a verb, has various meanings. As a noun, it may mean a plan or scheme, an intention or aim, something planned for, or an outcome aimed at, or it may just mean a pattern or decoration. It also means the arrangement of parts, details, space, shape, form, color, texture, etc., so as to produce a complete and artistic unit. The relationship of parts to the whole with regard to function, activities, structure, materials, engineering, technology, etc., is still another series of meanings of this word. For our purposes, all of these meanings are quite acceptable.

Design, as a verb, is still more difficult to define clearly. Most definitions refer either to its meaning

2
A design on a Sari. Here design means a pattern of various shapes and how they are put together.

1
The shaping of an environment may include both architectural and landscape architectural design considerations.

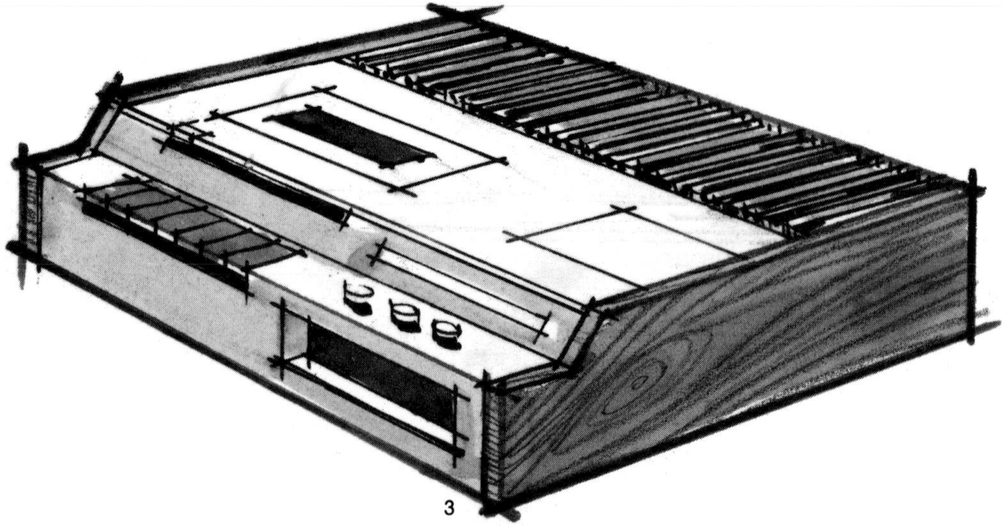

3
As new technology becomes available, new products—and consequently new design problems—appear.

4
Fashion design is a type of problem solving that requires synthesis of utility, craftmanship, and social values at any given time.

as a noun (an outcome) or to the physical behavior of the designer. Very little reference is made to the mental process involved in design even though design is more a mental task than a physical one. This is because we had very little information available on which scholars could agree with regard to the mental faculty as it relates to design. However, in the recent past, an increased amount of attention has been drawn to the rational understanding of the act of design.

PROBLEM SOLVING

Design can be viewed as a problem-solving process. Regardless of whether the aim is artistic or strictly utilitarian, it is the process of problem solving that characterizes the act of design. In the case of a painting, the aim may be to achieve a certain visual harmony. However, in the mind of the artist, this aim is transformed into a series of problems which he then can attempt to solve. It is through this act of problem solving that he arrives at a certain solution or solutions and thus "creates" his masterpiece. He goes through the process of problem seeking and then resolving those problems that he has conceived in his mind. For the designer of a pen, the aim may be both artistic and utilitarian. But whatever the aim, the designer translates it into or envisions it as a series of problems and then tries to solve each one. His arrival at a specific design is the result of a problem-solving process. Likewise, the designer of a residence, park, office tower, airport, dress, or minicomputer, is a problem solver.

STEPS IN THE PROCESS

This problem-solving process can be divided into a number of steps. When a designer is confronted with a problem, in his conscious or unconscious

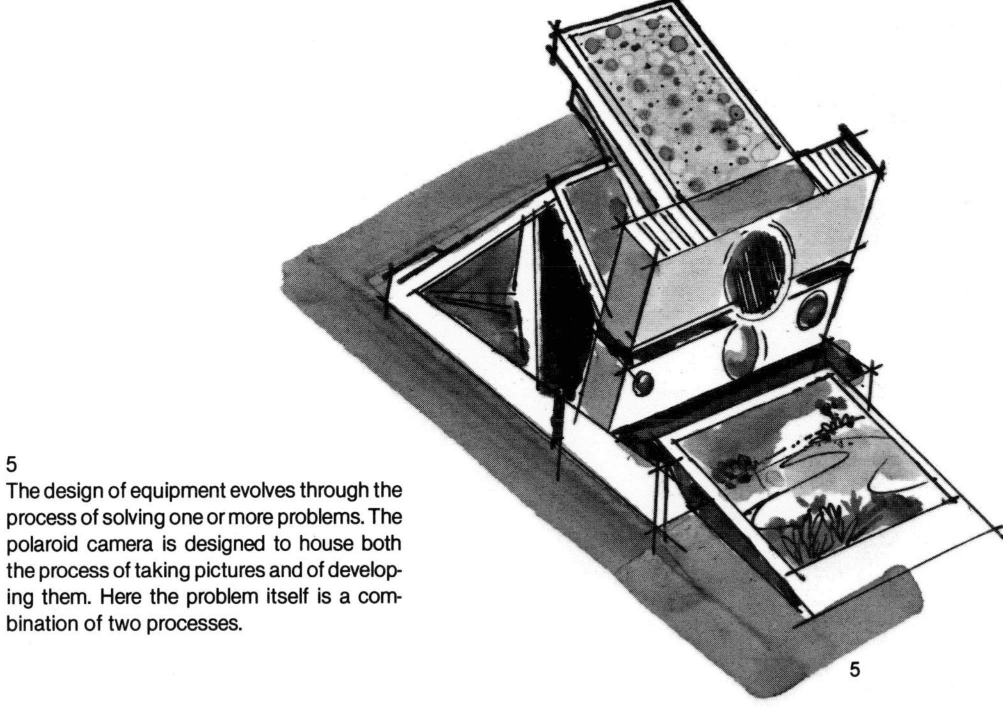

5
The design of equipment evolves through the process of solving one or more problems. The polaroid camera is designed to house both the process of taking pictures and of developing them. Here the problem itself is a combination of two processes.

5

6
As the environment or context of the problem changes, so does the design.

6

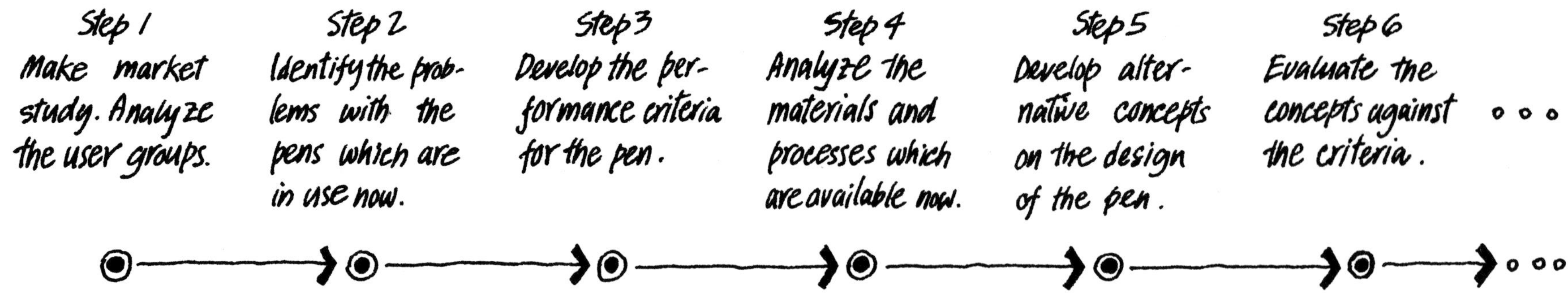

7
A problem can be divided into a number of steps or smaller problems for ease of solving.

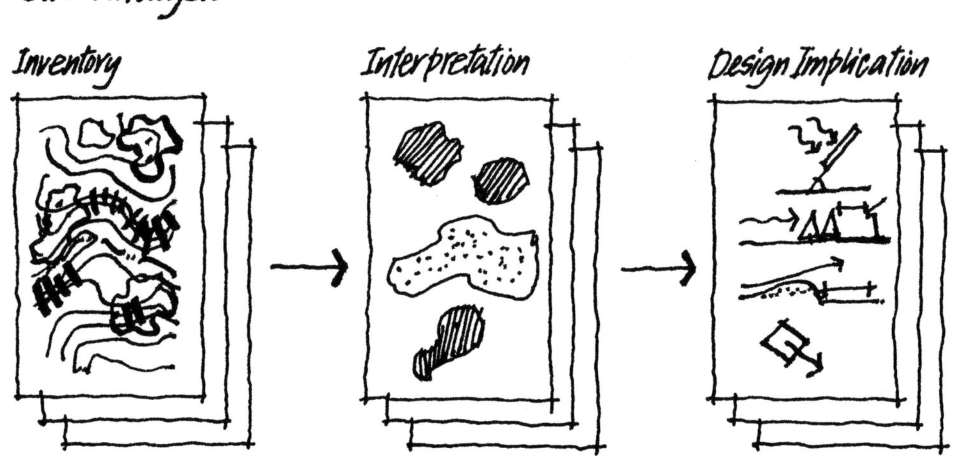

8
A site analysis can be broken down into a number of steps while the site analysis itself is one of many steps in environmental problem solving.

mind, he divides the problem into a series of smaller problems and arranges them into a sequence of steps. He does this because it is easier to deal with the smaller problems one at a time. The sequence of steps is, of course, also very critical. The larger the number of steps in the process, the smaller is the problem at each step. Each step can then be dealt with in greater depth and with more careful thought. This way a greater number of issues can be considered for the problem at hand. Thus, a problem having a large number of issues must be broken down into a large number of steps.

For additional ease, each step can be further broken down into smaller steps, and thus greater consideration can be given. This process of breaking down steps into smaller and smaller steps can be continued for still larger problems.

FEEDBACK

A step-by-step problem-solving process allows for feedback. As the problems in a single step are being dealt with, new problems may be generated that require rethinking of the previous step or steps. This rethinking prompts evaluation and serves as feedback in the process. *Feedback* is a process of discovery in problem solving and is necessary to arrive at a workable solution. Evaluation and discovery prompt necessary adjustment in understanding the problem, and form an integral part of the problem-solving process.

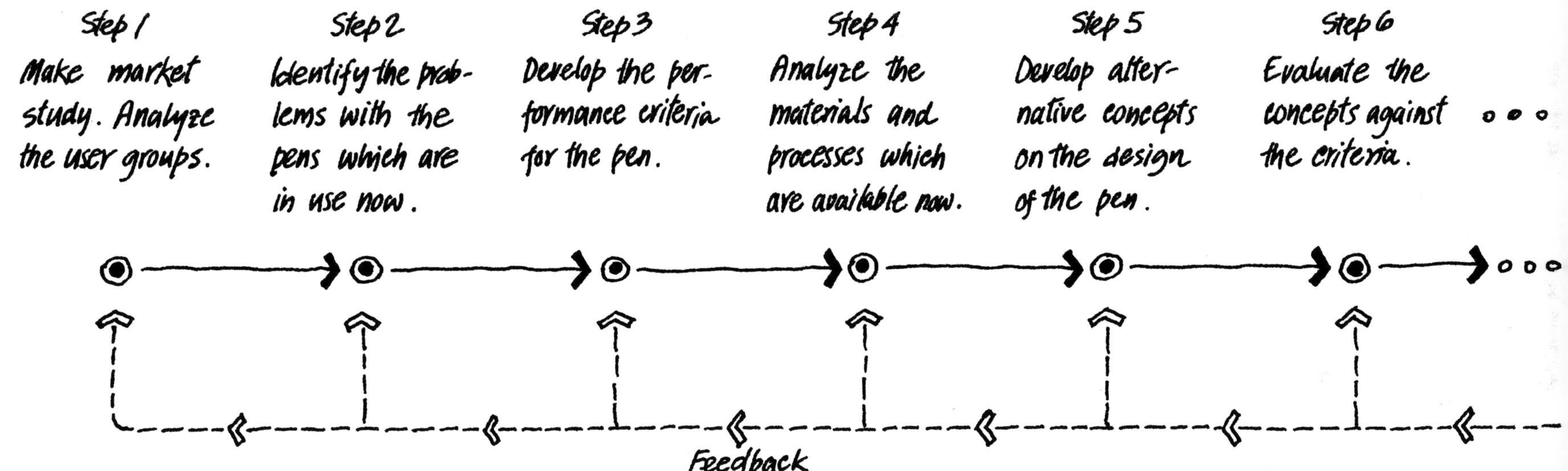

9
Feedback allows evaluation and rethinking and is necessary to arrive at a workable solution.

BIOLOGICAL PROCESS

The biological world is dynamic. It is a world of growth and propagation. Every second new cells are created; new genetic combinations are generated, stored, and transmitted by DNA, RNA, and enzymes, causing cell differentiation, producing new forms, shapes, colors, textures, and new combinations thereof. It is the ultimate of creative processes. To make things happen smoothly, the feedback mechanism is present here, especially in those areas where creative activities are in full swing.

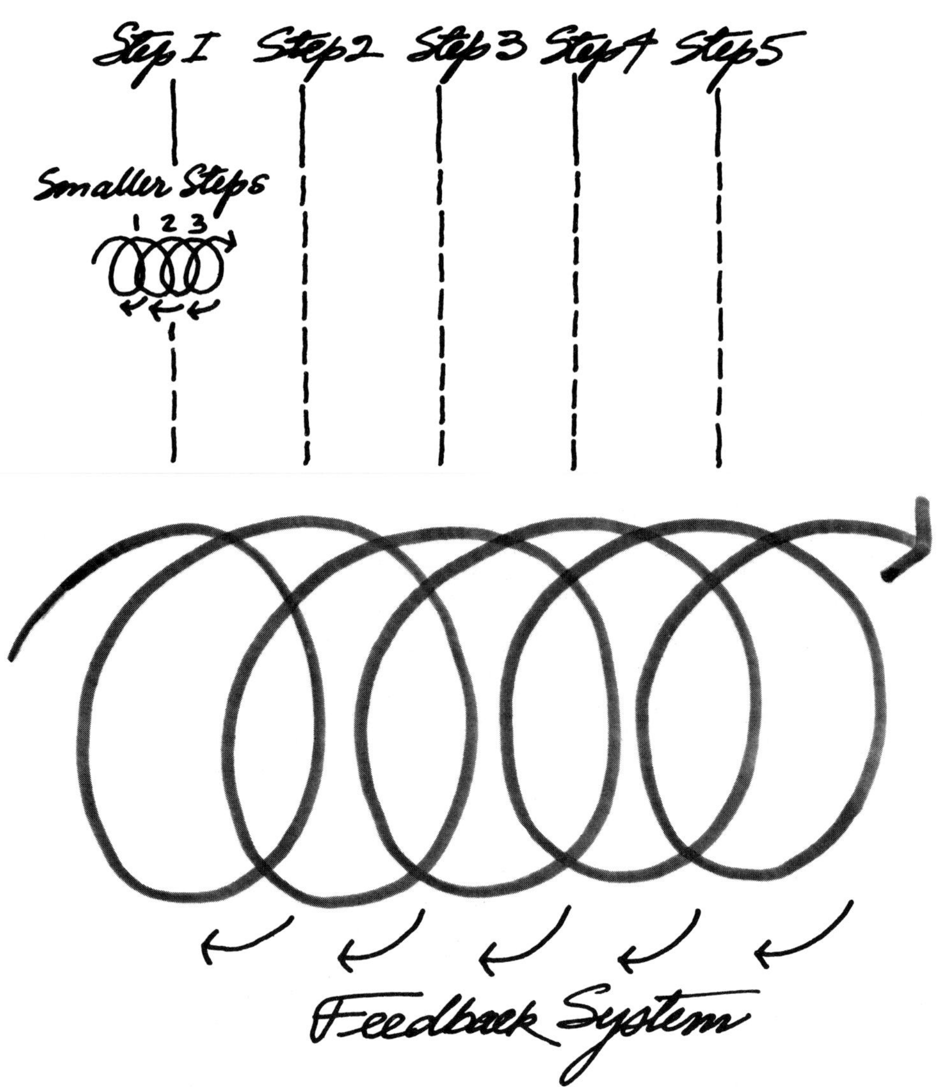

CYCLICAL PROCESS

Biological evolution is a brilliant example of a creative process involving mistakes and feedback systems. The evolution (or the design) of new species is nothing but an accommodation of corrections prompted by previous mistakes. The dynamics of our evolving environment made this process very challenging and thus highly creative, producing enormous variety to meet the needs of new situations. This planet, together with its changing environment and ever evolving living world, make up a gigantic creative process.

Design or creative problem solving is similar to the biological process. It is not rigid or strictly linear. Instead, it is a cyclical process progressing with continuous feedback and necessary adjustments as new information becomes available. With such a process allowing for feedback and adjustments, the problem begins to take new shape—its own unique shape—and direction, and the solution becomes an evolutionary rather than a formulaic answer.

10
A creative problem-solving process is a cyclical one allowing for continuous feedback, rethinking, and redefining at various steps.

2

Communication: A Tool for Problem Solving

Communication is a tool for survival in the biological world. The information flow from the gene to the entire cell system through the enzyme is an on-going process. This process is central to growth, maturation, aging, decay, and thus to the cycle of life. It is a complex network, always at work and responsible for the systematic functioning of the body. There are also other levels of communication systems in the body. The nervous system is a complex network reaching throughout the body and carries messages almost instantly to the brain. The cardiovascular system carries nutrition to remote areas of the body. At the cell level, there are fascinating

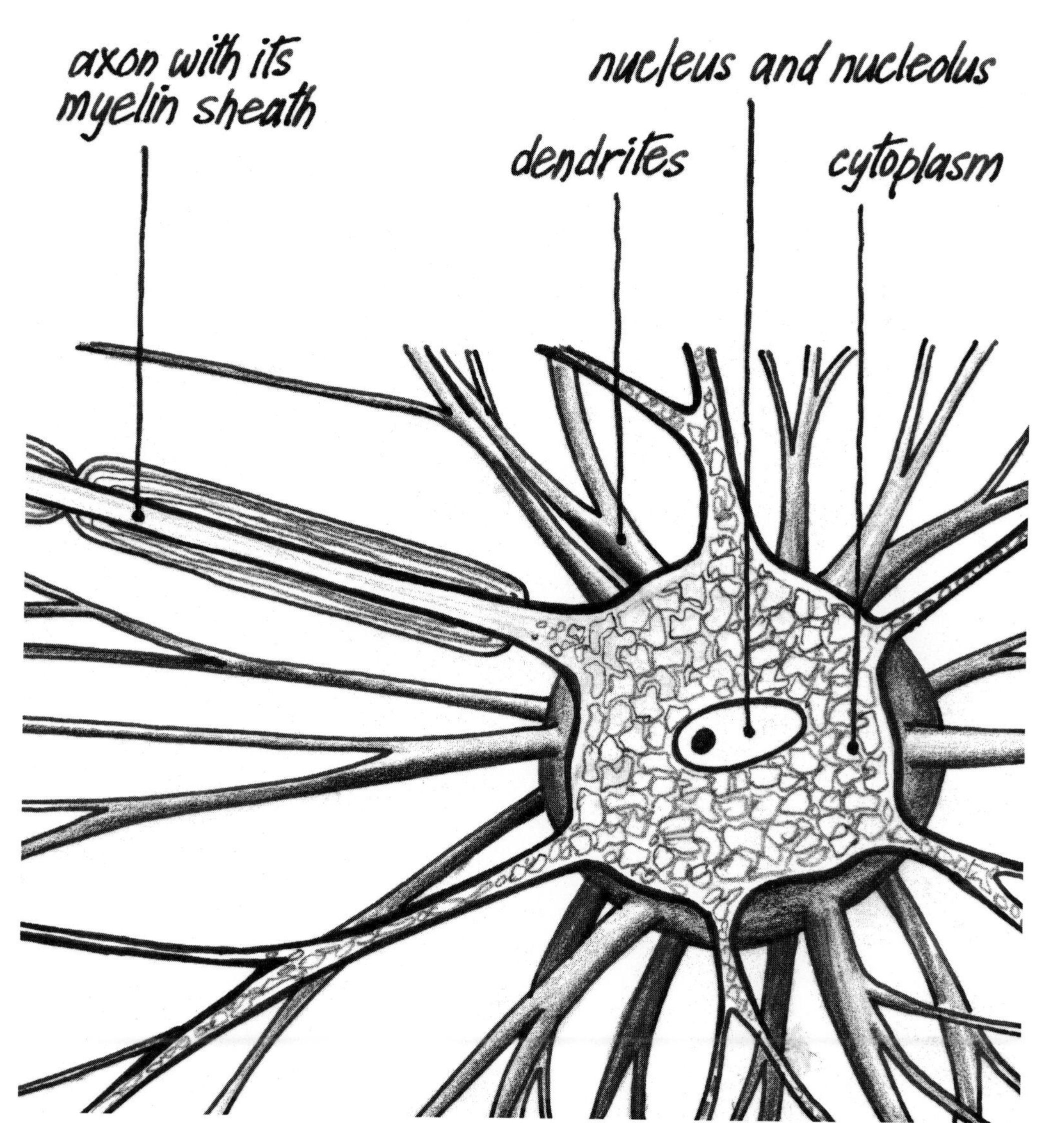

11
A nerve cell receives and sends messages almost instantly through its dendrites and axon.

12–13
The endoplasmic reticulum is a series of concentric cavities and serves to transport synthesized proteins.

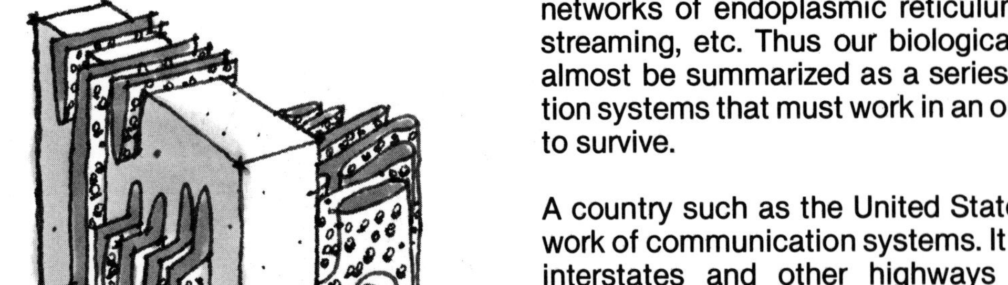

12

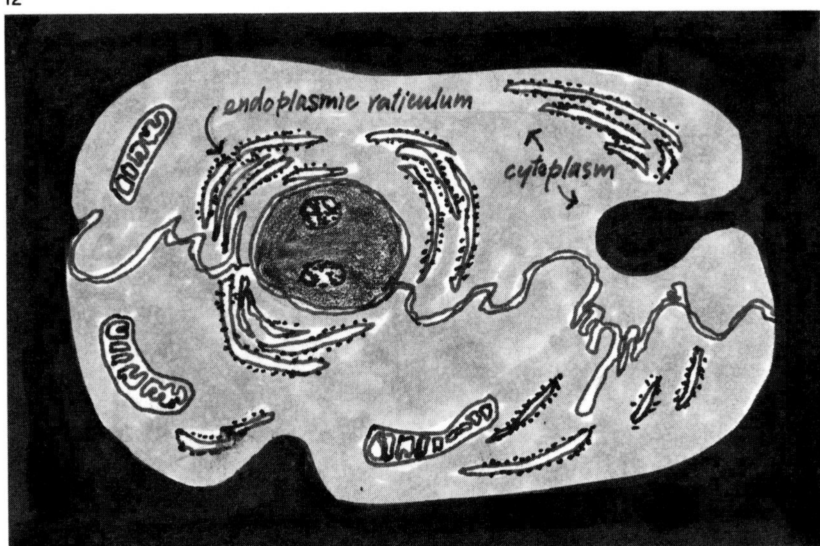

networks of endoplasmic reticulum, protoplasmic streaming, etc. Thus our biological existence can almost be summarized as a series of communication systems that must work in an orderly way for us to survive.

A country such as the United States is also a network of communication systems. It is connected by interstates and other highways through which various distribution systems, including that of food, are at work, and they must function well in order for people to obtain daily necessities. Air routes, telecommunications, power distribution, etc., form another series of communication systems the country is heavily dependent upon. Any prolonged disruption of these systems would put this country into a severe crisis. Communication systems are almost the lifeline of the country.

GRAPHIC COMMUNICATION

Anthropologists tell us that, unlike most of the animal kingdom, speech is a special gift to human beings. It is special not only because we can label things and concepts with it, but also because we can use these labels to communicate.

Graphic communication is another gift to human beings, but for the average person, it is mostly an unexplored frontier. Traditionally, we have left this gift for artists to explore. Except for a handful, most of us never develop graphic skill and thus never enjoy the use of its potential in our everyday lives. Graphic communication is a much stronger tool for comparing situations between two points in time, and for the development of choices and alternatives for creative decision making. We have always left this task to the linear, verbal, and logical self.

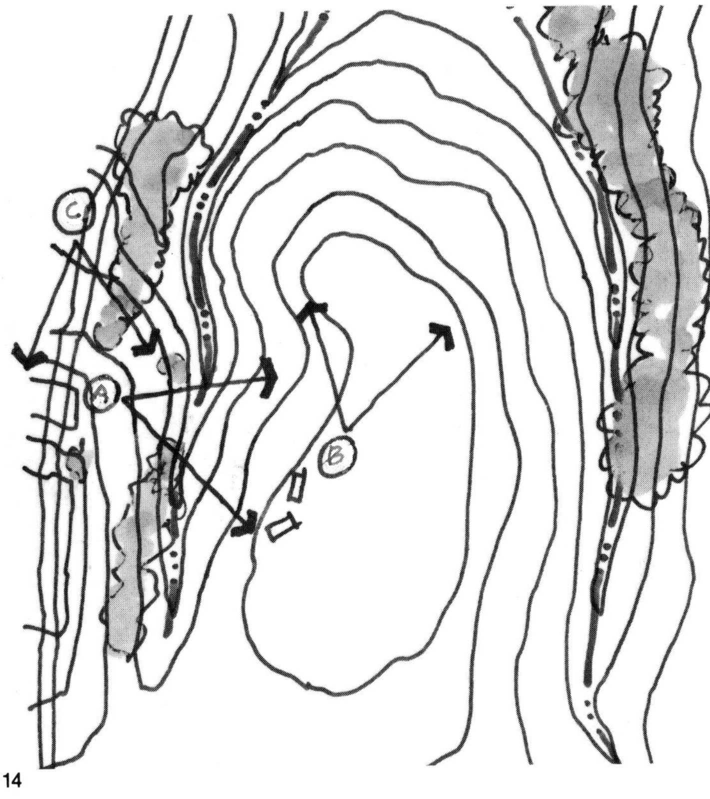

14

A

15

B

16

C

17

14–17
Comparing situations at various points in time can be effectively aided by graphic communication and thus can help analyze visual, spatial, and sequential qualities. Three sketches drawn from three spots on the site aid in spatial comparison.

18
As opposed to the old belief, recent findings show that both hemispheres of the human brain are engaged in highly cognitive functions, each specializing in a mode different from the other.

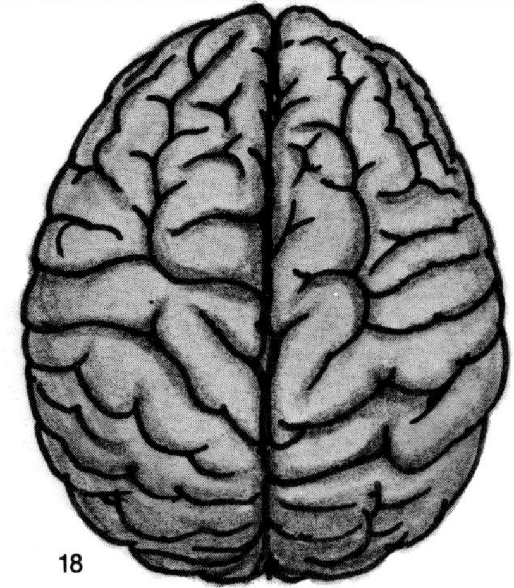

18

19
Graphic display provides greater communication between steps and thus aids the feedback process.

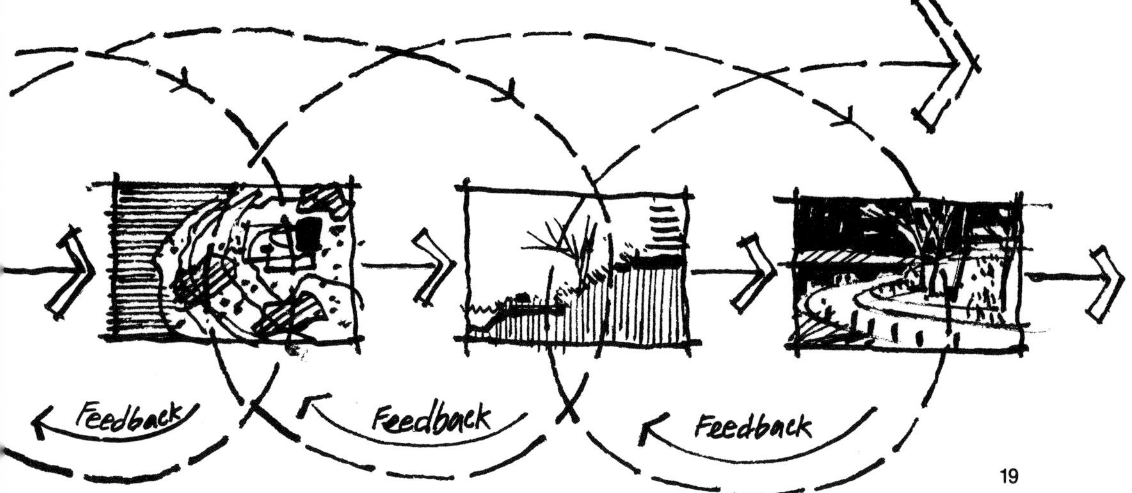

19

HEMISPHERIC ASYMMETRY

For quite some time, we have been aware of the hemispheric asymmetry of our brains, but recent research confirmed certain interesting facts in this area. The fact that the left side of the brain, in the majority of people, is responsible for speech and language, which are in turn linked with reasoning and thinking, is why nineteenth-century scientists named it the major hemisphere, meaning that it is dominant over the right side of the brain, which they named the minor hemisphere, attributing subordinate value to it. Recent findings confirm that both hemispheres of the brain play roles in higher cognitive functioning, the right hemisphere specializing in spatial, graphic, and holistic behavior, the left in linear, verbal, and analytic behavior. In the past, visual and graphic communication did not receive much attention as an important apparatus for higher cognitive behavior, and, consequently, its full potential was not uncovered. Later in this book, we will discuss more about hemispheric asymmetry.

As we have seen earlier, design can be viewed as a problem-solving process, which in turn can be broken down into steps for ease of solving. New information that becomes available at various steps needs to be displayed and communicated as feedback to earlier steps. In our day-to-day decision making, which is a kind of problem-solving process, we satisfy such communication needs through a language and speech apparatus. We may not actually be saying words, but our verbal self silently per-

20–22
Graphic feedback allows greater evaluation in the design process. Here the plan, section, and perspective provide feedback to each other.

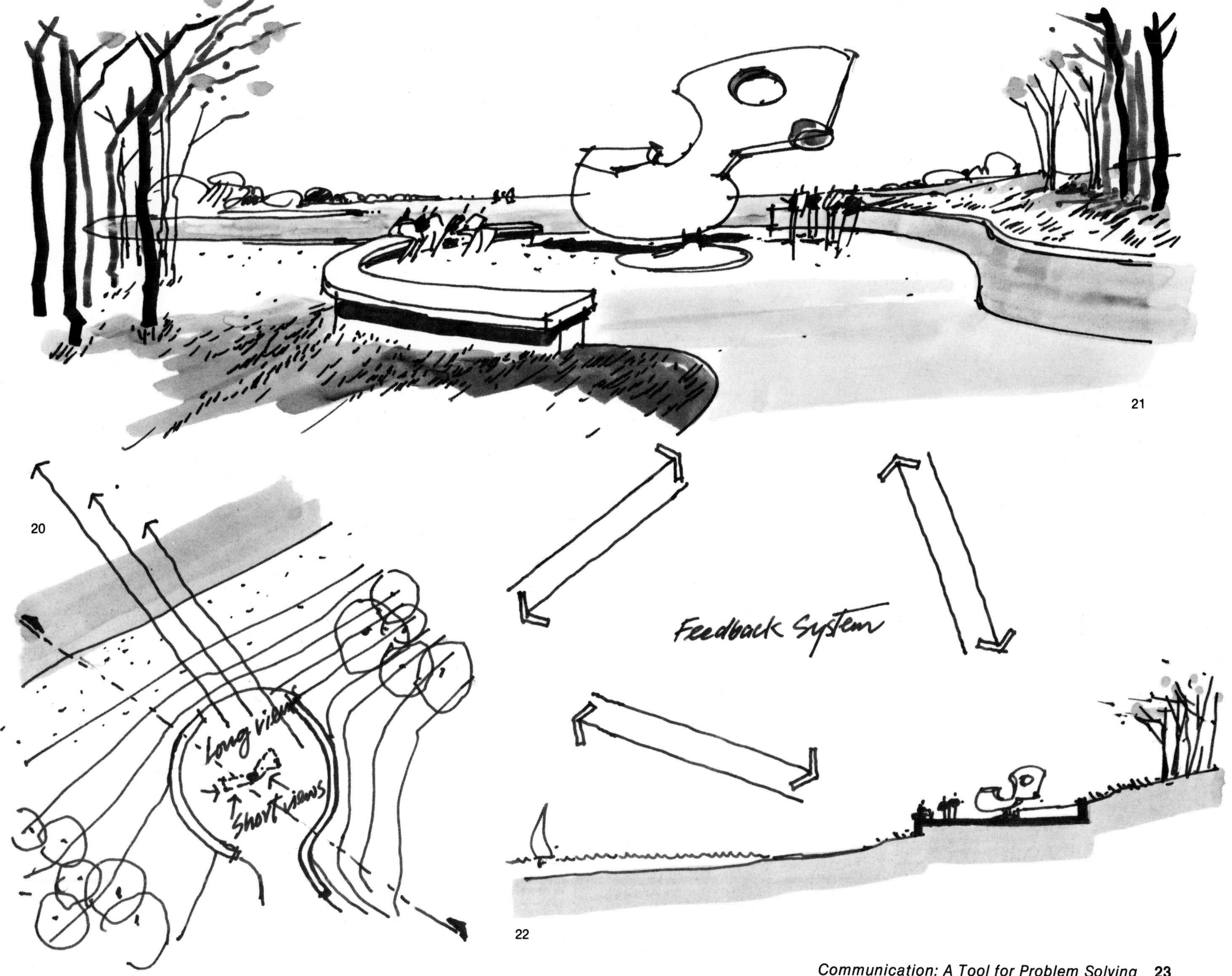
Long views
Short views
Feedback System
20
21
22

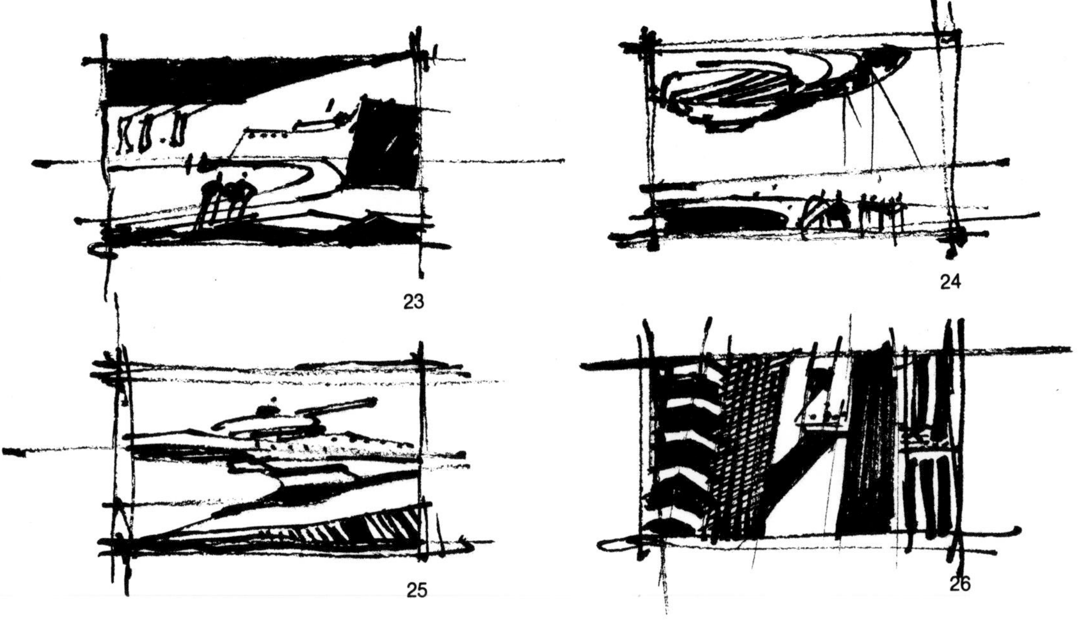

23–26
Thumbnail sketches help to study the design of scenes and their sequence in a science fiction film. Here graphic communication is serving a very important role in the problem-solving process.

forms this task with the help of logic and reasoning, which we name *thinking.* This is done almost automatically as an unconscious decision. The left hemisphere, being linear and sequential, does a poor job of it. If the problem is a complex one, it cannot handle it and then calls on the right side of the brain for visualization, which, of course, should have been done in the first place.

Graphic communication can perform the task of communicating between steps of problem solving more effectively. Both in displaying the "total picture" and in making connections, graphic visualization is very helpful. It is a higher cognitive task appropriate for the right hemisphere of the brain. As this function is natural for the right side of the brain, it can perform the task most efficiently.

Predominantly in the West and, in recent times, also in certain parts of the East where western intellectual influence has permeated, an average "educated" adult develops the capabilities of the left side of the brain, i.e., the linear, verbal, logical, and analytic faculties. On the other hand, the capabilities of the right side of the brain are underdeveloped. The intuitive and nonlogical approach of this half of the brain has been considered intellectually poor. Consequently, we have a tendency to indiscriminantly give all tasks to the left side of the brain regardless of whether it is appropriate for it or not.

3

Design as a Communication Problem

DESIGN AND DISCOVERY

For a given situation, for a given set of constraints and resources, you could almost say that the design is already there; what the designer needs to do is to discover it and communicate the discovery. His task is that of a communicator, both to himself and to the outside world. He must take into consideration the givens, constraints, and resources. Through the use of communication skills, he must then analyze them, uncover the choices or alternatives, evaluate them, and select the optimum solution. The

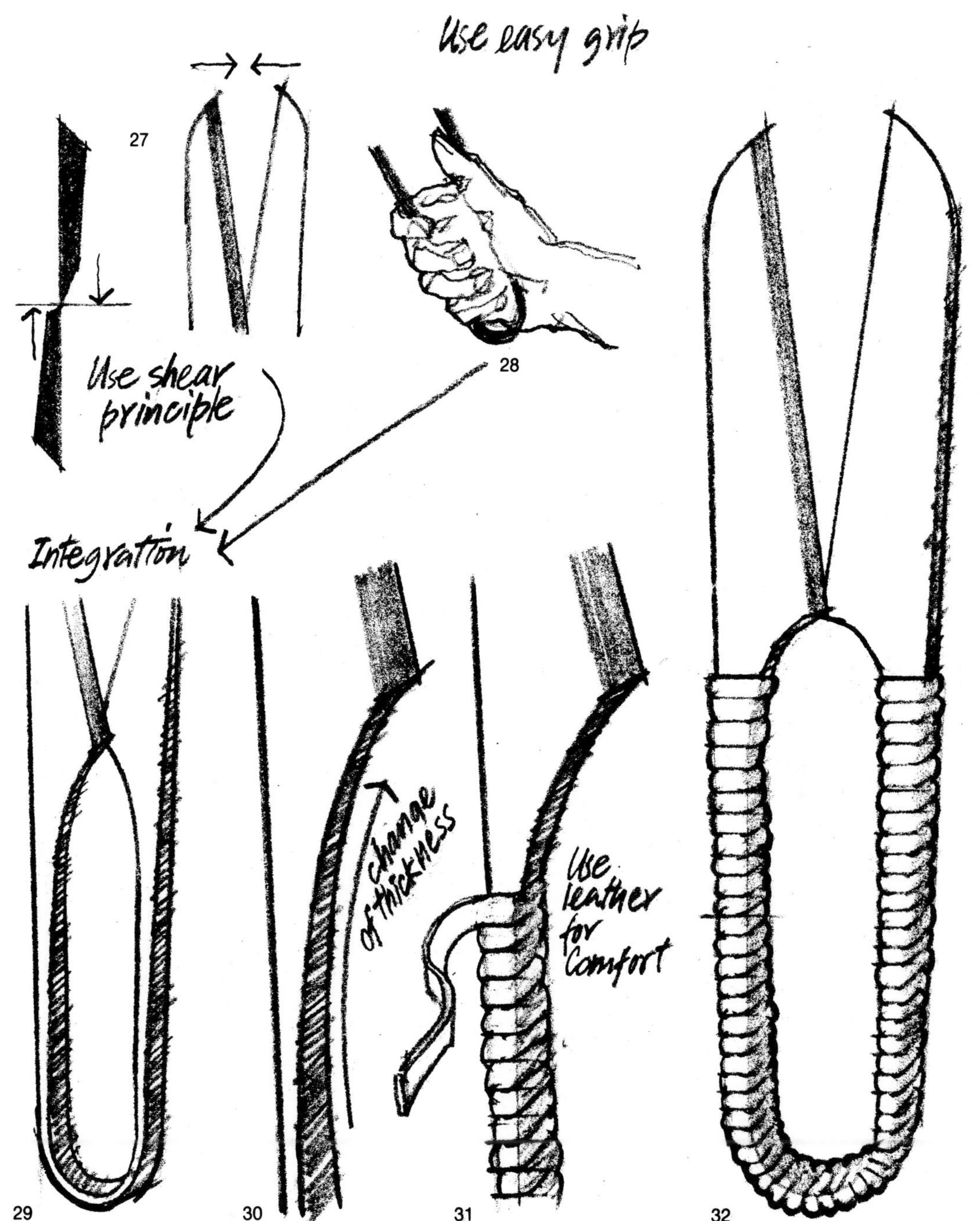

27–32
Problem solving can be considered a discovery process. The shear principle (27) and an easy grip (28) are two constraints, which are articulated in this solution by using one piece of metal (29) and by varying thickness (30). Comfort—another constraint—is achieved by using leather for the grip (31). Thus, the final solution (32) evolved from the given constraints.

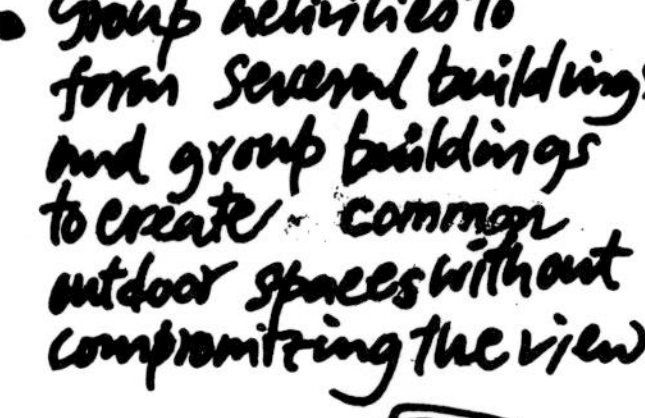

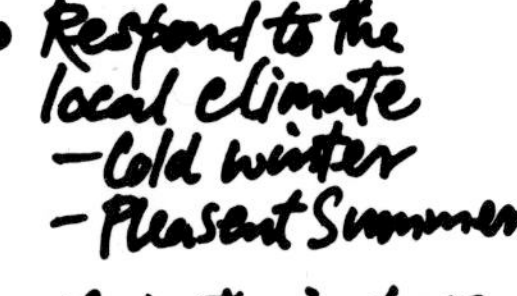

33

stronger his communication skills, the more thorough his analysis and alternatives become. This results in a superior final solution.

The designer's role is that of finding the design that is already there, waiting to be discovered through the use of his communication skills. If the design is already there and he is merely discovering it, one may ask, then where does his creativity lie? His creativity lies in the effectiveness of his communication skills both in the discovery process and in giving expression to his discovery. Two designers

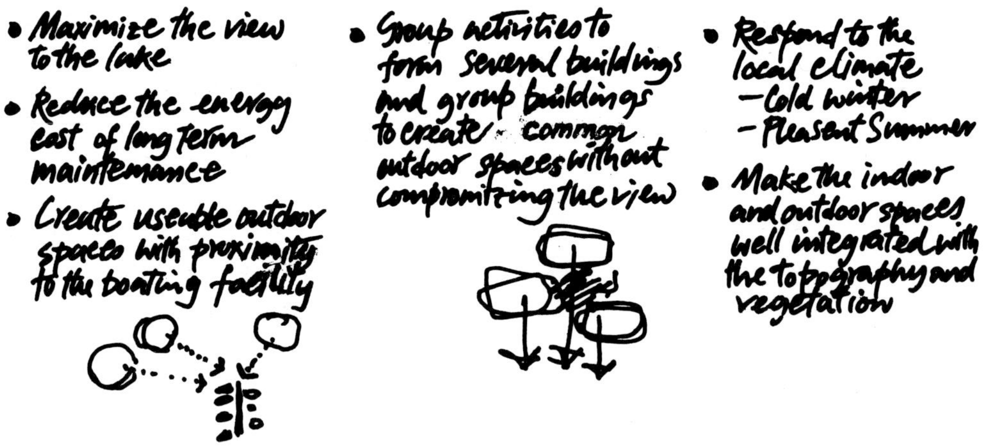

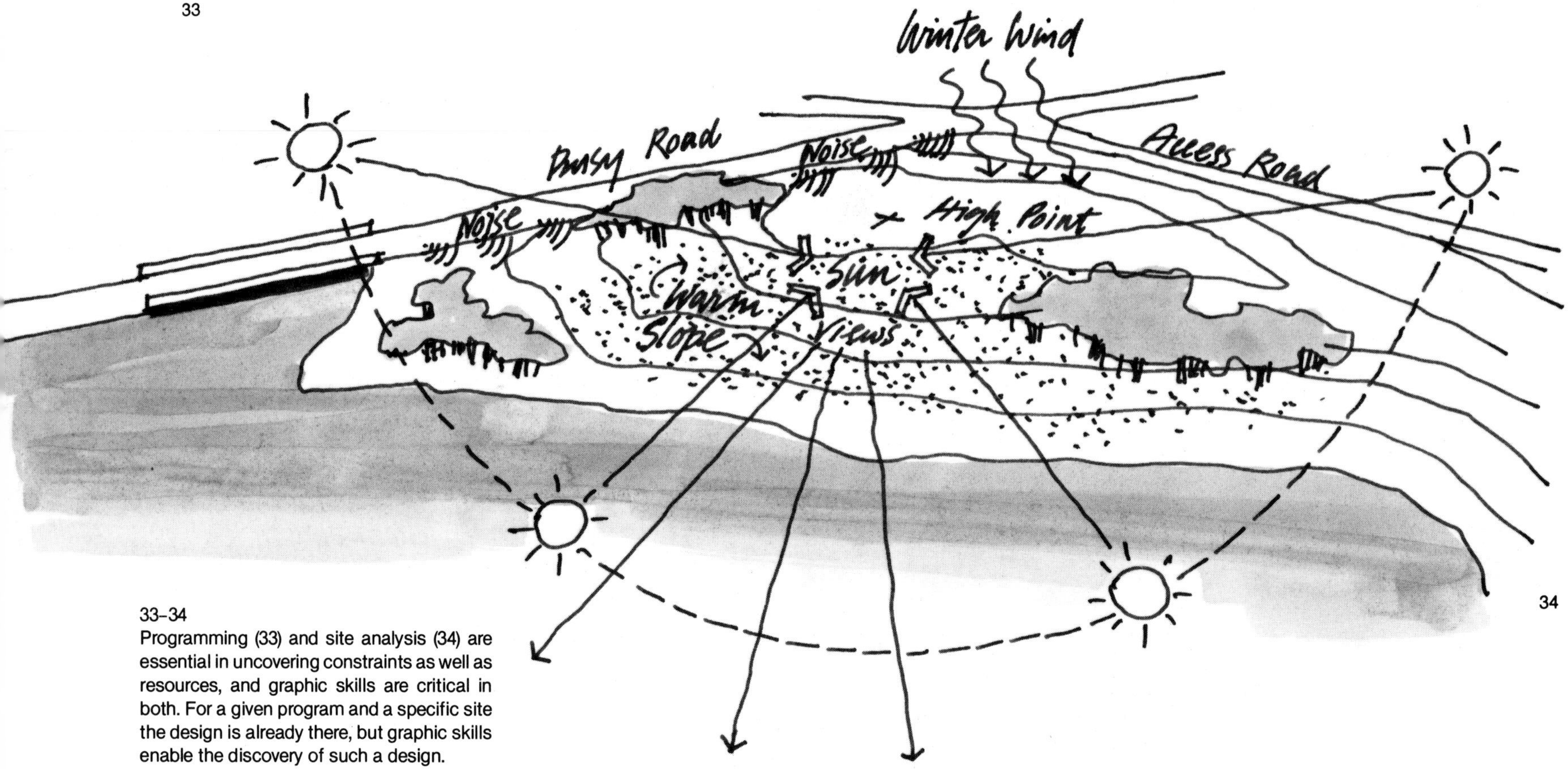

34

33–34
Programming (33) and site analysis (34) are essential in uncovering constraints as well as resources, and graphic skills are critical in both. For a given program and a specific site the design is already there, but graphic skills enable the discovery of such a design.

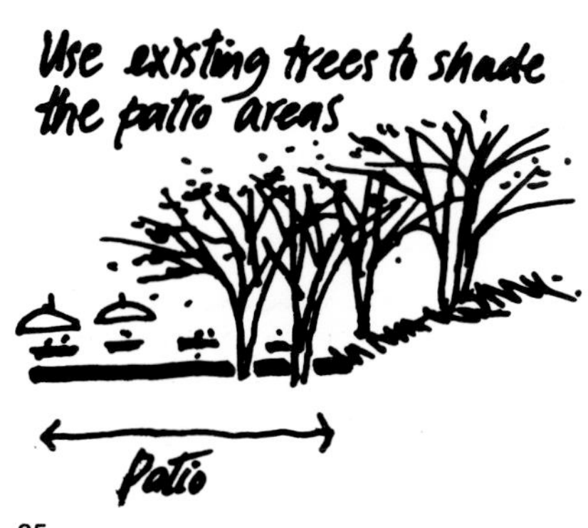

35

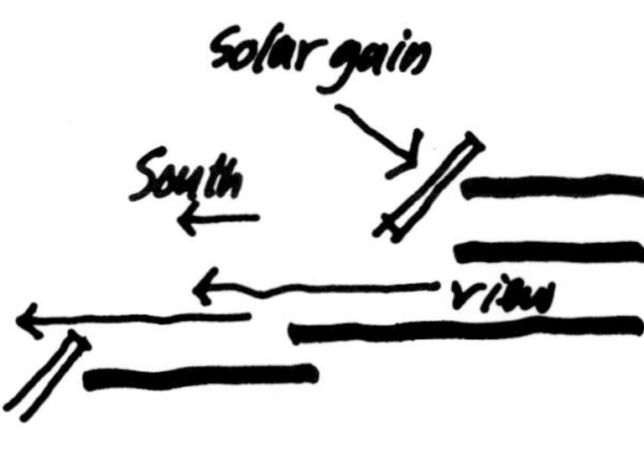

36

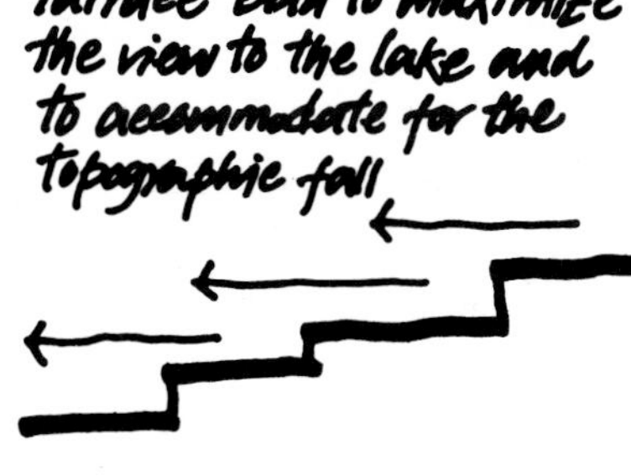

37

38

working on the same problem will "discover" differently and will give different expressions to their discovery. It is the critical skill of communication that separates them and adds personality to their solutions.

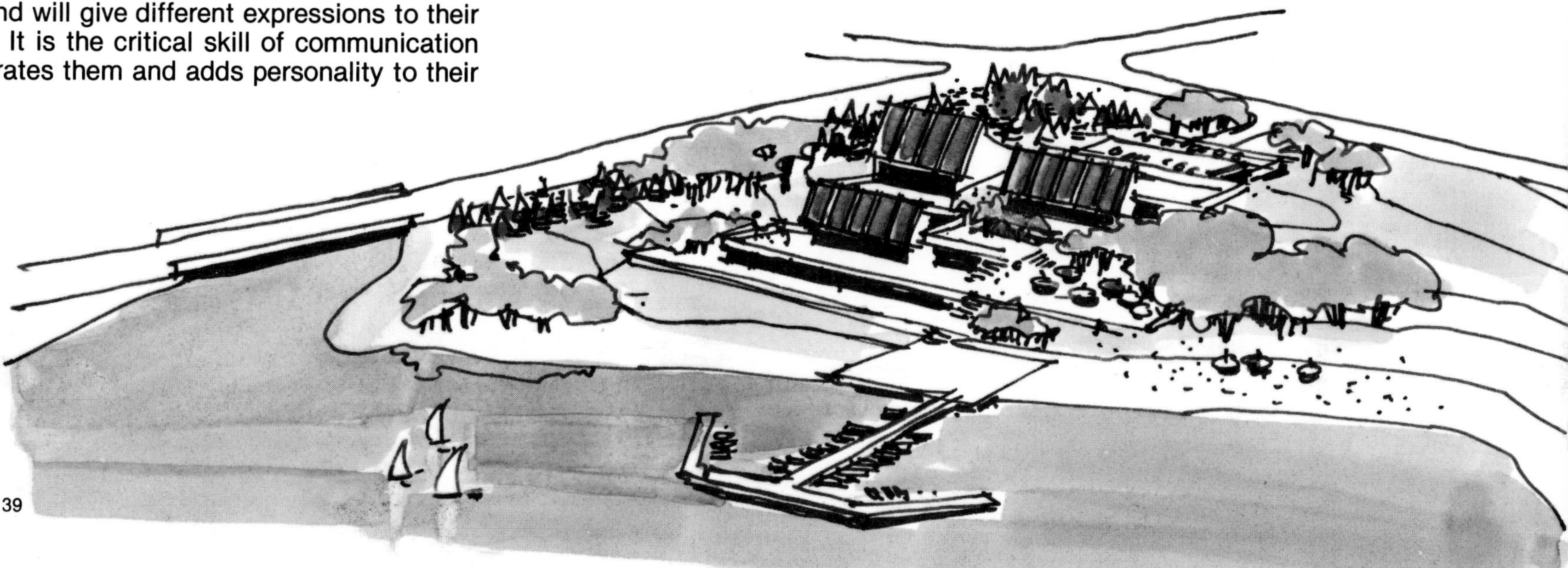
39

"Discovering" the design is no different than discovering the physical laws of nature. Scientific discovery also requires communication skills. In the case of a physicist, the communication medium may be predominantly mathematical, whereas for an architect the predominant medium may be graphic. But in both cases, mastery of communica-

35–39
The analysis of the program and site resulted in a series of design conditions that are articulated graphically (35–38). A design solution (39) is a discovery through graphic assimilation and articulation of these design conditions.

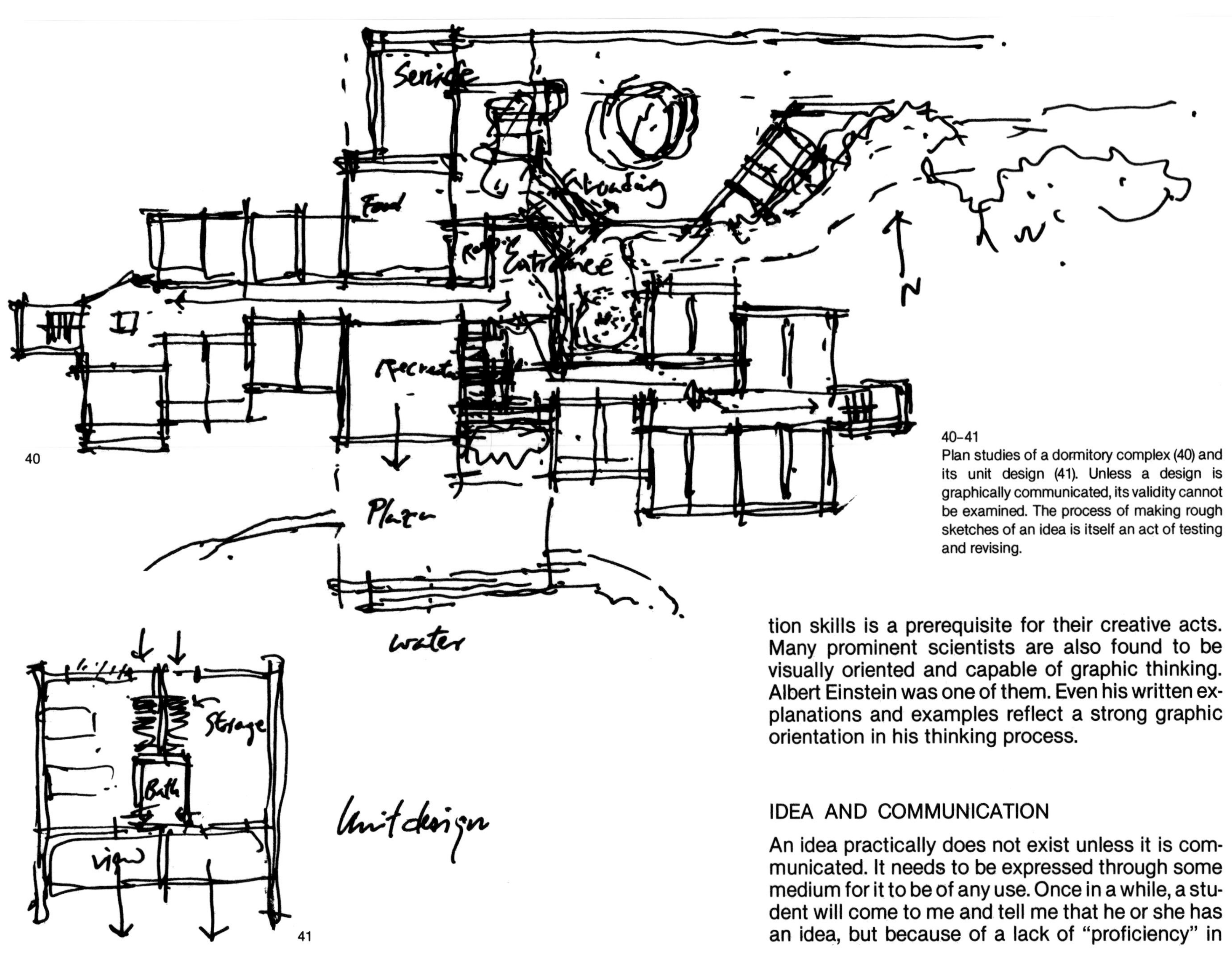

40

41

40–41
Plan studies of a dormitory complex (40) and its unit design (41). Unless a design is graphically communicated, its validity cannot be examined. The process of making rough sketches of an idea is itself an act of testing and revising.

tion skills is a prerequisite for their creative acts. Many prominent scientists are also found to be visually oriented and capable of graphic thinking. Albert Einstein was one of them. Even his written explanations and examples reflect a strong graphic orientation in his thinking process.

IDEA AND COMMUNICATION

An idea practically does not exist unless it is communicated. It needs to be expressed through some medium for it to be of any use. Once in a while, a student will come to me and tell me that he or she has an idea, but because of a lack of "proficiency" in

42

graphic communication, it could not be expressed. In such a case, the problem is not so much the proficiency level in graphic communication as it is the incompleteness of the idea or the inability to visualize it in his or her mind. An idea is incomplete unless it can be visualized or communicated. Communication is the test of whether there is really any idea; unless the idea is a sound one or at least has potential of becoming one, it is hard to visualize or communicate. Too many times we are tempted to confuse an idea with a vague notion of one, or, sometimes, even with a hope of one. Graphic proficiency, or the ability to draw, is dependent upon the ability to see or visualize, and on the clarity of the concept or idea to be drawn. Regardless of how

42–43
The freehand perspective sketch (42) and section (43) can be used to examine the three-dimensional aspect of the design concept.

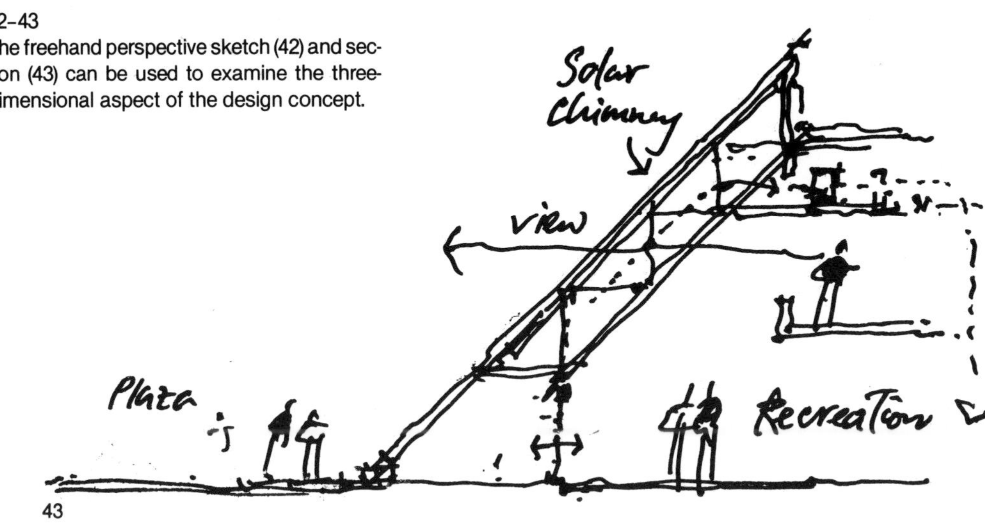

43

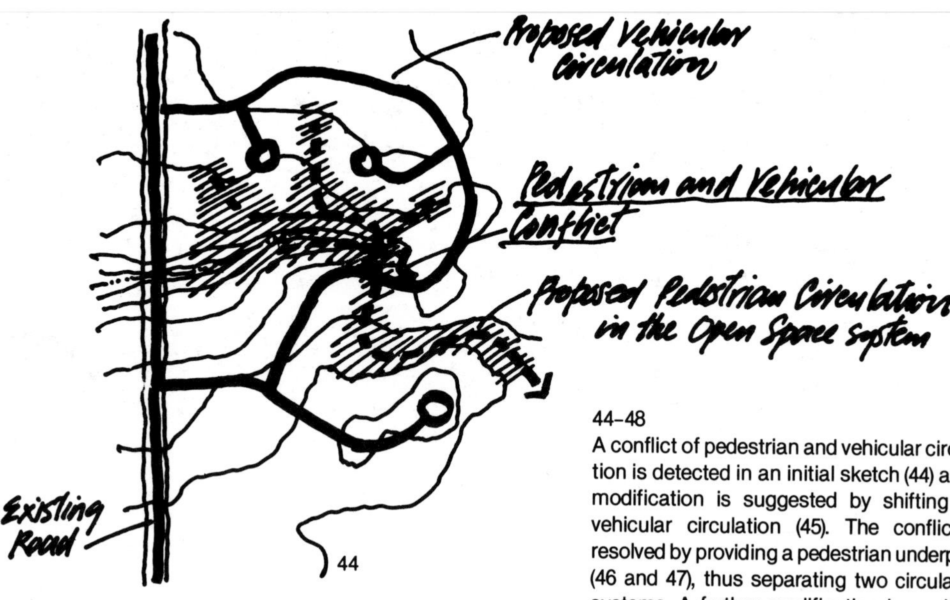

44–48
A conflict of pedestrian and vehicular circulation is detected in an initial sketch (44) and a modification is suggested by shifting the vehicular circulation (45). The conflict is resolved by providing a pedestrian underpass (46 and 47), thus separating two circulation systems. A further modification is made by widening the underpass (48) to allow for more light and a drainage ditch.

poor you consider your ability to communicate graphically, if your idea is well thought out, you should be able to draw it. The difficulty may stem from your reluctance to make a commitment because you are afraid of making yourself vulnerable to criticism, or from incompleteness of the idea.

A design solution is the communication of an idea. It is the way in which the idea is communicated. The act of communication, its nature, its style, and the very level of its involvement, are deeply linked with design. Such a design solution is a statement made by the designer in his own personal way of communicating. It is an expression of the designer's creative communication. The art of communication is inseparable from design.

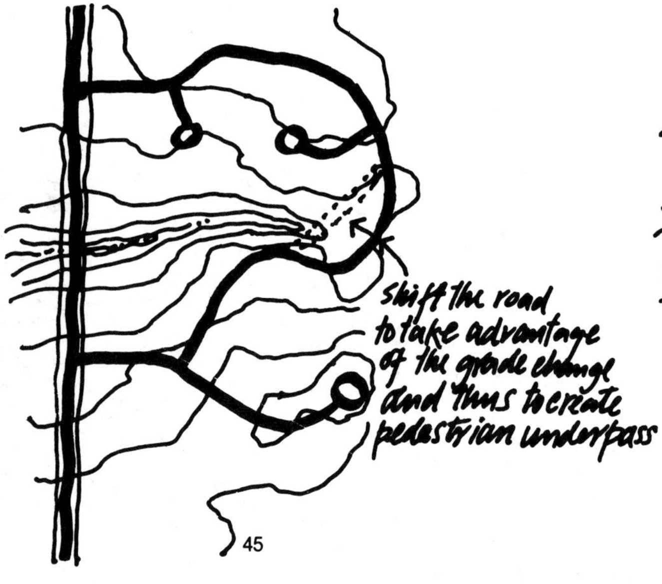

Shift the road to take advantage of the grade change and thus to create pedestrian underpass

45

Pedestrian Underpass

46

Too dark widen

Provide drainage ditch

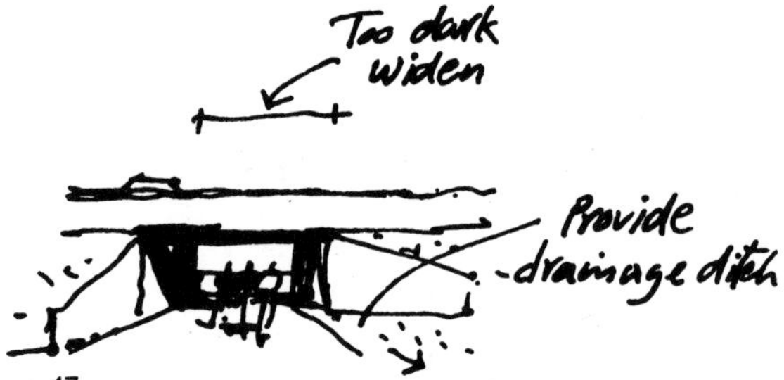

47

48

Part Two

Visual Thinking

Visual Thinking and Problem Solving

51

52

53

54

51–54
Comparing images between two points in time or place is a critical human experience which triggers new ideas and innovations by creating links between them.

In the evolutionary process, man's ability to compare a past situation with the situation at hand is a remarkable milestone. This enables him to examine situations other than the present one and thus provides him with greater choices for creative decision making. Remembering what is out of sight and dealing with such absent situations has undoubtedly provided man with an edge over the rest of the animal kingdom. This has also equipped him with

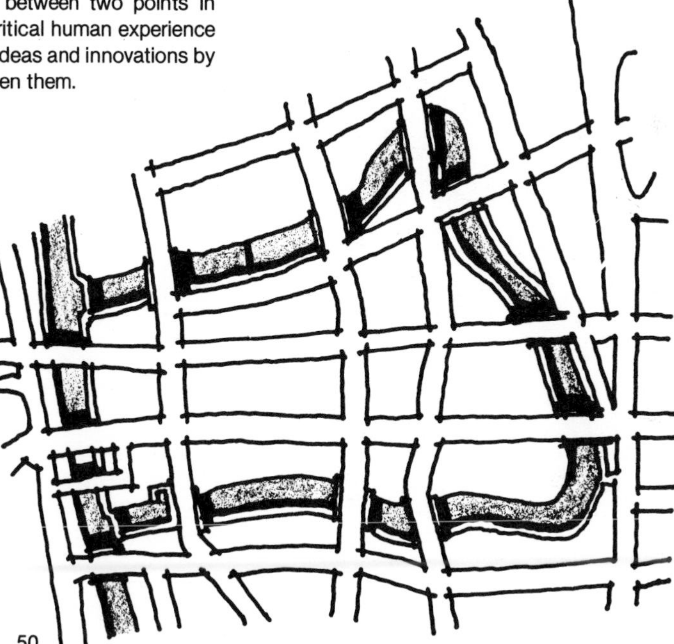

50

49–50
The San Antonio river walk (49) is a superimposition of three distinct systems—downtown streets, pedestrian circulation, and the river (50). They are cunningly integrated to produce a series of pleasant spaces. Each of these systems belongs to a separate world of images, and our natural tendency to compare these contrasting images is what evokes the excitement of these spaces.

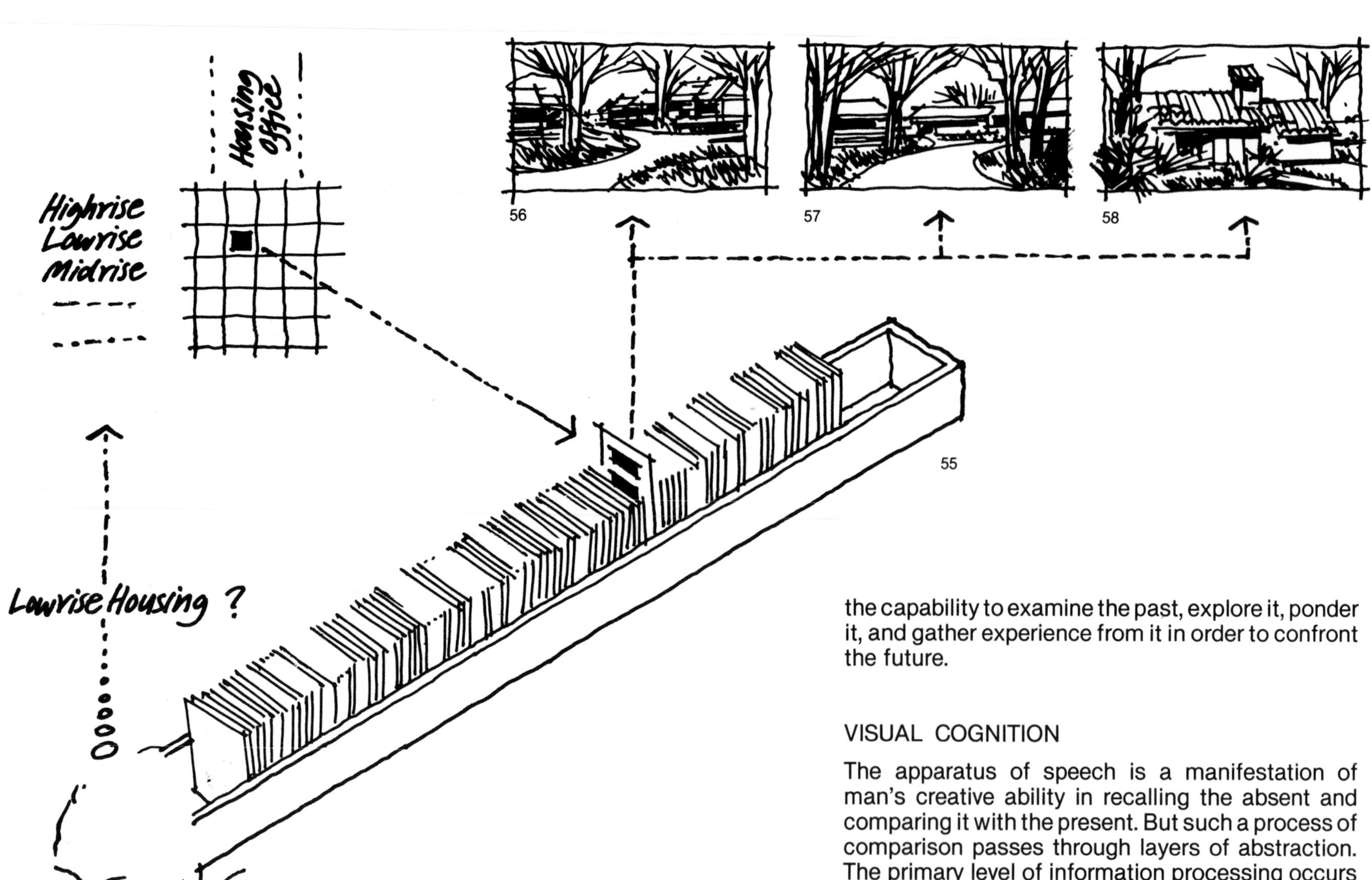

the capability to examine the past, explore it, ponder it, and gather experience from it in order to confront the future.

55–58
To recall the past we look through the mind's eye into the catalog of pictures and images we accumulate over the years (55). The primary level of information processing is visual. Our perception of "low-rise" housing is what we are able to retrieve pictorially by the words "low-rise" and "housing" from our catalog (56–58).

VISUAL COGNITION

The apparatus of speech is a manifestation of man's creative ability in recalling the absent and comparing it with the present. But such a process of comparison passes through layers of abstraction. The primary level of information processing occurs through the senses, among which our visual sense plays a dominant role. When we try to recall a past situation, we try to see it through the mind's eye. In such a process, our mind looks for it through the catalog of pictures and images, and actual search and identification happens at the visual level. Remembering the absent situation is seeing through the mind's eye and recognizing it.

"DARŚANA"

Throughout the world, the act of thinking has been associated with the act of *seeing.* The Greeks regarded philosophy as a kind of sightseeing adventure. In Sanskrit, the world for philosophy is "darśana," meaning "to see." It is seeing past, present, and future situations side by side and comparing them that makes thinking a creative process.

CHILDREN'S IMAGINATION

As children, when we heard fairy tales, we pictured them in our minds. As the story advanced, our minds drew up newer pictures of images and their backgrounds. For each of the characters, palaces, houses, and landscapes, we had a definite picture in our minds. We understood the story through these pictures, we related to the story through them, and we remembered the sto y through them. When our turn came to tell the story, we went back to those mental pictures and images of the characters, palaces, houses, and landscapes. The perceptual world of fairy tales is highly visual. This is why children love books that have a lot of visual information.

The realm of imagination is highly visual. It is filled with visual images, and new images are continuously being created by adding, subtracting, and manipulating the old ones. For the mind, it is a world of adventure in visual experience. Children experience this adventure continuously through their imaginations. You can give them anything—a cardboard box or a piece of lumber—and they will fill in the rest with imagination: they will turn it into a ship, a house, a bridge, or a car. They will add sounds and motion to reinforce their imagination and visualization process.

When it comes to creative imagination the adult

59
Stories are understood, retained, and told with the help of pictorial mapping in our minds. Adding pictures or sketches to stories reinforces such mapping; this is why children (as well as grownups) love story books that have plenty of visual images.

60
The beauty of pictorial images is that they are highly plastic and can be easily manipulated to create worlds of fantasies and imaginary creatures and landscapes.

61
Visual images are vivid and can set specific moods in a story.

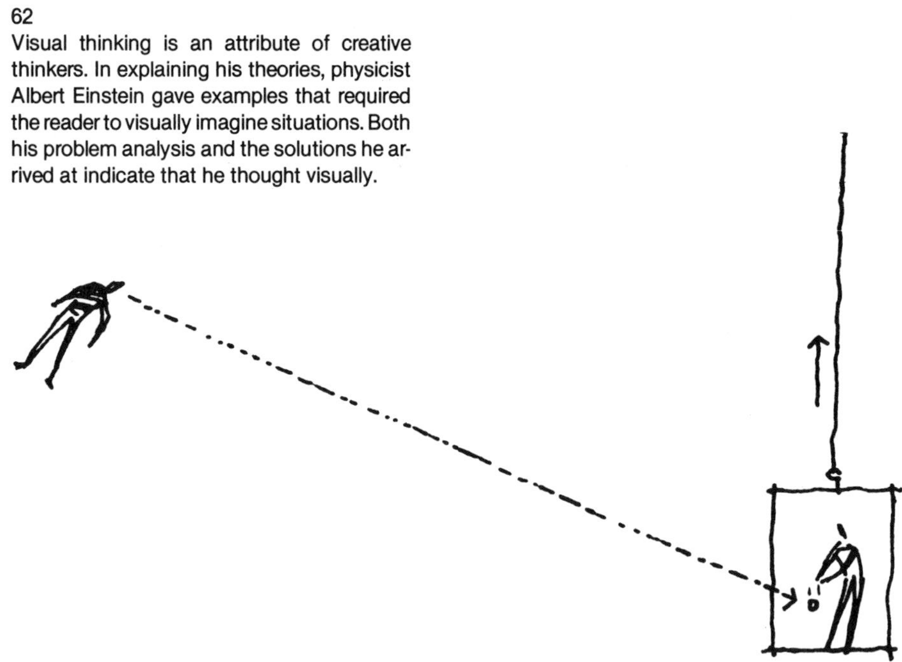

62
Visual thinking is an attribute of creative thinkers. In explaining his theories, physicist Albert Einstein gave examples that required the reader to visually imagine situations. Both his problem analysis and the solutions he arrived at indicate that he thought visually.

world is no different from that of children. It, too, is filled with adventures in visual experience and visualization. It is interesting to note that both the words *imagination* and *visualization* have an origin that has to do with the sense of *sight.* This is so because we receive almost nine-tenths of all information through our eyes, and thus the visual sense plays a dominant role in the information-processing and retrieval system.

VISUAL THINKING AND CREATIVITY

Biographical study of the famous physicist Albert Einstein shows that he had difficulty with his verbal ability during childhood. His verbal development was delayed. Even as an adult he had problems with language skills. But his strength was in nonverbal, spatial, and visual thinking. He thought visually. His perception of problems was nonlinear, graphic, and spatial, and he responded to them through visual thinking. This is evident from the way he gave examples in explaining his theories. His examples are filled with visual images and situations requiring the reader to imagine them visually. He analyzed problems visually and got down to the fundamentals without cluttering his mind. He was in direct touch with the visual concept without worrying about the "labeling" or verbal side of it. Visual thinking is an attribute of creative thinkers.

64
Light rays from two simultaneous lightnings *A* and *B* will reach the midpoint *M* on the embankment at the same time. Will the lightnings also appear simultaneous to the observer on the moving train at point M_1, which is the corresponding midpoint at the time they occurred? Einstein posed this type of question, which requires visual thinking.

63
Albert Einstein suffered delayed verbal development in his childhood, but his strength was in nonverbal, spatial, and visual thinking.

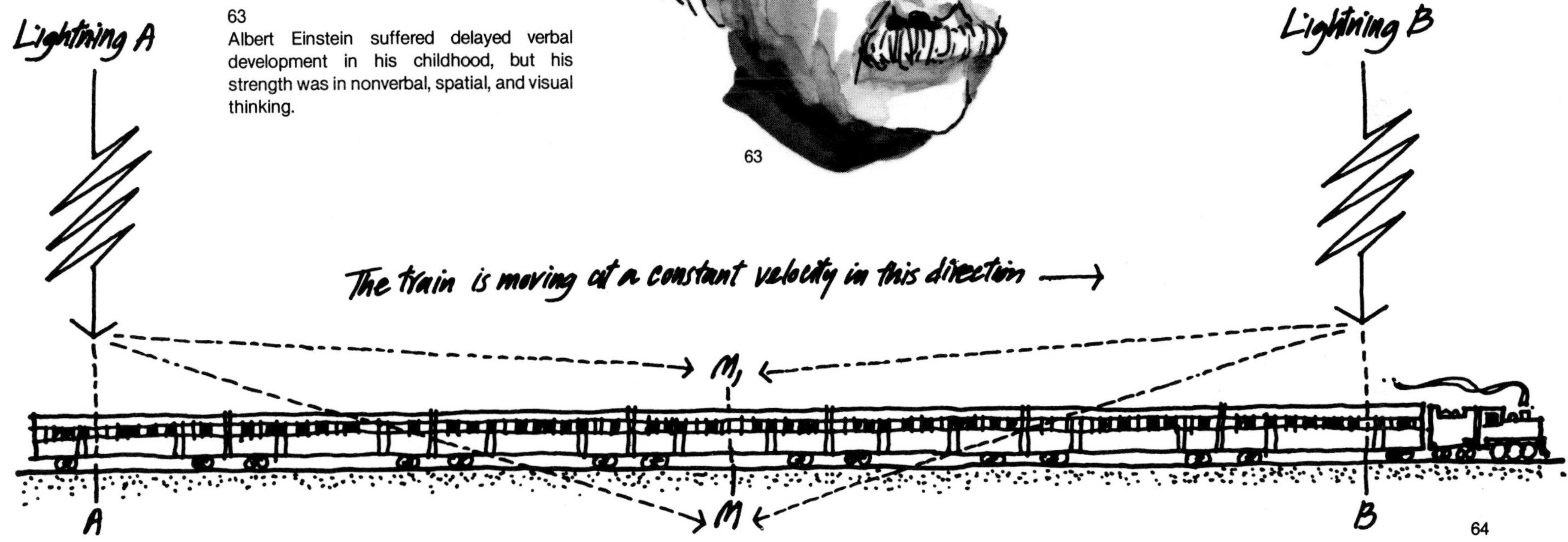

63

64

Visual thinking is spatial, i.e., multidimensional, as opposed to verbal thinking, which is linear. This difference is critical in so far as problem solving is concerned. Visual thinking is closer to the real world, which is spatial in nature, because of the fact that it is multidimensional. It also presents us with direct choices and possibilities, and thus makes the problem-solving process a more creative one. On the other hand, making a similar exploration through verbal thinking can obscure important choices and possibilities with the clutter of "labeling," i.e., verbal language.

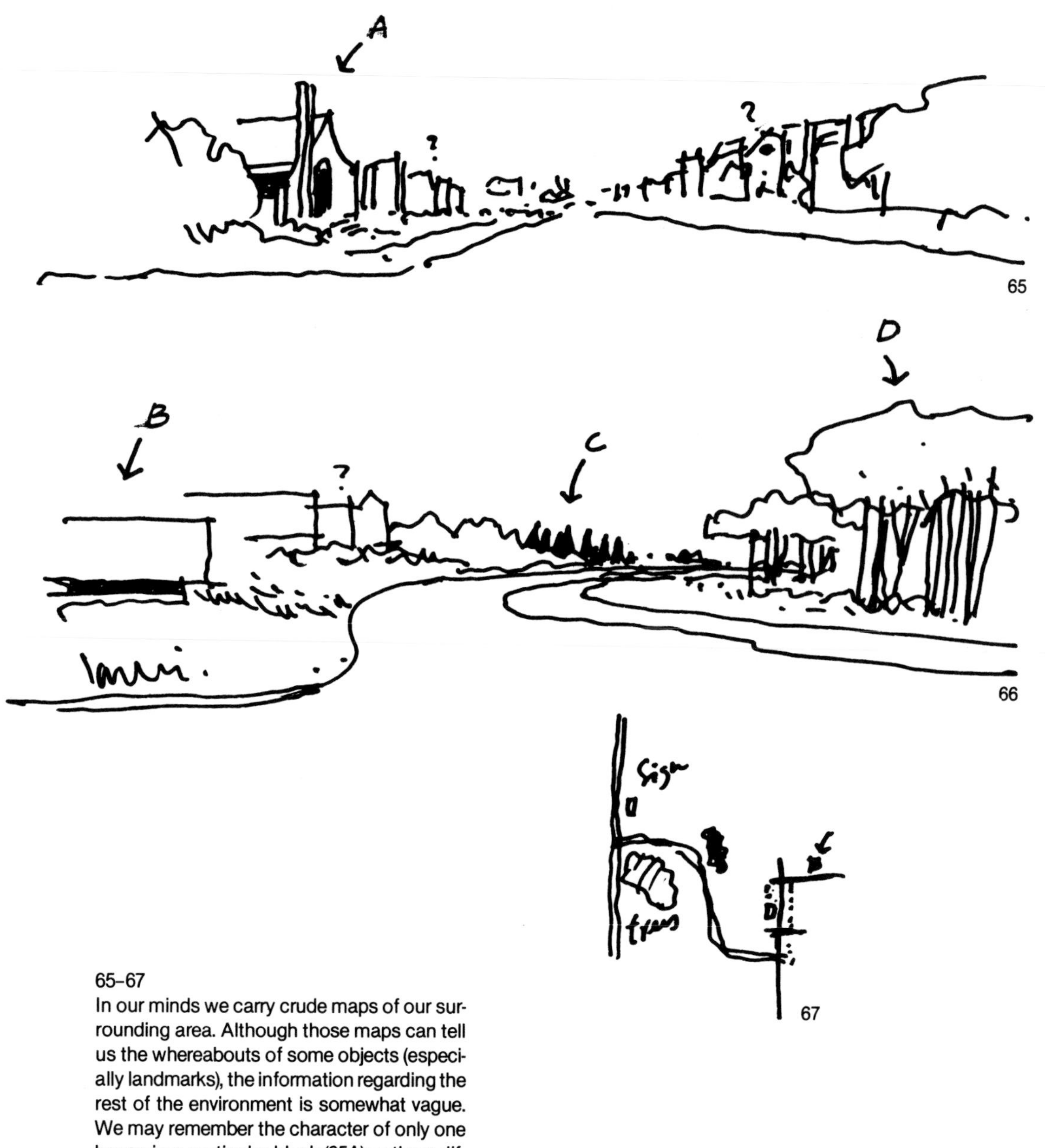

65–67
In our minds we carry crude maps of our surrounding area. Although those maps can tell us the whereabouts of some objects (especially landmarks), the information regarding the rest of the environment is somewhat vague. We may remember the character of only one house in a particular block (65A) or three different features of another area (66B, C, and D); the mental map is made up of such particular features. Comparing a real map with the mental map can reveal our visual and perceptual biases.

MENTAL MAP

Most of us use visual thinking to some degree. Since we are not normally aware of it, we do not develop higher visual thinking skills. For example, in our minds, we carry a kind of map of our surrounding area in visual form, and we use it every day with a great deal of confidence even though we do not know the names of streets or block numbers. We do know the whereabouts of various objects and buildings through spatial perception. We find it hard to describe such a map in words, and we realize this when we try to give directions over the telephone to a first-time visitor. Direction giving becomes easier when it is in person, for that way gestures can be used as a part of visual communication. In doing so, we sometimes draw a crude map in a hurry to support our verbal information. A simple exercise of taking some time to record our mind's map of the surrounding area on a piece of paper and then comparing it with an actual map of that area can give us clues as to the level of visual perception, and such similar repeated exercises can improve our visual capability.

5

Graphic Tools for Visual Thinking

The natural and obvious medium for expressing visual thinking is graphic communication. Since it is the direct transfer of a mental picture or image, very little information is lost during such a transfer process. Graphic communication is multidimensional, as is visual thinking. Thus, it can depict the content of visual thought most accurately.

GRAPHIC REINFORCEMENT

Verbal communication, being linear in nature, becomes long, tedious, and often boring when trying to communicate visual thought. In such a situation, we feel the natural urge to reinforce our verbal communication with graphic communication, and, if such reinforcement is made, communication becomes clearer and more straightforward. Graphic communication also gives confidence to the communicator, for it sends feedback to him immediately.

It takes many words and sentences to describe a

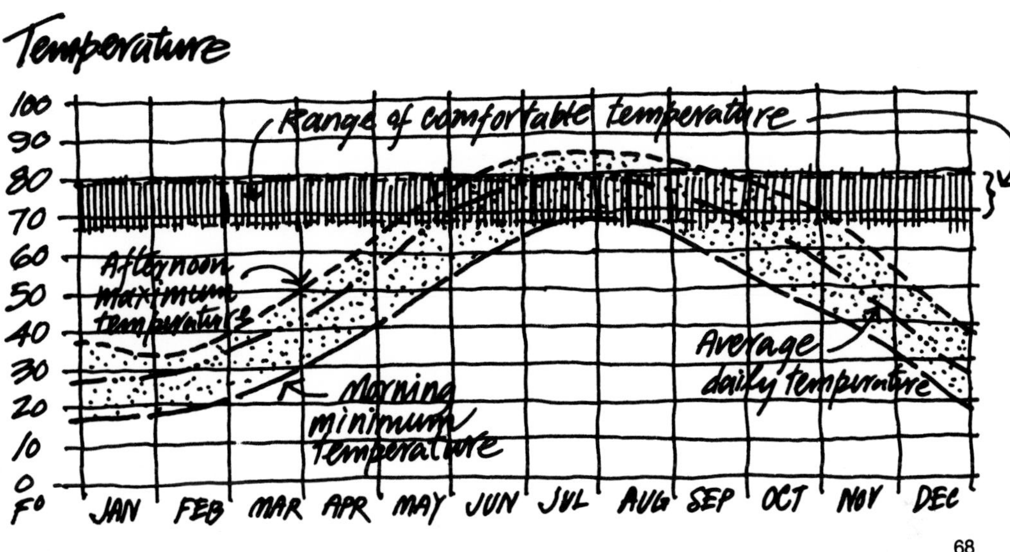

68

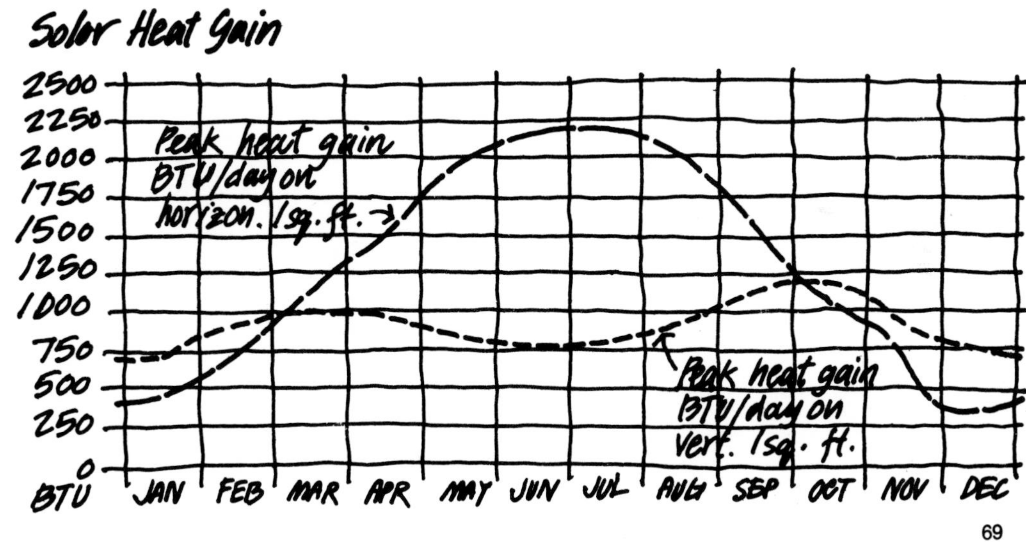

69

68–69
Graphs and charts are two-dimensional, and if they are added for reinforcement, they can significantly improve verbal communication, which is one-dimensional or linear.

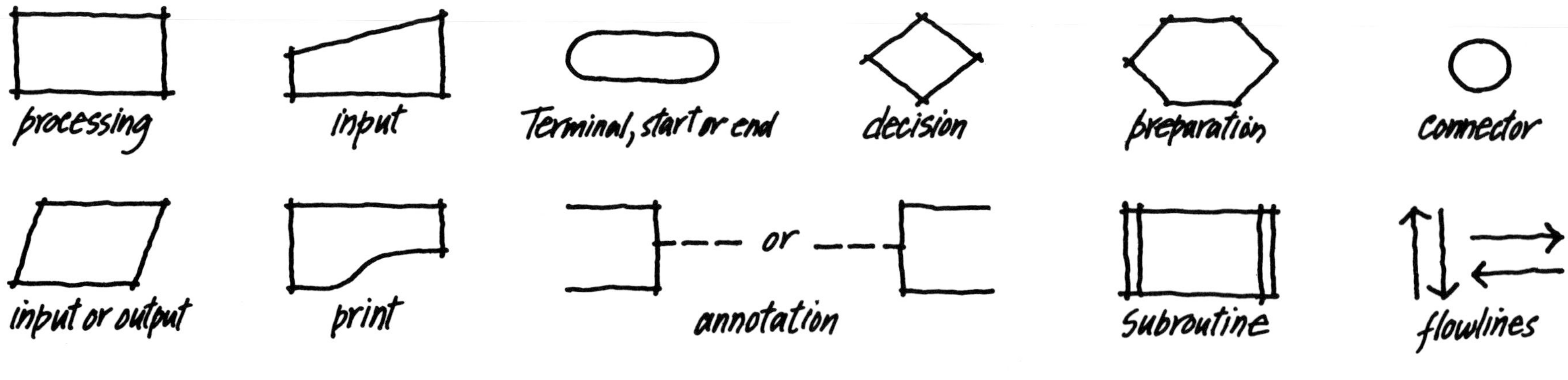

70
In computer science these graphic symbols are given specific meaning and are very effective visual tools in communicating an algorithm.

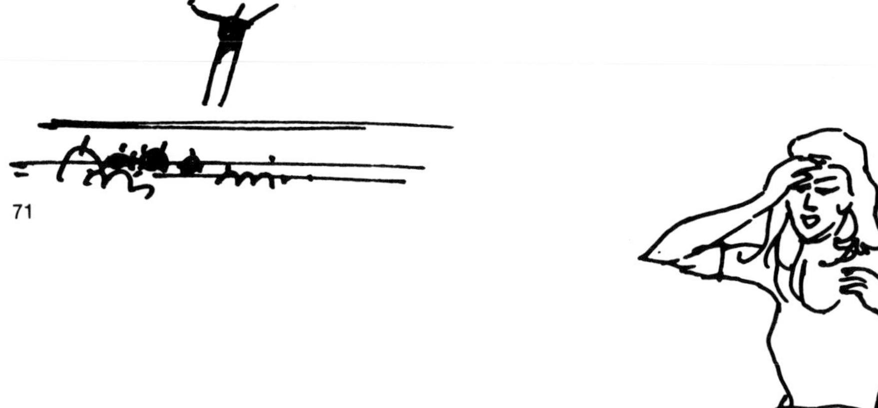

71

73

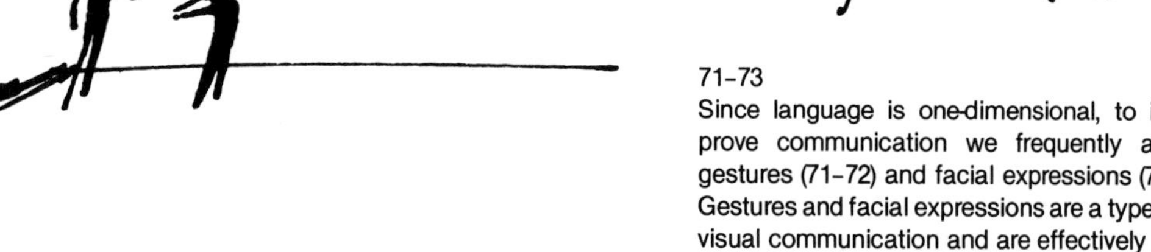

72

71–73
Since language is one-dimensional, to improve communication we frequently add gestures (71–72) and facial expressions (73). Gestures and facial expressions are a type of visual communication and are effectively articulated in sign language.

picture, and we do not grasp the whole picture until such a description is completed. Even then, our perception of the picture may be different than what is being communicated because our individual interpretations of the words are different. On the other hand, the same picture, when graphically communicated, can send a great deal of information almost at a glance.

Our information retrieval system also works at the visual level. As a matter of habit, we even make various eye movements during the information retrieval process. In fact, certain kinds of eye movement are associated with certain types of information retrieval. Since mental cataloging is in pictorial form, in the verbal communication of images, we use facial expressions as well as movement of the eyes, hands, and body to compensate for the information lost during transfer from the visual to the verbal level.

74–75
The mental picture of a cypress is an ideal version and may not be an exact picture of an individual specimen. Such an image plays an important role in the picture catalog of the mind and can be viewed as a kind of abstraction.

VISUAL ABSTRACTION

Our mind is continuously receiving visual stimuli, but it makes visual abstractions out of them. Abstraction is a process of simplification. We have seen many trees, but our mind has recorded only a few simplified versions of them, representing various types of trees. For example, the mental picture of a cypress is a simplified or ideal version of this species. This particular mental picture may not exactly resemble any individual cypress, but it represents all cypresses in the picture catalog of our mind. This kind of abstraction is a natural and continuous process and goes on in our mind for cars, houses, furniture, and everything else.

74

75

76–81
There can be various levels of abstraction. An abstraction of a tree may be made up of the light pattern (76) created by it or its characteristic lines (77). The branching of the tree (78) can be another level of abstraction, while representing only the main structure (79) is a higher abstraction. A still higher abstraction may reduce the tree to a symbol (80–81).

LEVELS OF ABSTRACTION

Visual abstraction can occur at various levels. We may have one level of abstraction representing all weeping willows or another level of abstraction representing all deciduous trees or all evergreens. We may have a still higher level of abstraction representing all trees. Thus, abstraction levels may range from very narrow to very broad.

Graphic communication occurs at one level of abstraction or another. Even a realistic drawing is a form of abstraction in the sense that it is removed from the actual object, which is capable of transmitting much more information and feeling than its

82
A realistic drawing of a tree is also a form of abstraction since to a certain degree it is removed from the actual object.

graphic form. Of course, diagrams, charts, graphs, etc., are higher levels of abstraction and are far removed from the actual objects, organizations, or systems.

GRAPHIC COMMUNICATION TYPES

The problem-solving process requires various levels of abstraction, and thus various types of graphic communication are needed; the type depends on the content of visual thought, the audience to whom it is communicated, and the purpose of such communication.

Functional diagrams, system or process diagrams, charts, graphs, etc., being of higher abstraction, are useful in communicating general or central concepts. They are normally used to explain a trend or the relationship between the parts and the whole. In these types of graphic abstractions, conflicts, problems, and inconsistencies that can otherwise be easily obscured are readily visible. Since they are

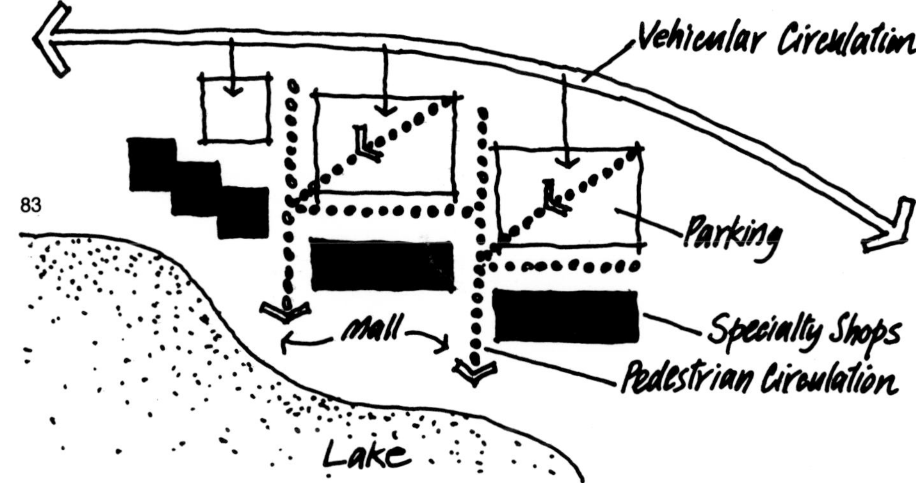

83
A conceptual diagram can be a two-dimensional abstraction and be effective in showing space utilization and circulation systems.

Circulation Core
84

Vertical Circulation:
2nd to 20th floors
21st to 40th floors
85

84–85
A diagrammatic plan (84) and section (85) can be combined to communicate a concept.

86
Flow charts can be effective in visualizing and identifying the critical path in a process.

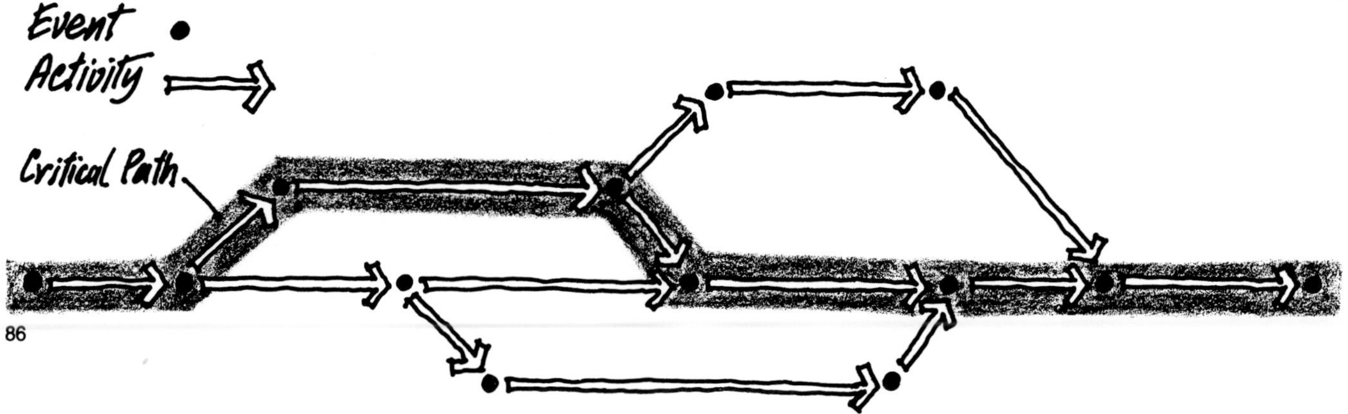

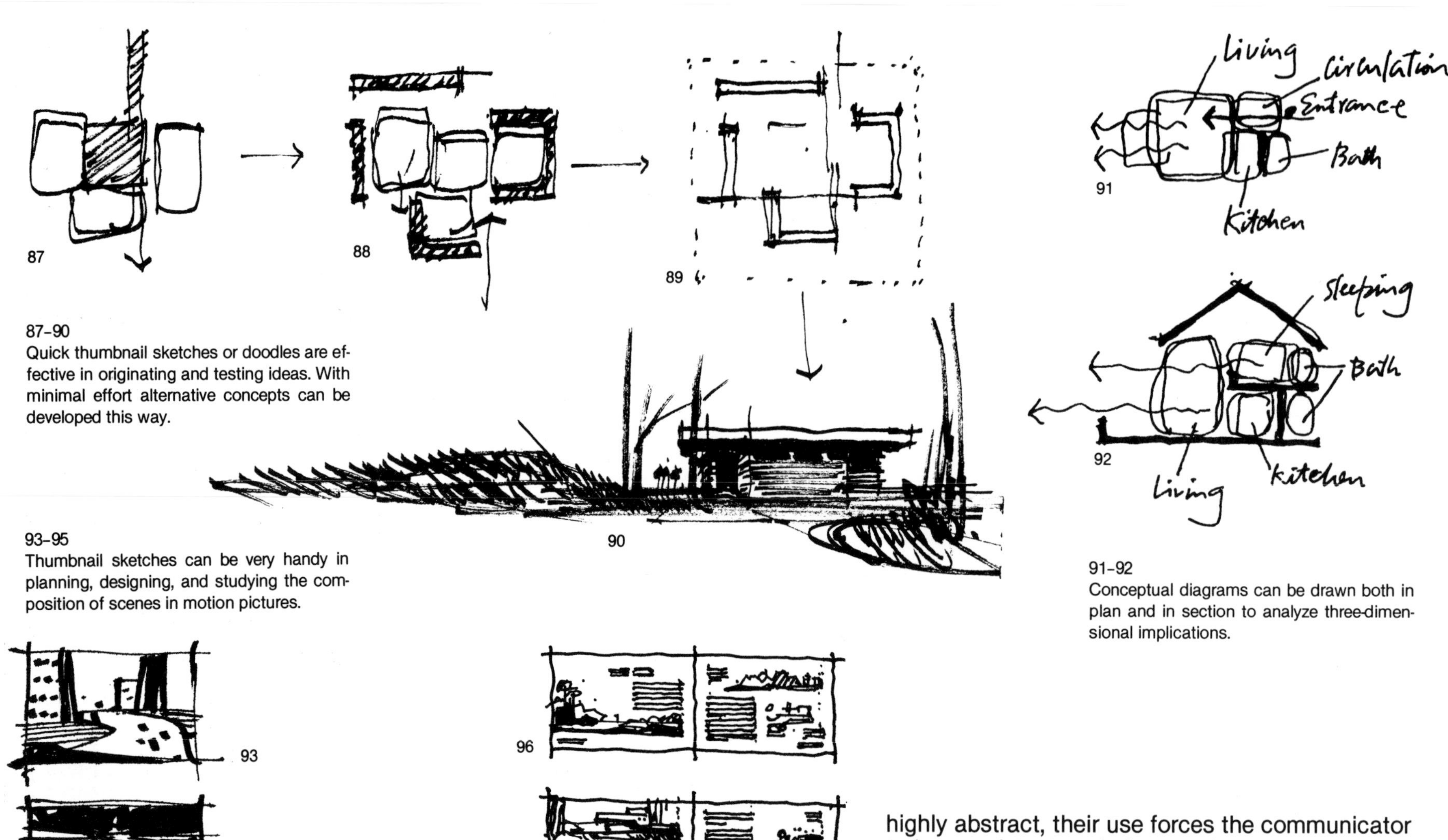

87–90
Quick thumbnail sketches or doodles are effective in originating and testing ideas. With minimal effort alternative concepts can be developed this way.

91–92
Conceptual diagrams can be drawn both in plan and in section to analyze three-dimensional implications.

93–95
Thumbnail sketches can be very handy in planning, designing, and studying the composition of scenes in motion pictures.

96–97
Initial tiny sketches used in the study of layout design can give quick feedback as to the quality of composition.

highly abstract, their use forces the communicator to be consistent and clear, and to make the communication direct and straightforward.

Architects' and designers' doodles are scribble-like drawings generated by the visual thought process. They are a kind of thinking aloud and thinking graphically. They are idea originators, thought stimulators, and are produced quickly. They are scribbles, bubbles, two-dimensional diagrams, or three-dimensional representations. They are what

98
Freehand sketches can be used to study topographical change and its implications upon the space relationship among natural and built objects on the land.

99–101
Freehand drawings are used in developing a plan for a townhouse unit. Grouping the units to form a building (99) offered an idea about possible shapes of the units. The circulation and functional requirements were transformed into a possible organization (100), which in turn crystallyzed into a tentative floor plan (101).

98

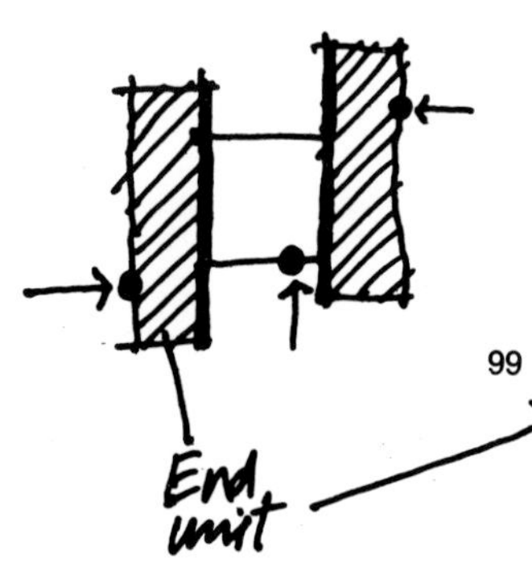

99

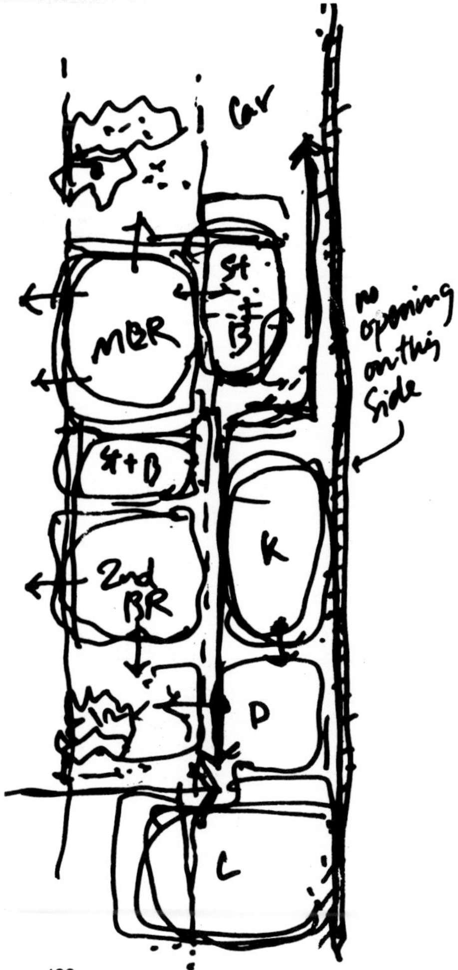

they are; they are doodles. They are a kind of direct contact with the visual self and multidimensional thought process.

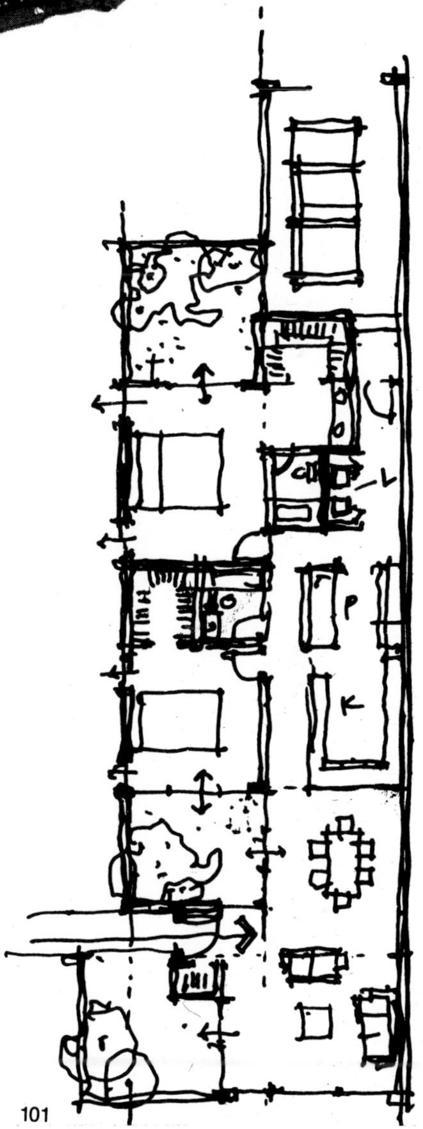

Freehand drawings are very useful in testing concepts or ideas to see whether they work. They can be in the form of bubble diagrams, plans, sections, elevations, top views, side views, oblique views, and perspective views. They are tentative and drawn very quickly. They are meant for the review process. Changes and modifications can be made on them

100

101

102

103

102–104
Freehand perspective sketches not only depict three-dimensional appearances, but also convey feeling, emotional quality, or mood, regardless of whether it is a design of a jacket (102), an exterior environment (103), or an interior (104).

104

by the designer himself or by others. A designer produces plenty of such drawings and sketches, and continuously reviews them until he is satisfied with the design and the design meets all criteria.

Making quick sketches such as perspective and oblique drawings of what the designed space or product will look like is important for several reasons. These sketches not only describe the physical appearance but also depict the atmosphere, essence, and feeling of the space or product. Three-dimensional sketches are capable of capturing these qualities, for they are direct transfers from visual imagination.

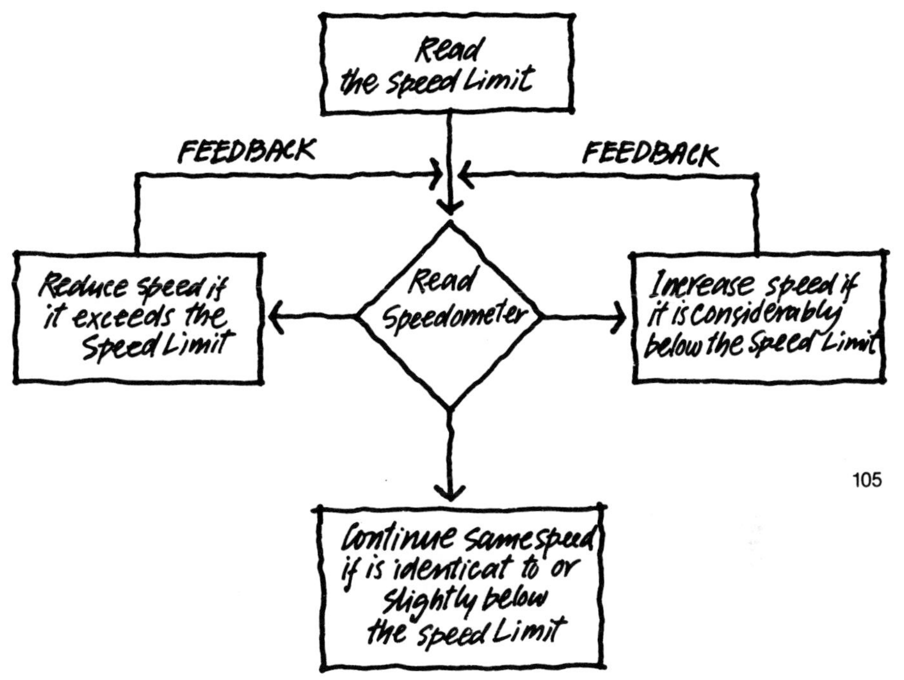

105

Graphic Communication as a Feedback Mechanism

Driving an automobile involves several feedback systems. Watching the speed of the cars that are ahead and along side, watching the speed limit, maintaining a certain speed on the highway, watching the stoplight signals, shifting gears in a standard car—each of these entails a feedback system, and each must work well for smooth driving. The

105–106
Watching the speed limit and maintaining speed accordingly involve a feedback system (105). Driving also involves other feedback systems (106).

106

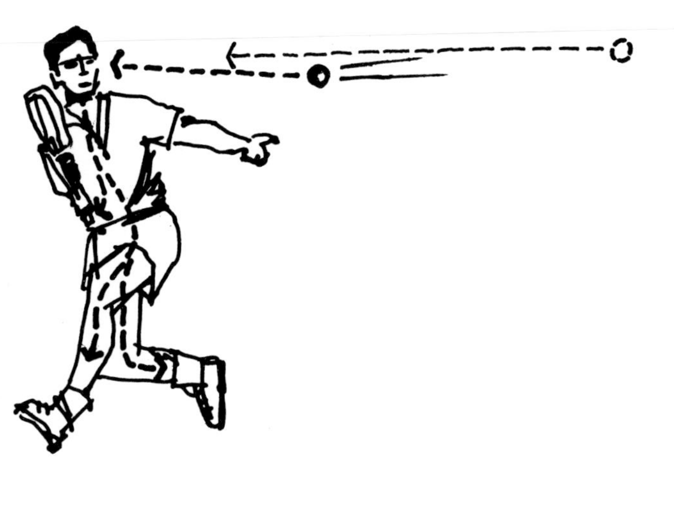

107–108
When a tennis player hits the ball or a baseball player catches the ball, he uses a feedback system in estimating its path. This enables him to continuously adjust his position and the position of the racquet or mit.

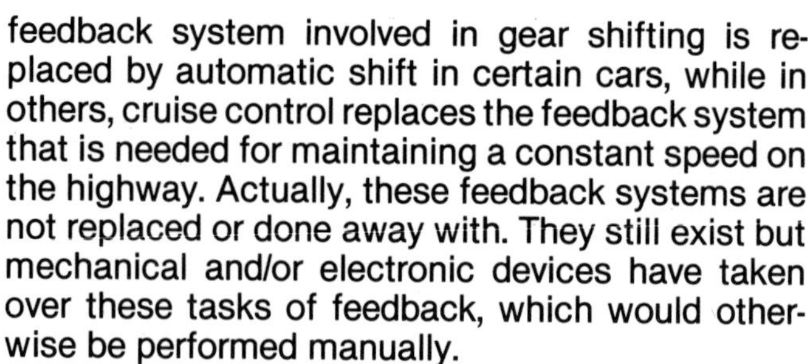

feedback system involved in gear shifting is replaced by automatic shift in certain cars, while in others, cruise control replaces the feedback system that is needed for maintaining a constant speed on the highway. Actually, these feedback systems are not replaced or done away with. They still exist but mechanical and/or electronic devices have taken over these tasks of feedback, which would otherwise be performed manually.

When a baseball player is catching the ball, he uses a feedback system. In such a situation, his eyes continously measure the angle, direction, and speed of the ball and give feedback to his brain in order to make appropriate changes in his position and the reach of his hand. On a windy day, his body feels the wind velocity and direction, and he makes the necessary corrections in estimating the path of the ball in the air.

In the mechanical and electronic world such as computer technology, any sophistication is associated with having a better feedback system. Sometimes, working out the appropriate feedback system becomes the most critical problem, and its resolution generally results in improvement.

CREATIVE PROCESS

Feedback mechanisms are cardinal to any creative process. Without them, the process is a static one and thus, with its progression, fails to account for new situations, new findings, and discoveries. In any creative process, all specific problems or decisions which it will confront at every step are unknown at the outset although we may have some ideas and direction about them. To make it creative, the process must be an open one, allowing for the flow of new information and appropriate adjustments. In a sense, a creative process is a learning process, learning new situations, new problems or new combinations of problems, and then responding to them accordingly. Thus, the response or resolution becomes appropriate, new, and unique. It is an evolving process, and that is the beauty of it.

GRAPHIC FEEDBACK

Graphic communication displays the thought process in a manner that can be perceived easily and immediately. It provides feedback both to the originator or designer himself, and to the user or client. Graphic feedback is very effective because it sends messages at the spatial or multidimensional level, which is the very nature of visual thinking.

A sketch, drawing, or diagram displays itself through numerous points at the same time. All these points together establish its unity. Its multidimensional nature avoids any boredom. Es-

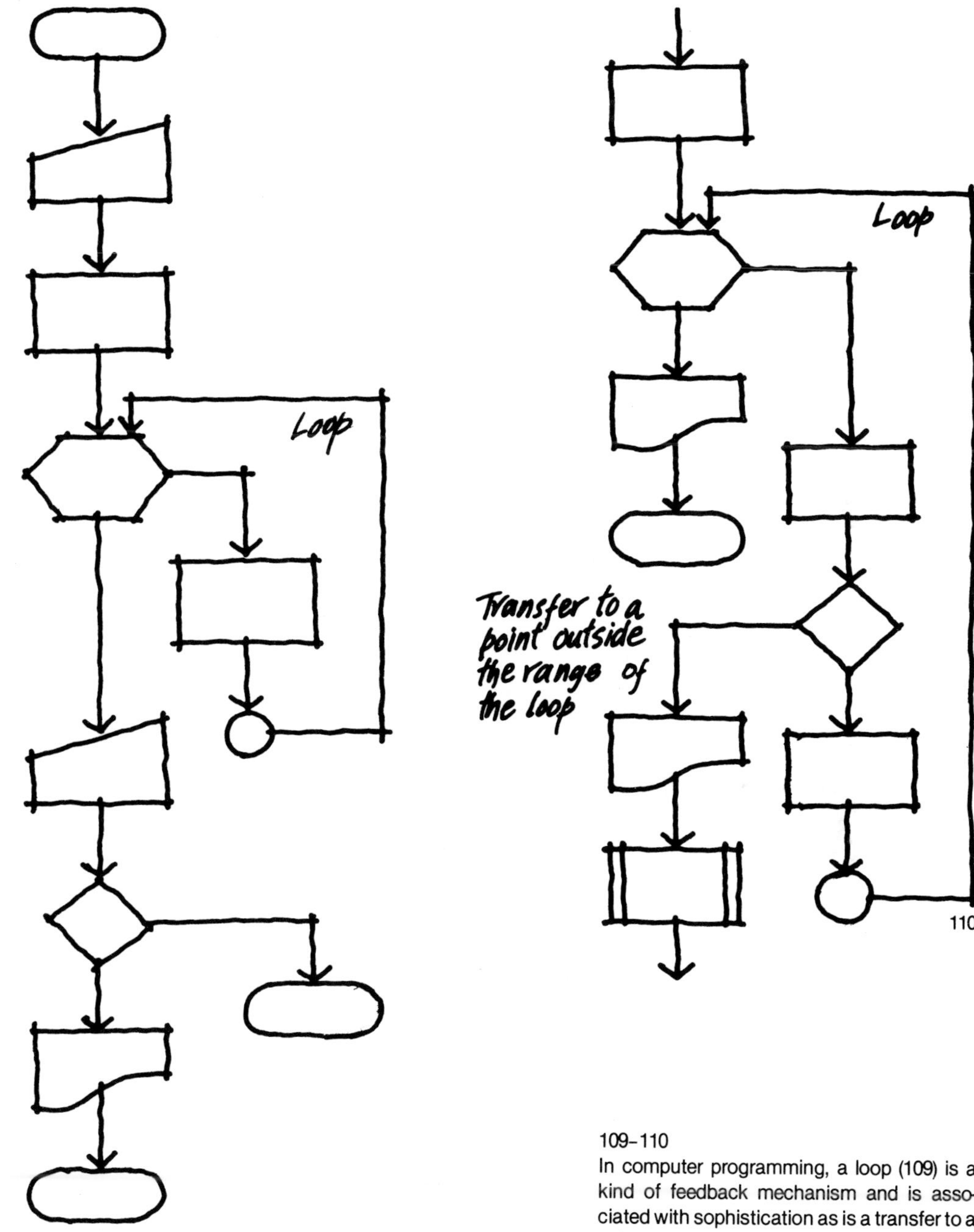

109–110
In computer programming, a loop (109) is a kind of feedback mechanism and is associated with sophistication as is a transfer to a point outside the loop (110).

111

111–113
Since a sketch (111) is not linear, one can begin reading it at almost any one of numerous points (112). However, we absorb information from the sketch in a random sequence (113) rather than from one side to the other. This allows the viewer the choice of sequence, and thus prevents any boredom.

112

113

sentially, one can start reading the drawing at any of these points. There is no specific starting point. This allows the viewer freedom to choose the vantage point in receiving information. His eyes can move freely through various points until it begins to make sense, which he does in a relaxed way.

FEEDBACK CYCLE

Inspiration from the brain makes the hand produce the drawing and thus creates the opportunity for the eyes to see and evaluate it. The evaluation process happens in the brain after receiving the information from the drawing through the eyes. At the end of the evaluation, the brain sends new information or inspiration through the hand, to change, modify, or redraw it, and thus, continues the feedback cycle. At the initial stage, what the brain sends as a message and what the hand draws, it is a tentative proposal. Whether it works, whether it has any conflicts or problems, or whether it is simply an impossibility is not yet fully known. It is a kind of adventure projecting into the world of imagination. Every such attempt is an exploration in the frontier of new ideas. It is at the fringe between the possible and the impossible, between rationality and irrationality, between the probable and improbable, between assurance and uncertainty.

Brain to hand, hand to drawing, drawing to eyes, and then to brain, this feedback cycle can be completed within seconds or even in a fraction of a second. As soon as the hand starts drawing, the feedback cycle also starts and begins to give continuous feedback during the process of drawing. Changes begin to occur already long before the sketch, drawing, or

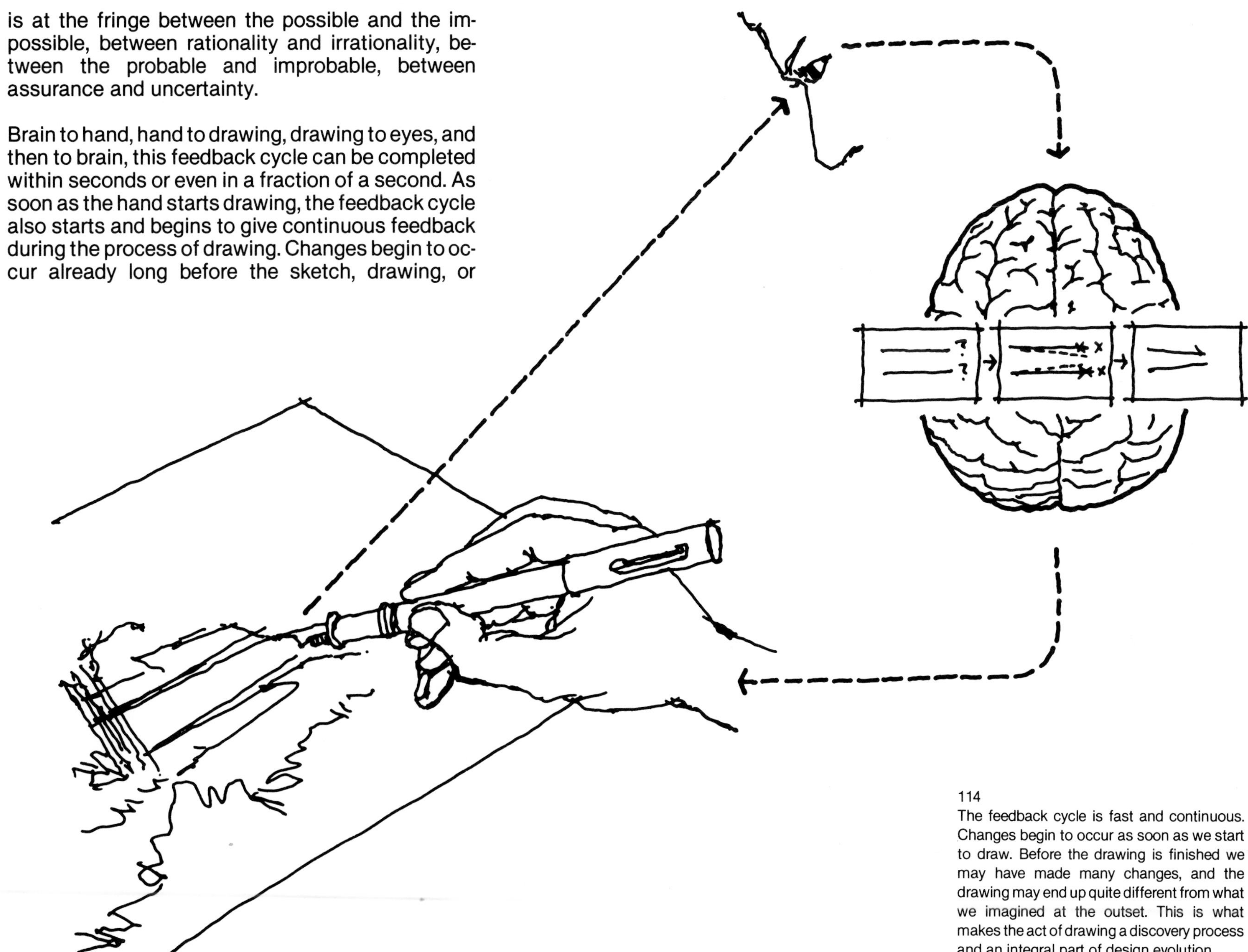

114
The feedback cycle is fast and continuous. Changes begin to occur as soon as we start to draw. Before the drawing is finished we may have made many changes, and the drawing may end up quite different from what we imagined at the outset. This is what makes the act of drawing a discovery process and an integral part of design evolution.

115
Graphic feedback is essential for design teams. It can improve fresh new ideas as well as trigger another series of new ideas in the minds of the team members from the imperfections, mistakes, or conflicts of the graphic presentation of one idea.

diagram is finished. With sufficient practice, this feedback mechanism can be internalized, and thus it can become a part of our intuition.

GRAPHIC FEEDBACK AND DESIGN TEAMS

In team situations, where various experts contribute toward a common design goal, graphic feedback serves as an important tool. Not only can fresh new ideas be improved by it, but often new ideas are triggered in the minds of team members from imperfections, mistakes, or conflicts in the graphic representation of one idea. Members of the team may be highly talented and expert in their respective areas, but unless there is clear communication among them, their efforts toward a design goal become futile. A team can be highly creative only when its members transmit and receive information effectively. To this end graphic feedback is very useful.

Part Three

Hemispheric Asymmetry and Problem Solving

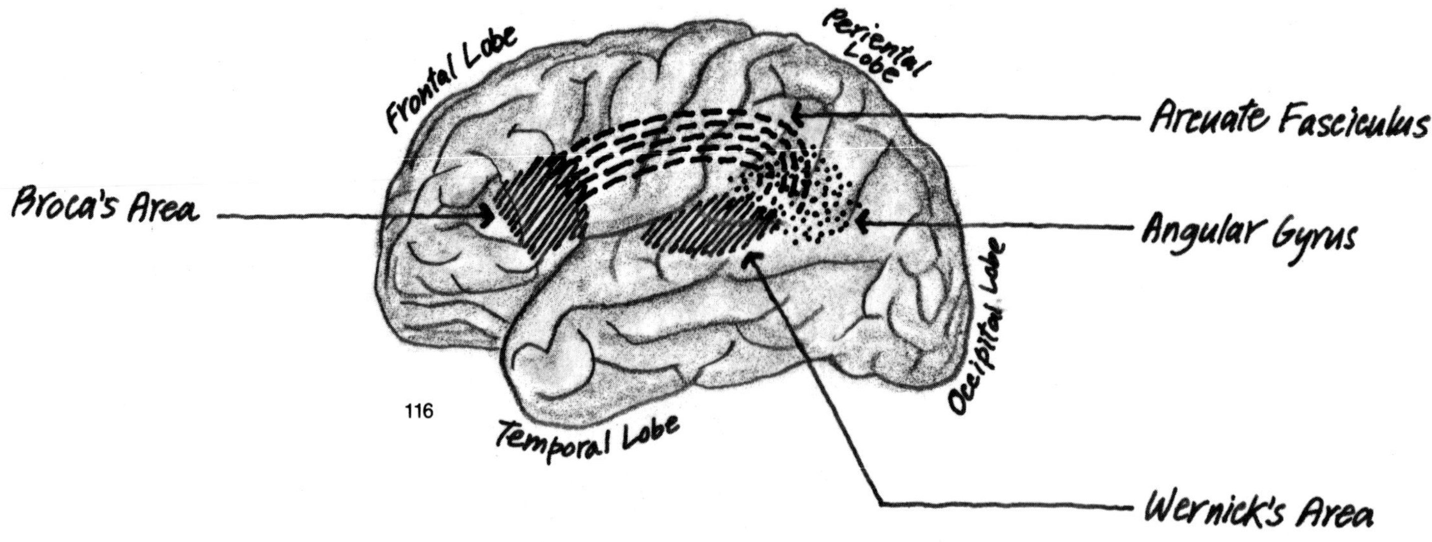
Frontal Lobe
Periental Lobe
Arcuate Fasciculus
Broca's Area
Angular Gyrus
Occipital Lobe
Temporal Lobe
Wernick's Area

7

New Frontier in Brain Research

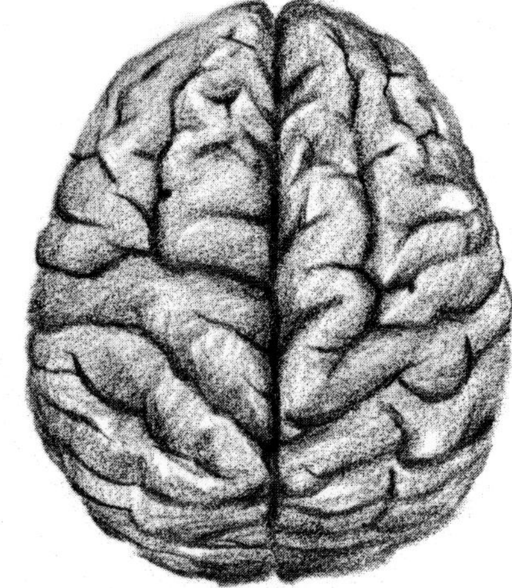

117

It is interesting to note that the 1981 Nobel Prize in Physiology/Medicine was shared by three scientists for research on the human brain. They are Roger Sperry at the California Institute of Technology, and David Hubel and Torsten Wiesel of Harvard University. During the last twenty years their work has prompted major revisions in the understanding of the human brain. The Nobel Prize committee cited Sperry for his contribution in "extracting the secrets from both hemispheres of the brain and demon-

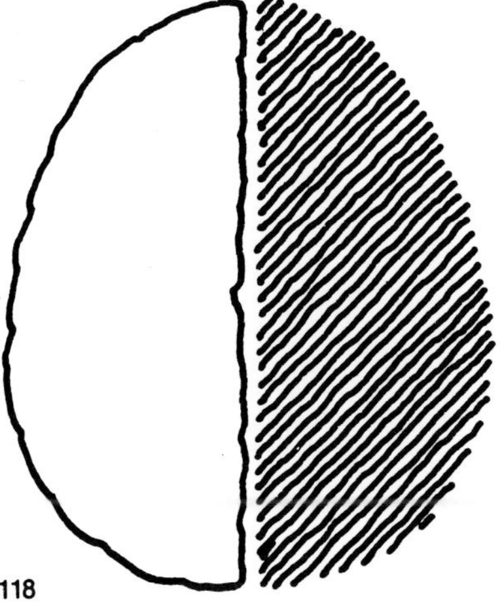
118

116
In the majority of people, the primary language region is located in the left cerebral cortex. Broca's area is responsible for the production of speech, Wernick's area is responsible for its comprehension and organization, and arcuate fasciculus maintains coordination between these two areas.

117–118
The human brain consists of two halves, right and left hemispheres (117), and each of them is highly specialized. Recent research shows that the right hemisphere (118) performs many higher functions and is superior to the left in many ways, such as in concrete thinking, spatial consciousness, and comprehension of comlex relationships.

strating that they are highly specialized and also that many higher functions are centered in the right hemisphere." The committee also pointed out his research for bringing out new scientific knowledge that the right hemisphere "is clearly superior to the left in many respects, especially regarding the capacity for concrete thinking, spatial consciousness and comprehension of complex relationships." In recent years, the work of these scientists has triggered research by many other scientists in related areas, and thus a whole new expanse of information is becoming available with regard to the cognitive aspect of the human brain.

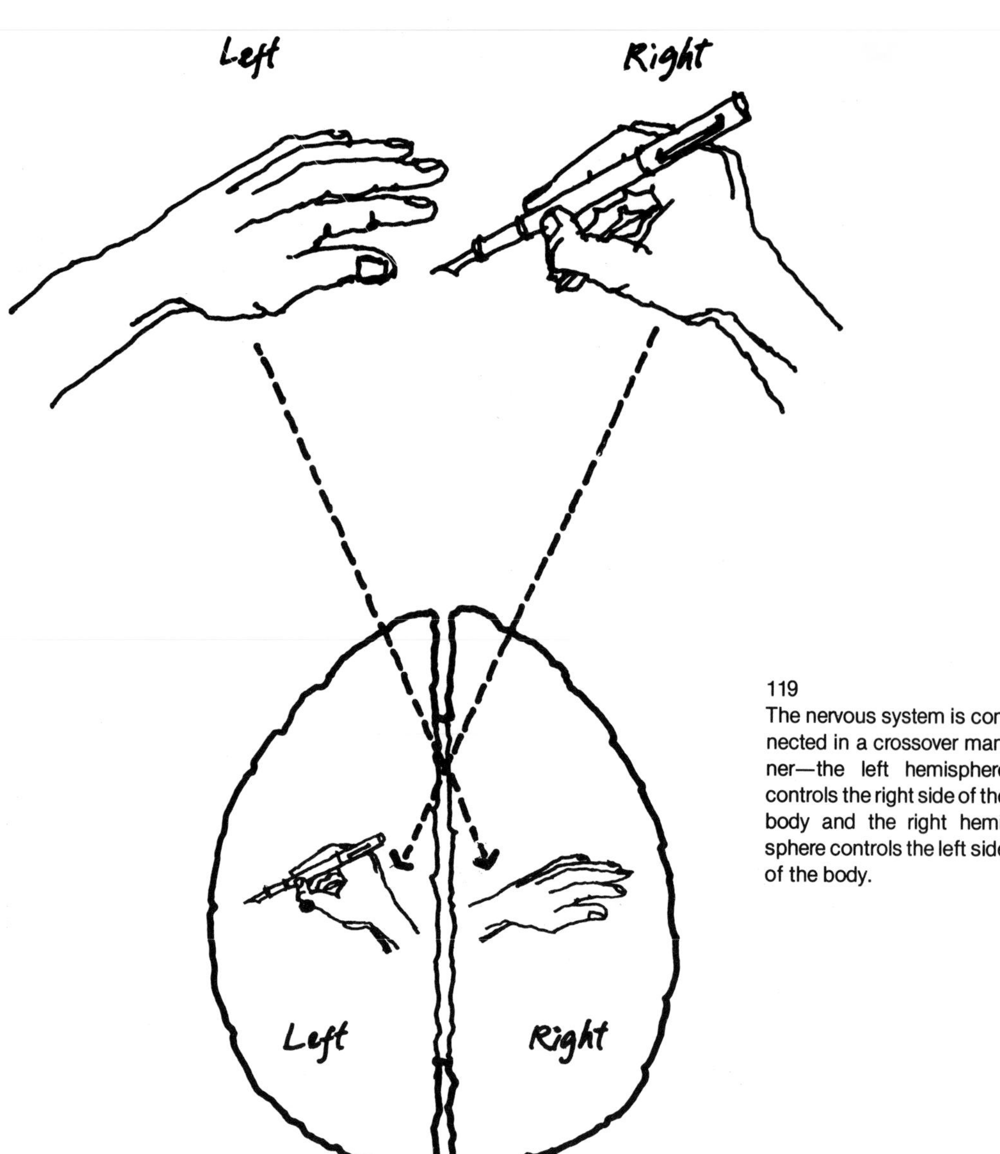

119
The nervous system is connected in a crossover manner—the left hemisphere controls the right side of the body and the right hemisphere controls the left side of the body.

THE BRAIN HEMISPHERES

The human brain consists of two halves, the left hemisphere and the right hemisphere, and they are connected by the corpus callosum, a bundle of interconnecting nerve fibers. Our nervous system is connected in a crossover manner, the left hemisphere controlling the right side of the body and the right hemisphere controlling the left side of the body. For example, the right hand is connected with the left hemisphere and the left hand with the right hemisphere.

In the majority of individuals, i.e., 90 to 99% of right-handed individuals and 50 to 70% of left-handed individuals, the left hemisphere is the seat of language-related functions. This was known to scientists for about a 150 years. Such knowledge became evident mainly from brain injury cases of unilateral damage. For example, damage to the left side of the brain was associated with loss of speech in the majority of cases.

THE OLD VIEW

Since language functions are connected with logical thinking and reasoning, nineteenth-century scientists theorized that the left hemisphere was the major or dominant one, whereas, the right hemisphere was the minor one, subordinate to the former. This view was held as true for decades. Our education, especially in the West and many parts of the modern East where western influence has permeated, is centered around language, reasoning, and analytic skills. Thus, through a kind of cultural conditioning, we attribute advanced qualities and extremely high cognitive values to the left hemisphere, which houses those skills. On the other hand, the right hemisphere was thought to be less advanced, mute, and endowed with capabilities of lesser significance.

NEW RESEARCH

In the 1940s, it was discovered that surgical division of the corpus callosum, the connecting cable between the hemispheres, can reduce the severity and frequency of epileptic seizures in patients for whom other measures have failed. Thus, a group of patients went through surgical division of the corpus callosum, known as commissurotomy. Commissurotomy patients (split-brain patients), in contrast to patients having unilateral brain damage, have two relatively normal hemispheres. The ability to test the hemispheres separately provided a new opportunity to better understand their functional differences. Experiments conducted by A. J. Akelaitis during the 1940s were disappointing in that they showed no significant difference between split-brain patients and normal subjects. Such failure, as discovered afterwards, was mainly due to inadequacies in the testing procedures. Later, it was established that the role of the corpus callosum is to maintain inter-hemisphere communication, i.e., to transmit infor-

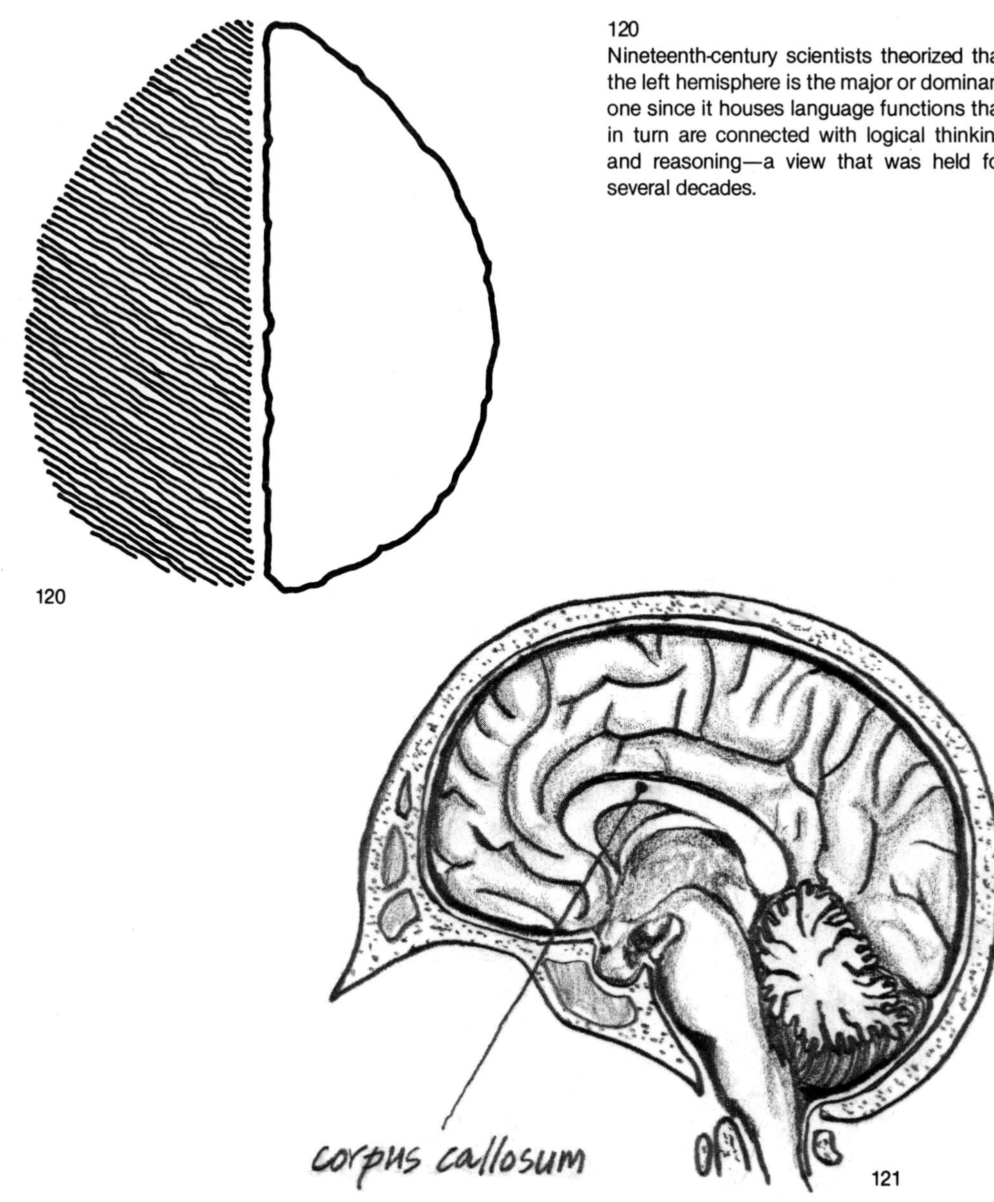

120
Nineteenth-century scientists theorized that the left hemisphere is the major or dominant one since it houses language functions that in turn are connected with logical thinking and reasoning—a view that was held for several decades.

121
The two halves of the brain are connected by the corpus callosum, a bundle of interconnecting fibers.

mation and memory between the hemispheres of the brain. However, its surgical division still allows the hemispheres to function independently. Through highly sophisticated tests in Sperry's laboratory, it was discovered that although there are

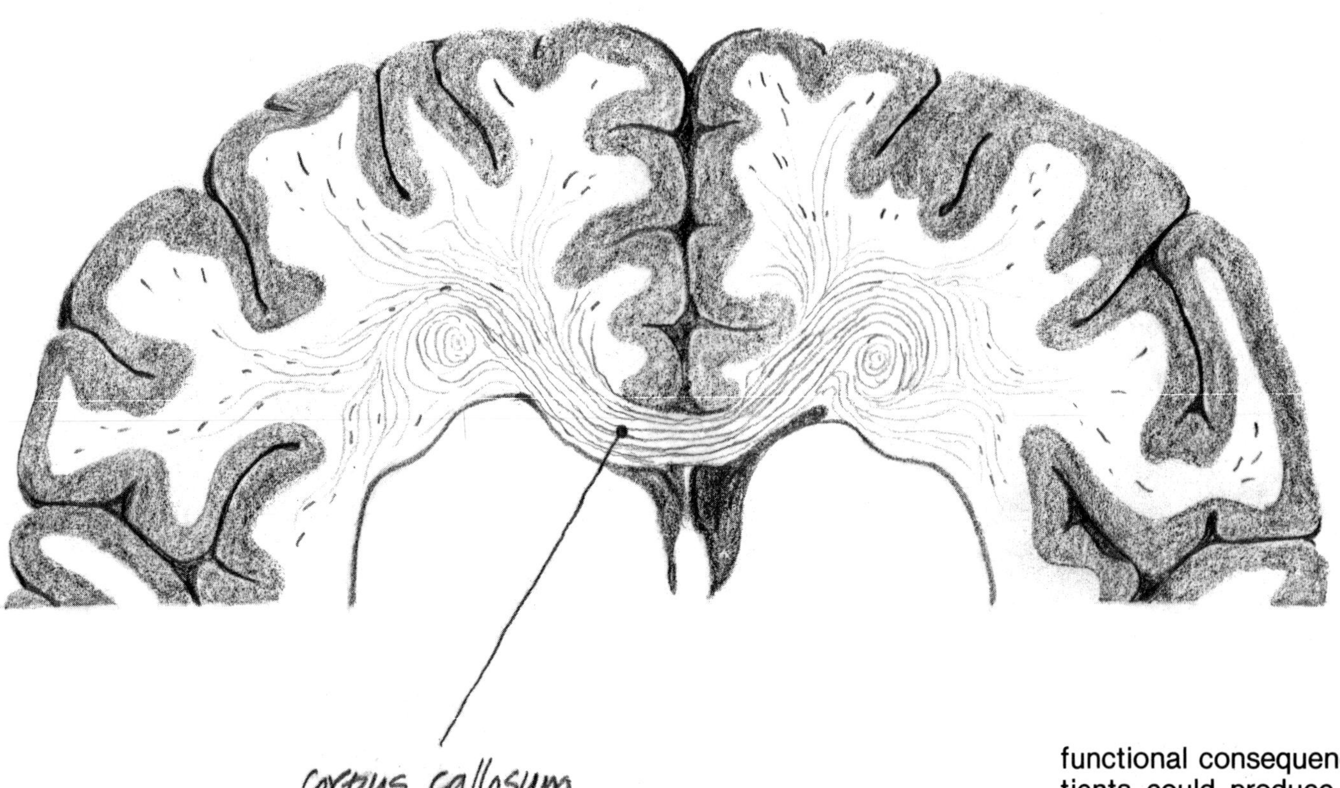

122
Commissurotomy is the surgical division of the corpus callosum, the connecting cable between the brain hemispheres. Split-brain patients (commissurotomy patients), having two relatively normal but disconnected hemispheres, provided an opportunity to understand the functional differences between the brain halves.

functional consequences of commissurotomy, patients could produce essentially normal behavior patterns through a variety of mechanisms. Experiments reveal that each hemisphere specializes in a different type of thinking, and both types are highly cognitive.

SPLIT-BRAIN EXPERIMENTS

Sperry's and other scientists' research with split-brain patients reveals various interesting facts about the cognitive aspects of each brain hemisphere. These findings are of special significance to the fields of graphic communication and problem solving, and how the two fields relate to each other.

In one experiment, the subject was asked to gaze at the midpoint of a screen. Then two different images were flashed on the screen, one on each side of the midpoint, i.e., one within each of the subject's right and left visual fields. The projection of the images was done very quickly so that the subject could not move his eyes to scan the images using both visual fields. Thus, each brain hemisphere received a different image; the right hemisphere received the image flashed on the left visual field, and the left hemisphere received the image flashed on the right visual field.

In one example, a picture of a spoon was projected on the left visual field and a picture of a knife on the right. When the subject was asked to name the object, he answered, "knife." But when he was requested to grasp the object with his left hand from a group of items hidden from his view, the subject picked up a spoon.

In a similar example, when a dollar sign was projected on the left visual field and a question mark on the right, the subject responded in the same peculiar way. When he was asked to draw with his left hand what he had just seen on a paper without

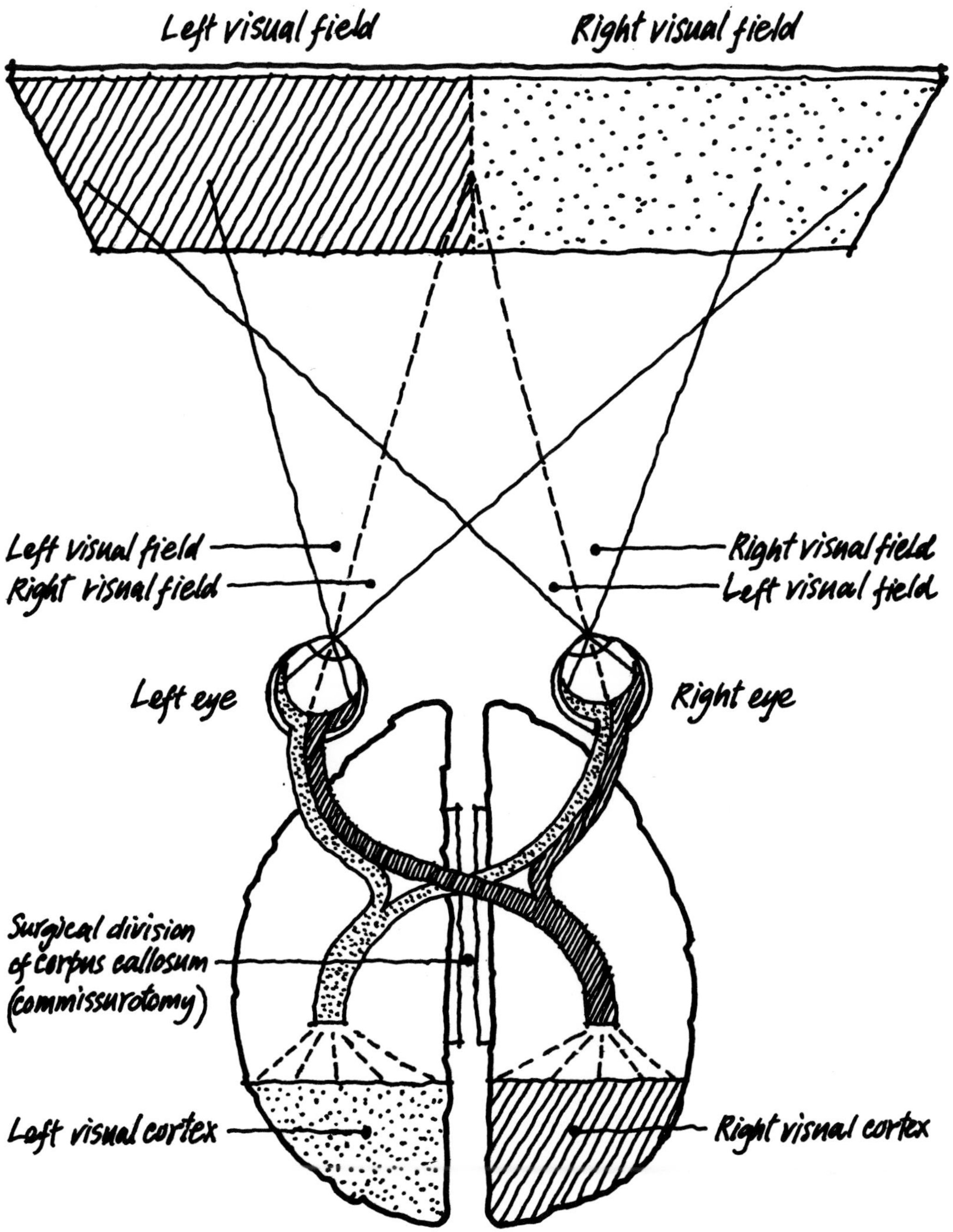

123
Each eye has two visual fields, right and left. Information from the right visual fields of both eyes is received by the left hemisphere while information from the left visual fields of both eyes is received by the right hemisphere.

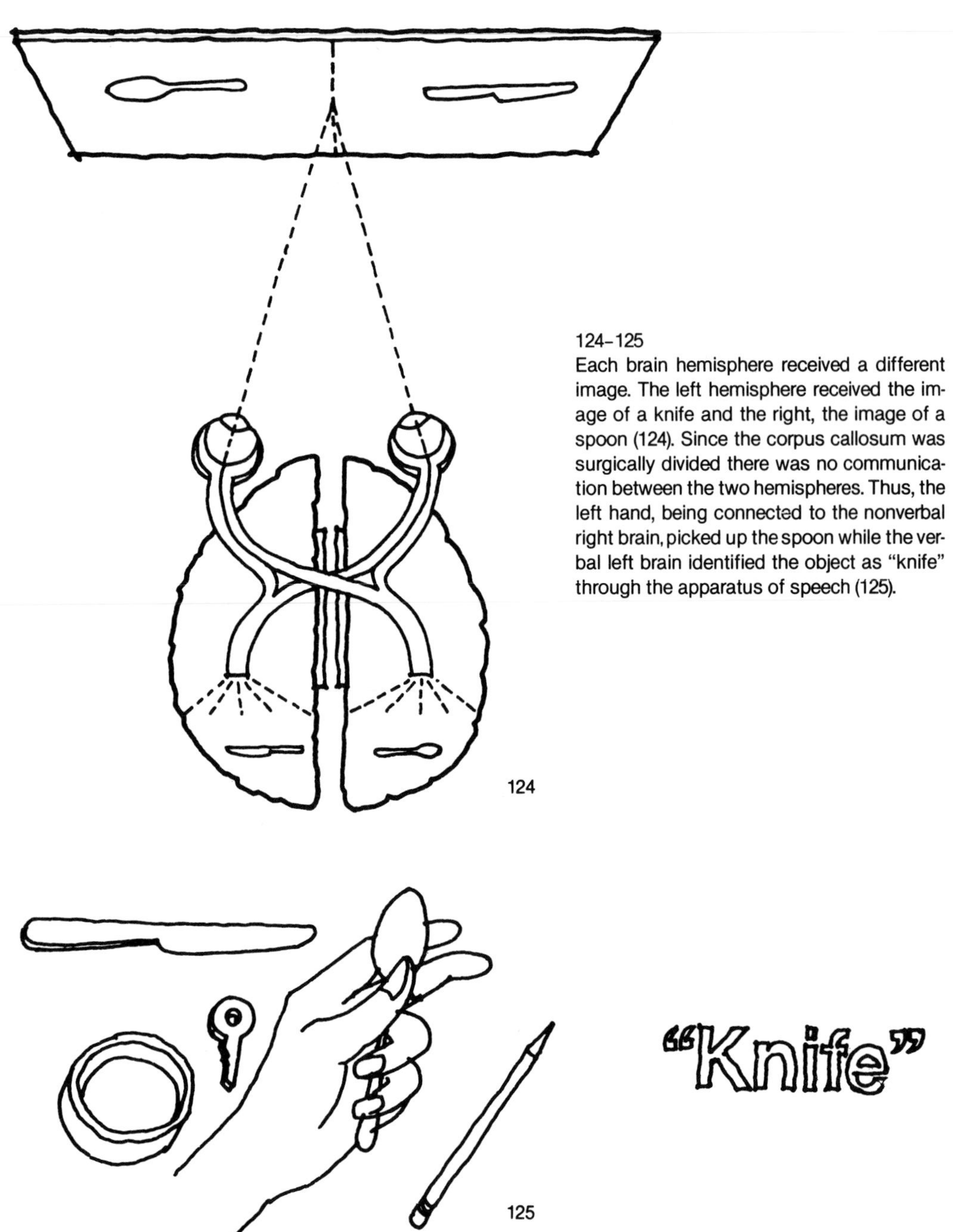

124–125
Each brain hemisphere received a different image. The left hemisphere received the image of a knife and the right, the image of a spoon (124). Since the corpus callosum was surgically divided there was no communication between the two hemispheres. Thus, the left hand, being connected to the nonverbal right brain, picked up the spoon while the verbal left brain identified the object as "knife" through the apparatus of speech (125).

looking, he drew a dollar sign. But when he was asked to name what he had drawn, he replied, "a question mark."

The explanation of this peculiarity is that the language hemisphere recorded information different from what the spatial hemisphere recorded because each hemisphere received a different message from its respective visual field. The verbal hemisphere (the left in the majority of individuals) recorded the knife or the question mark while the spatial hemisphere recorded the spoon or the dollar sign. Since, in these patients, the corpus callosum had been surgically divided, there was no transfer of information or communication between the two hemispheres. Each hemisphere "learned" through its own mode of learning. Thus, the left hand, which is connected with the right hemisphere, could identify the object or image by tactile inspection with respect to shape and form, or by drawing only the information which was stored in the right hemisphere while being ignorant of what was stored in "label" form in the left hemisphere. But when the apparatus of speech was used to identify the object or image, the verbal left hemisphere came forward with the name or "label" while being ignorant of what was stored in "spatial" form in the right hemisphere.

Other experiments with split-brain patients confirm that the right hemisphere is superior in spatial relation tasks. The two hemispheres also employ different strategies in problem solving. While the right hemisphere can easily distinguish between choices having more visual differentiation, the left hemisphere performs better when choices are easier to describe verbally.

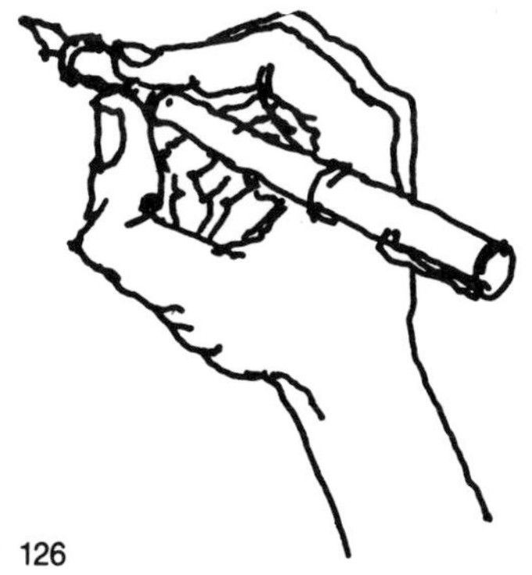

126

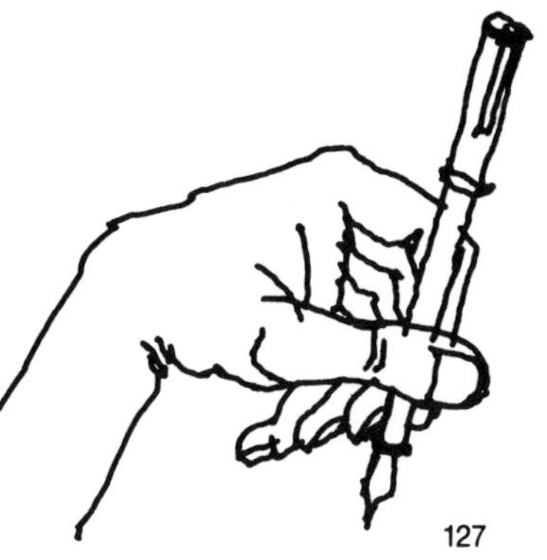

127

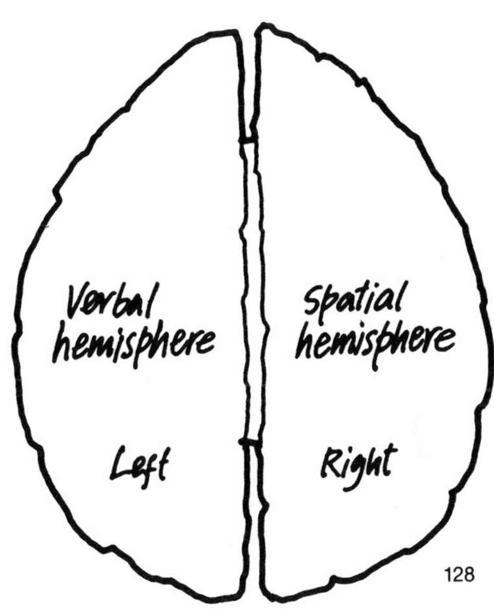

128

Two Cognitive Worlds

As we have seen before, in the majority of individuals, the left hemisphere specializes in language functions, and the right, in spatial tasks. In the remainder of individuals, cerebral lateralization is reversed, i.e., in them the right hemisphere houses language functions, and the left, spatial capability. Interesting research by Jerre Levy at the University of Chicago reveals a quick way to identify such cerebral lateralization among individuals: The language hemisphere is on the side opposite that of the writing hand in individuals who use the normal or noninverted hand position in writing. For those who use the inverted position to write, the language hemisphere is on the same side as the writing hand. Thus, for those right-handers who do not invert the hand position and those left-handers who do, the left hemisphere is the verbal one. Likewise, for those left-handers who use the noninverted position and those right-handers who use the inverted position, the verbal hemisphere is the right one. However, for the sake of convenience in our discussion, I will

126–128
The position of the writing hand can indicate the individual's hemispheric specialization. For those right-handers who use a normal or noninverted hand position (126) and those left-handers who use an inverted hand position (127), the left hemisphere is the verbal one (128).

refer to the left hemisphere as the language hemisphere since this is usually the case.

HEMISPHERE SPECIALIZATION

The brain hemispheres differ not so much in what they perform, but rather in their manner of thinking. The left hemisphere's approach is sequential, doing one thing at a time. It is linear and uses labels or names to keep track of things. Its way of knowing is through analytic, logical, and deductive processes. It employs a step-by-step, methodical strategy because it can store and retrieve only one item at a time, and it does so through its labeling system. Its syntatic faculty is a natural extension of such sequential capability.

On the other hand, the right hemisphere employs a holistic approach. It can perform parallel processing of information. It synthesizes, understands metaphoric relationships, and makes leaps of insight. Its perception is intuitive, spatial, and multidimensional. Its way of knowing is through gestalt. It has been suggested that it may be the seat of the "unconscious" as described by Sigmund Freud.

Recent experiments with split-brain patients show that the right hemisphere can also understand simple spoken or written words, but it has profound difficulty with the syntatical aspect of language. It is suggested that although the right hemisphere can derive meaning from spoken words, it does so through unanalyzed whole and acoustic gestalt. Its perception of language is very different from the syntactical analysis and understanding that the left hemisphere performs efficiently. The difference lies in how the hemispheres go about processing information. Certain nonlinguistic capabilities of the left brain also suggest similar conclusions. In processing pictorial information, the left hemisphere looks

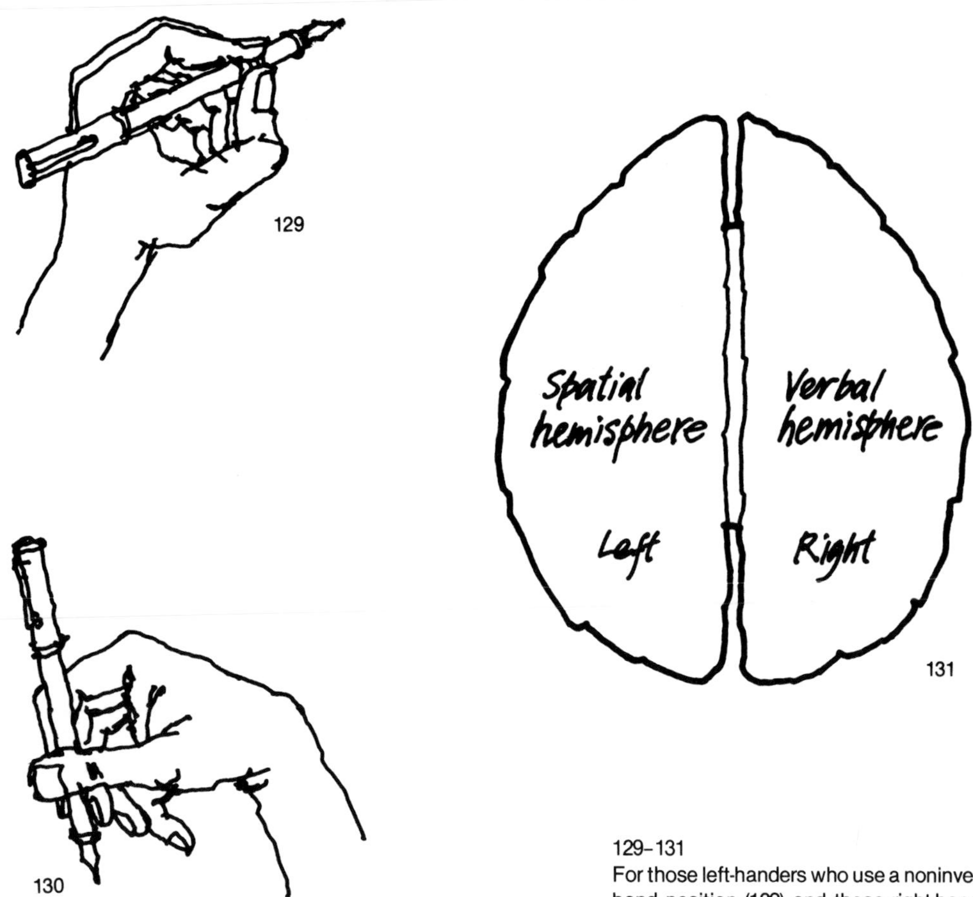

129–131
For those left-handers who use a noninverted hand position (129) and those right-handers who use an inverted hand position (130), the right hemisphere is the verbal one (131).

for distinctive features that can be verbally labeled, whereas the right hemisphere looks for congruity so that the stimuli can be understood as a whole. If the pictorial stimuli are a chain pattern, the left brain finds the task an easy one, which confirms its cognitive distinction with regard to sequential processing.

TWO COGNITIVE STYLES

The fundamental difference between the brain hemispheres is in their cognitive styles. They resemble two different streams of consciousness. Perhaps this is why, over the centuries, many philosophers have referred to the dual nature of the human being. In our everyday lives, we confront situations where something makes sense logically but our intuition or gut feeling senses otherwise. What actually happens is this: The left hemisphere accepts verbal and logical stimuli in order to make out the meaning while the right hemisphere makes parallel processing of clues from which it seeks the wholeness or gestalt. The conflict arises when these two streams of consciousness receive two opposing or different readings from the same situation. You have probably confronted situations when you went to someone for help, and the person sounded (verbal stimuli to the left brain) very helpful but the gestures, facial expression, and other nonverbal clues gave you the feeling (gestalt to the right brain) that the person really did not want to help you.

Since in the normal human brain, the corpus callosum is intact, an average person can maintain a sense of unity in spite of having two separate streams of consciousness. Interconnecting fibers of the corpus callosum enable communication between the brain halves. In a given situation, each hemisphere processes information suitable to its

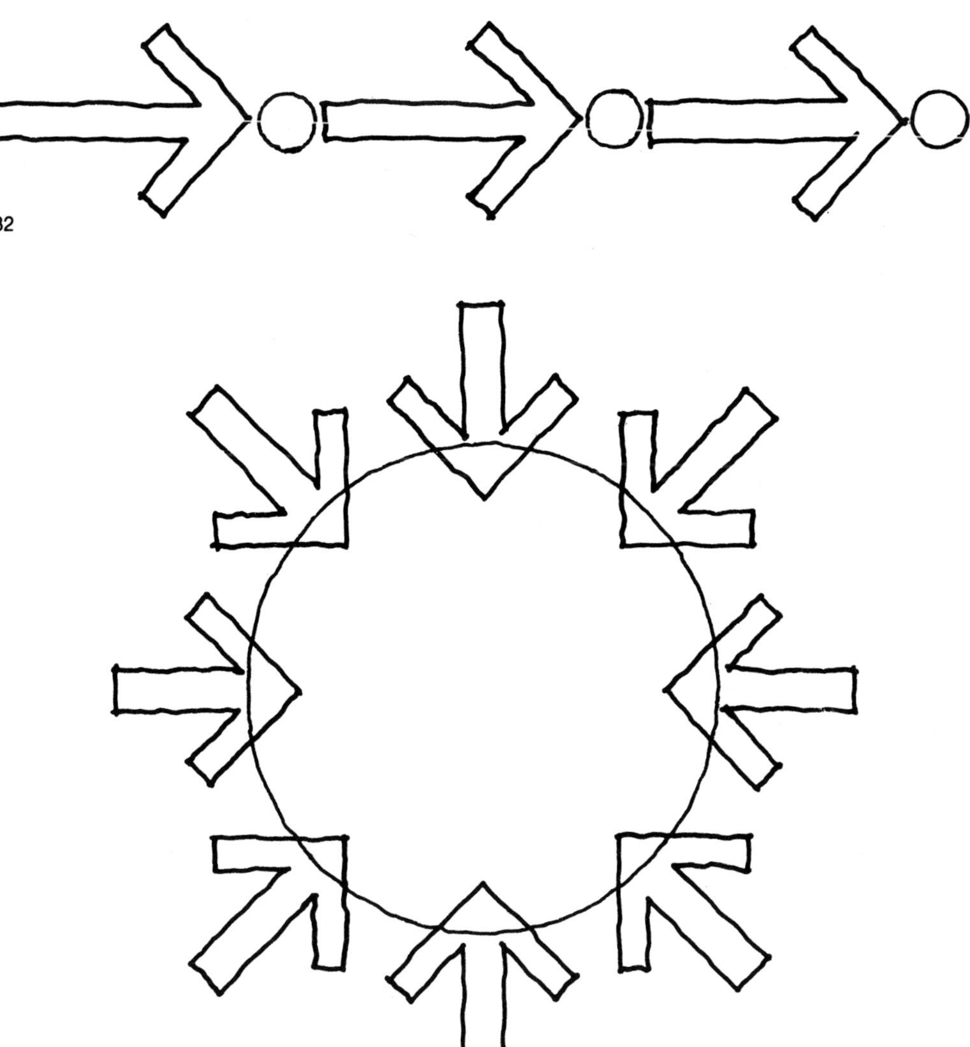

132–133
The left hemisphere's approach is linear and sequential (132), whereas the right hemisphere simultaneously processes information and seeks wholeness or gestalt (133).

Verbal
Logical
Linear
Temporal
Abstract
Methodical
Sequential
Syntactic
Numerical
Directed

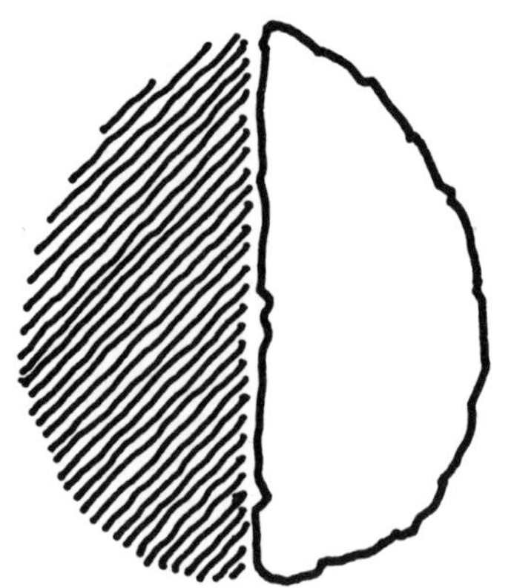

134
Certain adjectives can be attributed to the left hemisphere's approach to problems.

style. Sometimes, the left hemisphere, having the most training in the majority of individuals, tries to dominate and take over the task. Thus, in many situations, the right hemisphere is not even given the chance to utilize its potential.

Let us compare some of the specific differences in the modes employed by the left and right hemispheres in information processing:*

Left Hemisphere	**Right Hemisphere**
Uses verbal labels, words, definitions, and descriptions.	Uses mental images and introspective projections.
Uses logic and syllogistic deductions. Makes convergent conclusions.	Uses intuition, feelings, and visual clues. Requires no reasoning basis.
Takes a linear approach to problems. Looks for chain patterns and linked ideas.	Takes a holistic approach to problems. Seeks the overall pattern and gestalt.
Has sense of time. Employs successive and temporal order.	Has no sense of time but rather of space. Employs spatial order.

* Author's comparison modified after Joseph E. Bogen's "Some Educational Aspects of Hemispheric Specialization" in *UCLA Educator,* Spring 1975 and Betty Edwards' *Drawing on the Right Side of the Brain,* 1979.

Makes abstractions and reductions. Uses symbols.

Makes part-by-part analysis. Employs step-by-step methodical approach.

Sequentially processes information.

Uses syntactic analysis and relationships.

Uses numbers and counting.

Directed in approach. Processes relatively familiar information.

Perceives things as they are. Thinks in concrete terms.

Makes synthesis by putting parts into a workable or harmonious whole.

Simultaneously possesses information.

Uses metaphoric analysis and relationships.

Uses analogical relationships.

Free in approach. Can process relatively unfamiliar information.

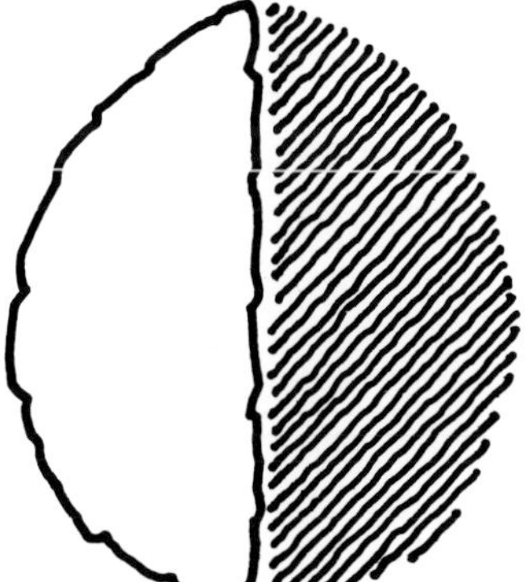

Imaginal
Intuitive
Holistic
Spatial
Concrete
Synthetic
Symultaneous
Metaphoric
Analogical
Free

DESIGN AND HEMISPHERIC SPECIALIZATION

The right hemisphere's ability to perceive form and spatial relationships is what helps us to draw. As we have seen, the capability to make holistic observations, synthesize parts into a workable whole, comprehend visual metaphor, and deal with the unfamiliar also belongs to the same hemisphere. Thus, it is deeply linked with our problem-solving faculty, especially if the problem is spatial in nature. Architects, landscape architects, interior designers, city planners, painters, sculptors, graphic artists, il-

135
Certain adjectives can be attributed to the right hemisphere's approach to problems.

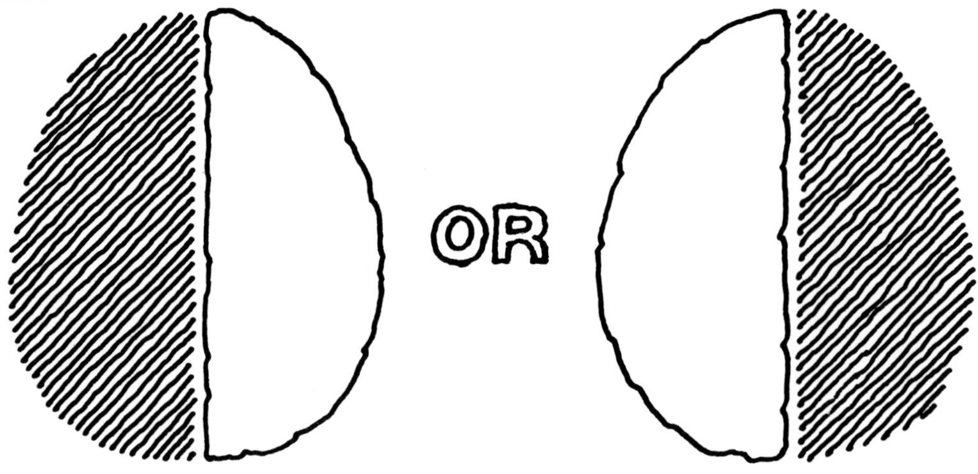

136
A hemisphere's imagined—rather than real —capability is what greatly influences whether it will dominate the other hemisphere. Thus cultural aspects play an important role in hemispheric dominance. Since our educational system is mostly geared to language-related functions, the left hemisphere seems to dominate our thought process. Balance between both hemispheres is ideal.

lustrators, and designers of furniture, garment, household or electronic products, office equipment, or theatrical sets, all deal with space and spatial manipulation in some form or other. Thus, use of the potentials of the right side of the brain is extremely important in the act of design. To draw with the aid of the right hemisphere is to be in touch with the spatial self, and this, then, leads to the development of its potentials.

HEMISPHERIC DOMINANCE

Since, in the majority of people, the verbal left hemisphere receives the most exercise and training, it uses its potential to a greater extent and tends to dominate the right. It becomes used to such dominance and tends to take over the majority of tasks, sometimes taking over those tasks that are more suited to the right hemisphere, and thus does a poor job of them. "Hemispheric dominance," says Jerre Levy, "seems to be more determined by a hemisphere's imagined than real capability." The next few pages will discuss how to deal with such hemispheric dominance and how certain strategies can be employed in unlocking the right hemisphere's potential for improving graphic skills.

Unlocking Right-Hemisphere Potential

We learn to write when we are children, and by the time we are adults, most of us write well enough to articulate our ideas, thoughts, and feelings. On the other hand, most people's graphic skills remain at a level no higher than those of an eight-year-old child. Although most individuals would like to be able to draw and they start drawing at a very young age, they fail to develop their drawing skills while becoming high achievers in other areas. When asked to draw, they lack confidence, feel embarassed, give excuses, apologize, and finally, when they do draw, get frustrated, restless, and feel sorry for themselves.

137
Young children (three to seven years old) draw with great confidence. Even though their drawings are sometimes nothing but scribbles and incomplete, they fill in the gaps with their imaginations.

138

138–139
Children draw for fun and challenge. It is almost an inborn instinct to draw—an urge to communicate.

Close examination reveals two important reasons behind this problem. First, although people begin drawing at an early age, they also quit early on, say, around age eight or nine. They quit because they felt frustrated at not being able to draw realistic pictures, and thus direct their energy to cartoon drawing or crafts. Second and more important, the problem lies in their approach to drawing. With the development of reasoning ability, they also begin to employ the left-hemisphere approach in drawing. They try to draw from their labeling system and reasoning rather than what the object appears to be, its spatial configuration, or how it occupies space. Their source of frustration stems from the left hemisphere's struggle with a task that is not suitable for its approach.

COGNITIVE BATTLE

An inexperienced hand suffers from the cognitive battle of the hemispheres where usually the left one wins and uses its labeling system to draw. The key is freeing the right hemisphere from the dominance of the left so that the right hemisphere can employ its strategy in "seeing" space. The following few paragraphs describe a few techniques for freeing the right side of the brain. Betty Edwards in her book, *Drawing on the Right Side of the Brain* (1979), explains how she found these techniques to be very useful for her students.

139

140
A realistic object intrigues our labeling system. The left brain wants to see things that have names.

141
A silhouette clearly shows how an object shares the same edges with the negative space around it.

142
Concentrating on negative space causes the left brain to abandon the task because it cannot use its labeling system; thus the right brain takes over by concentrating on shapes and spatial relationships.

NEGATIVE-SPACE DRAWINGS

The left hemisphere has no name for the empty space that surrounds an object. It can name and recognize the object itself, but the space around the object is nonsensical to it. We call these empty spaces "negative spaces." If instead of drawing the object, you attempt to draw the negative spaces, the left side of the brain, finding its shapes nonsensical, cannot handle the task. The task is then passed on to the right side of the brain, and the cognitive shift is thus accomplished. Through spatial relationships, the right hemisphere will read in all various shapes regardless of how nonsensical they appear, for it knows how to deal with the unfamiliar. If you have drawn the negative space around the object, you have then, in fact, drawn the object, for both the object and the negative space share the same edge.

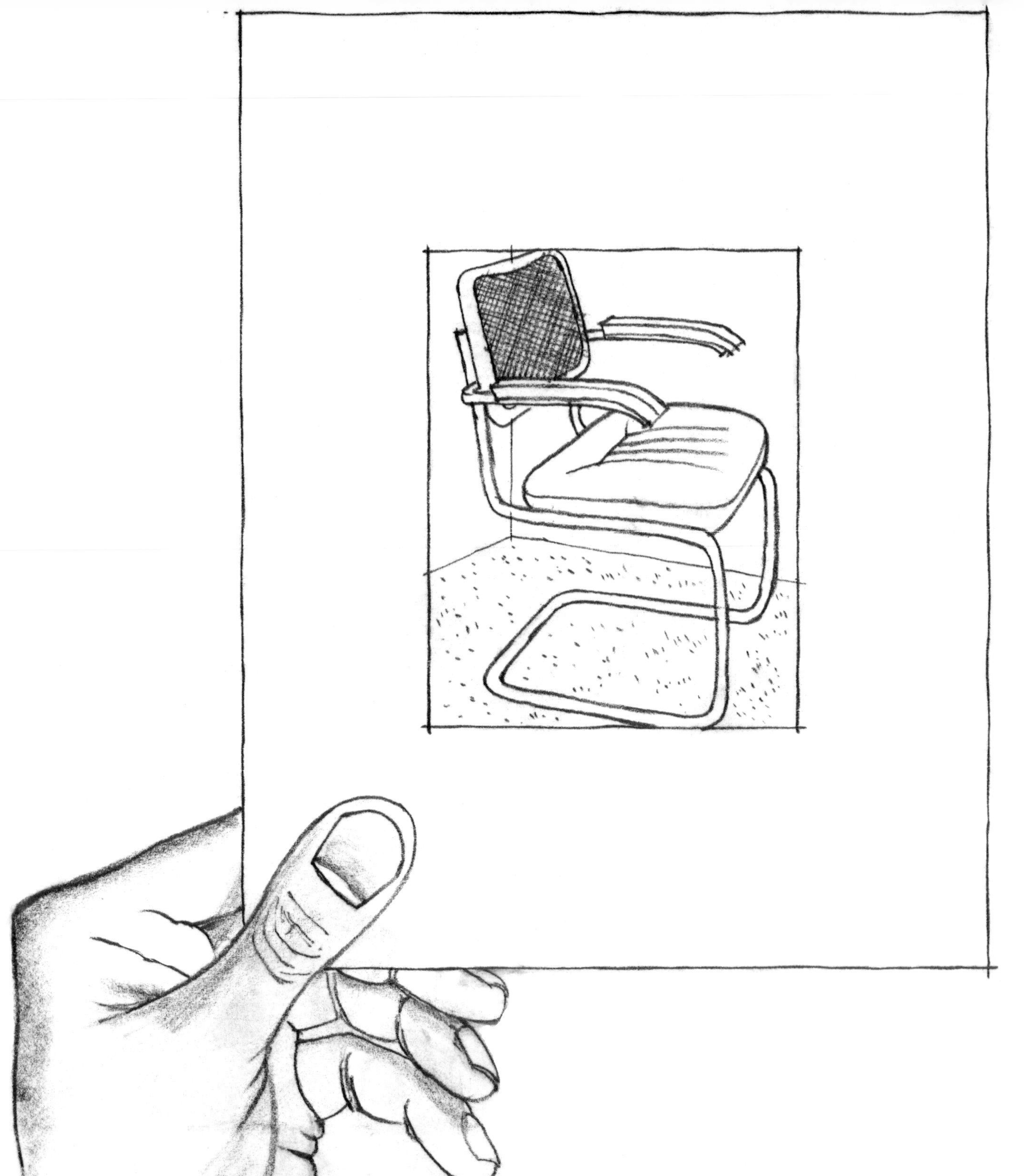

143
An object can be framed by closing or covering one eye and moving the viewfinder closer to or farther away from the object.

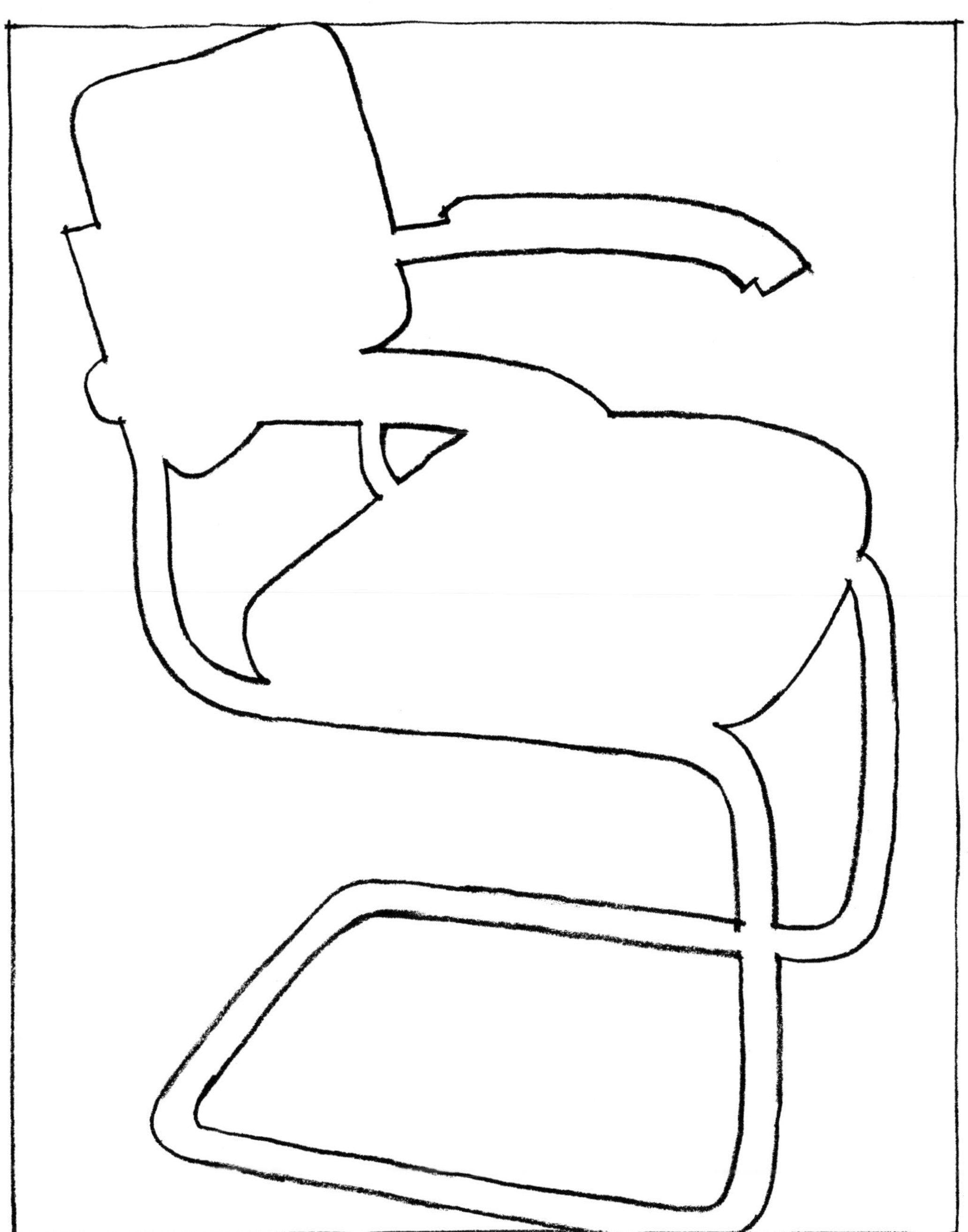

144
The negative space and the object share the same edges. Thus, drawing the shape of negative space amounts to drawing an outline of the object.

VIEWFINDER

Drawing is easier if the viewfinder is used to draw the negative space. A viewfinder can be made by cutting a rectangular hole in a piece of cardboard. The hole should be of the same proportion as the paper on which you will draw. You can look through the viewfinder, i.e., the rectangular hole, with one eye covered or closed, and by moving the viewfinder closer to or farther away from the object, you can frame the particular object you want to draw. Now you can simply draw the various shapes of negative space within the frame on the paper by causing the edges of the paper to correspond with the sides of the viewfinder rectangle: The picture is thus drawn. The reason it is easier to draw with the viewfinder is that it confines the negative space that tends to

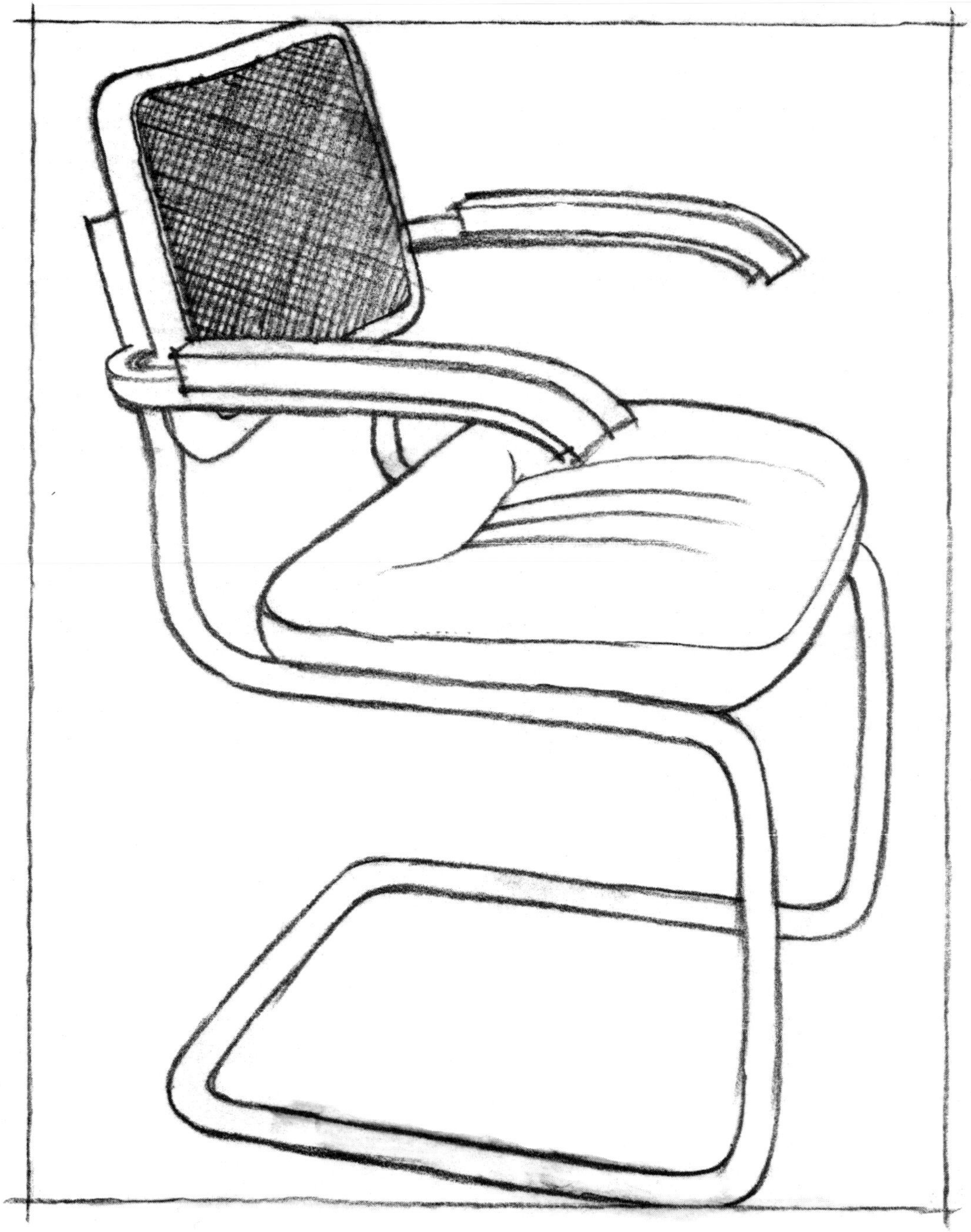

146
Negative space can be darkened with a pencil or ink to emphasize its shape.

145
After filling out the details, the negative-space drawing looks more realistic.

147

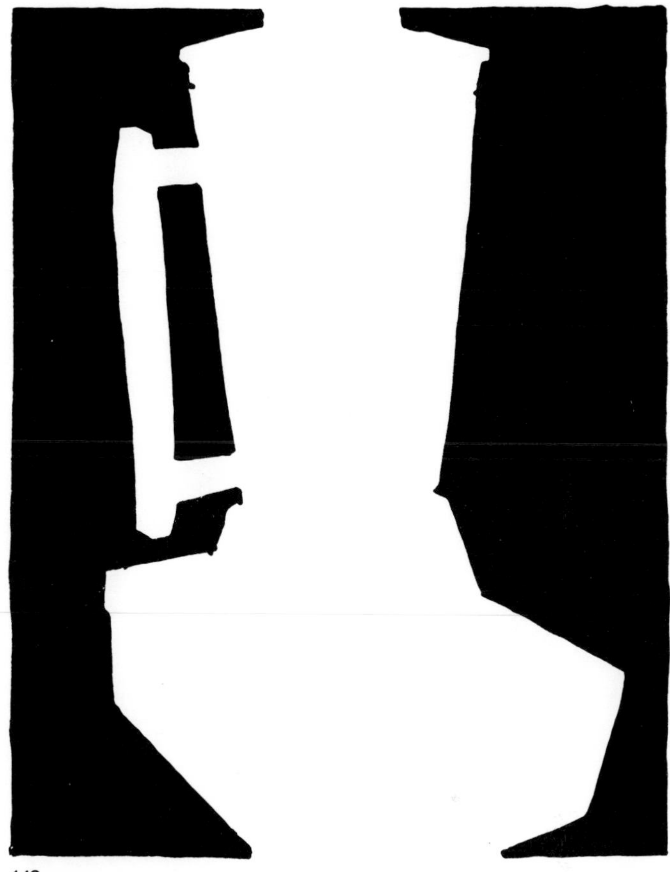

148

flow into the surrounding space continuum. Thus, the limited size of the drawing paper becomes more compatible with the framed area.

Darkening the negative spaces with a pencil or filling them in with black ink will emphasize their shapes. Negative-space drawings are pleasing to the eye perhaps because of the conscious display of positive and negative spaces, which gives a sense of unity or wholeness. The sense of composi-

147–148
Negative-space drawings can be read even though, lacking details, they look incomplete because the right hemisphere fills in the missing information.

tion is deeply linked with the perception of the negative space. An experienced designer thinks in terms of both positive and negative spaces.

UPSIDE-DOWN PICTURES

Another technique for achieving a cognitive shift may be used by drawing from an upside-down photograph or drawing. Frequently, if a drawing or photograph is upside down, the left hemisphere finds it harder to read because the object appears unfamiliar. Thus, the right hemisphere gets to process the information, and the drawing can be done simply, on the basis of spatial relationships.

CONTOUR DRAWING

In the 1930s, when Kimon Nicolaides was writing his book, *The Natural Way to Draw* (published in 1941, three years after his death), he was not aware of hemispheric specialization with regard to spatial cognition, as research in that field had not yet advanced to that extent. But he did realize that the act of drawing is deeply linked with spatial and tactile perception, and that to be in touch with such perception requires the employment of a certain approach. Thus, he introduced a technique called *contour drawing.* Contour drawing entails intense observation of the edges where "air" and the given object meet, or lines that separate planes within the

149
Contour drawing, which requires intense observation of the edges with reference to spatial and tactile perception, is in essence, a cognitive shift from the left hemisphere to the right.

150–151
The slow and tedious process of contour drawing puts intense emphasis on the sense of sight and touch, and thus makes one oblivious to the labeling system.

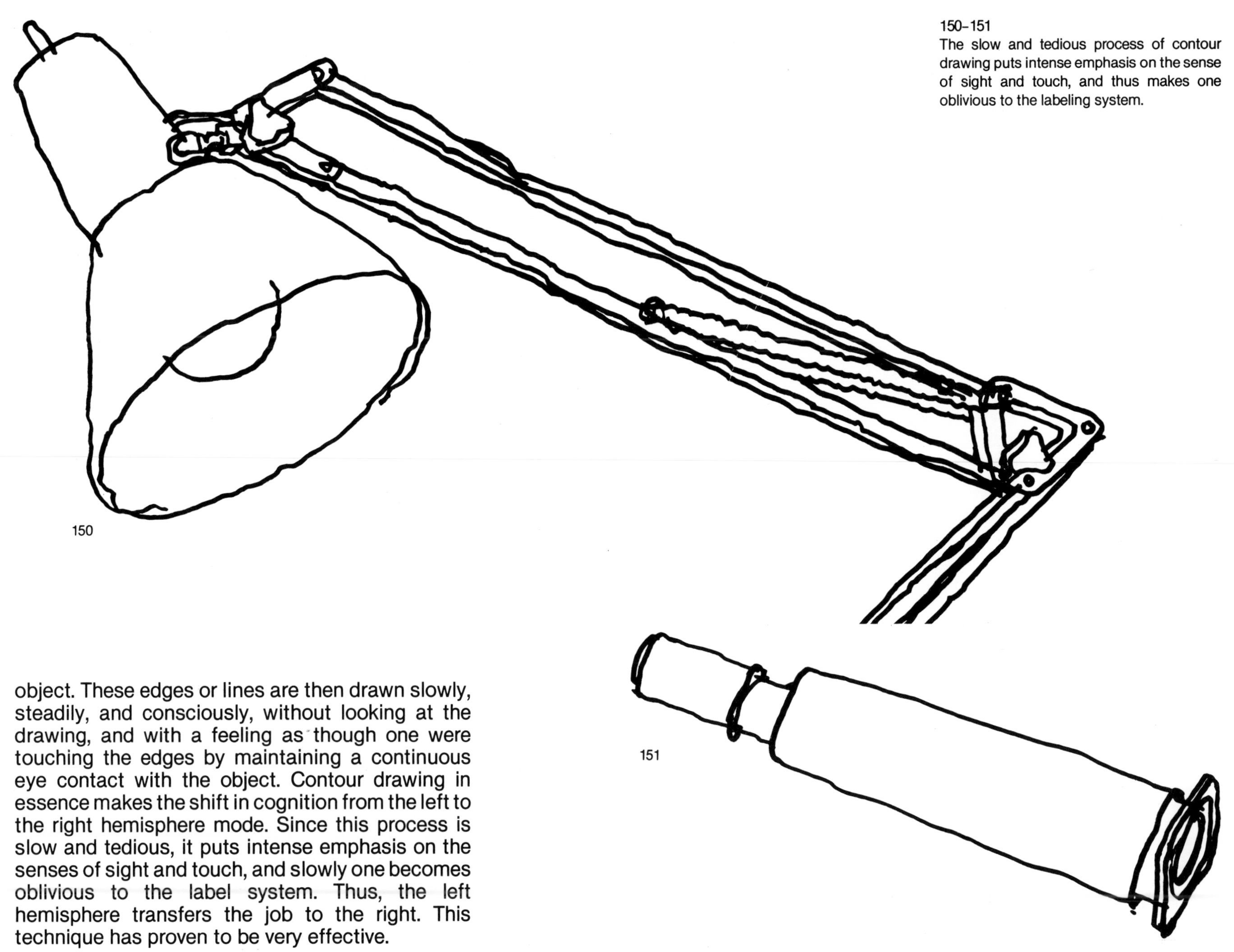

150

151

object. These edges or lines are then drawn slowly, steadily, and consciously, without looking at the drawing, and with a feeling as though one were touching the edges by maintaining a continuous eye contact with the object. Contour drawing in essence makes the shift in cognition from the left to the right hemisphere mode. Since this process is slow and tedious, it puts intense emphasis on the senses of sight and touch, and slowly one becomes oblivious to the label system. Thus, the left hemisphere transfers the job to the right. This technique has proven to be very effective.

SHADOW DRAWINGS

We recognize an object or space and its three-dimensional quality through patterns of light and shadow. Like negative spaces, shadow spaces also lack names and are thus ignored by the left brain. The situation here, too, can be turned around to make the cognitive shift to the right hemisphere.

152
Shadows form a pattern of shapes which by themselves are nonsensical.

153
Pictures can be prepared by simply drawing shapes of a shadow pattern.

153

If you look at the shadow and only concentrate on its shape, the right brain will take over the task since such shape is nonsensical to the left. Thus, you can perceive the shape of the shadow and draw it on a piece of paper. The area of the shadow can be

154

154–155
People with injuries to the right hemisphere of the brain have difficulty in reading certain shadow drawings.

155

darkened with a pencil or simply filled in with black ink. The portrait, object, space, or whatever you are drawing will quickly become apparent. Like negative-space drawings, shadow drawings are also pleasing to look at.

Recent research with brain injury patients reveals that the right hemisphere is responsible for making

156

meaning out of shadow patterns. It does so by leaps of insight, seeking wholeness in spite of missing pieces of information.

156–157
Shadow drawings are pleasant to look at for they leave out pieces of information and let the right hemisphere complete them by leaps of insight.

PROCESSING THE UNFAMILIAR

It has been remarked that the right hemisphere is capable of dealing with the unfamiliar. After the information has become familiar, the left hemisphere takes over, possibly because by that time it has established the new label or pattern through sheer exposure to it. This, incidentally, also confirms the reason behind certain of the left hemisphere's nonverbal capabilities.

Every single object or space is different. Its shape, size, color, texture, and spatial configuration are altogether unique. Each tree is different. So is each leaf on it. But when we say a "tree" we may mean each or any belonging to the category. Similarly, the word *leaf* refers to each or to any one of all leaves.

157

An abstraction, such as a "tree" or a "leaf," is the result of establishing the chain pattern and categorization by the left side of the brain through its familiarity with more than one tree or leaf. But when it comes to unfamiliar and unique situations, the right hemisphere processes such information.

The way a single object occupies a space is unique. Looking at it from a given point, i.e., its view from a given station point, creates a unique spatial configuration; the lines, angles, values, shades, and shadows, together make a unique spatial composition on the picture plane. The left hemisphere's attempt to draw from the name of the object is a form of abstraction, and is bound to result in a drastic departure from what the object or space actually looks like—the way its spatial configuration appears to be on the picture plane. Thus, the right hemisphere's ability to process unfamiliar information is what enables us to understand spatial relationships.

What there is for tomorrow is unknown. What the social, economic, ecological, political, or cultural situations will be is a matter of projection. But deep insight is required to make any meaning out of them. With new combinations and new situations, what will be or should be the shape of tomorrow's environment or material world is unknown. At least, we do know it will be different from what it is today. Leaps of insight are required for the designer to explore and examine the unfamiliar. To this end, the right hemisphere of the brain plays an important role in dealing with the world of dreams, imagination, and unprecedented situations.

158
The right hemisphere's ability to deal with the unfamiliar is what contributes to forming the new shapes of tomorrow.

Part Four

Graphic Analysis and Abstraction

10

Understanding the Nature of an Object

Our eyes are continuously moving, confronting various visual stimuli and taking a visual inventory. They are inspecting, evaluating, making judgements, accepting or rejecting, and thus making an assessment of the total environment. Normally, if a person visits a new place, during the first five minutes, he makes a visual inspection equivalent to more than what numerous still pictures would record. In the process of this visual survey, he may look in various directions—forward, backward, sideways, diagonally, upward, or downward— and probably focuses his eyes on many objects and details. But upon leaving the place, he is left with a general impression and can remember only a few details.

159
When a person visits a new place for a short time, he makes a thorough visual inspection of the environment, but he retains only a general impression of the place on departing.

160

161

163

162

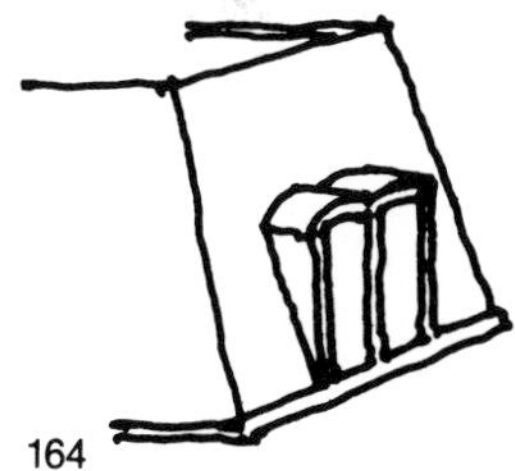
164

160–164
When we leave a place, we remember only a few objects, and they vary with our interests. Sketching forces us to notice details that we may otherwise ignore.

165
Our habit of visual inspection to warn us of hazards in the environment causes us to ignore the rest of the environment unless we have a special interest in certain types of objects or issues.

VISUAL SCANNING

Our behavior of continuous visual inspection can be thought of as a built-in mechanism to warn us of any potential danger or hazard in the environment, and thus serves a very practical purpose. Visual scanning is done in a great hurry covering as many objects or stimuli as possible. Such scanning is issue oriented. In this case, for example, the issue is to look for potential dangers or hazards. Consequently, during our visual inspection, only the items that seem to be possible sources of danger or hazard draw our attention, and we tend to act accordingly.

ISSUE ORIENTATION

The same is true about other kinds of issue-oriented visual scanning. Each individual has different in-

166–167
A person with an "issue orientation" toward automobile design notices the details of cars and may become so knowledgeable that he can name the model and make of a car by looking at the details of its front or back.

166

terests. Depending on his interests, each individual develops a specific issue orientation with regard to his visual scanning. For example, one individual may have an interest in the way people dress, and his visual scanning would then be oriented toward clothing and apparel. Thus, he notices and observes items that are in the realm of clothing and apparel, and ignores other things in the environment. Similarly, someone having an interest in the latest automobile models goes through automobile-oriented visual scanning. Form, size, detail, and color of automobiles attract his attention while other objects in the environment go unnoticed.

167

Aside from the specific interest or issue orientation, we seldom take time to look at objects in our environment and carefully analyze them as to how they work, how they are built, how the parts relate to

168

169

168–169
Sketching an existing building (168) makes us notice the concept, details, and reasoning behind its specific form and setting (169).

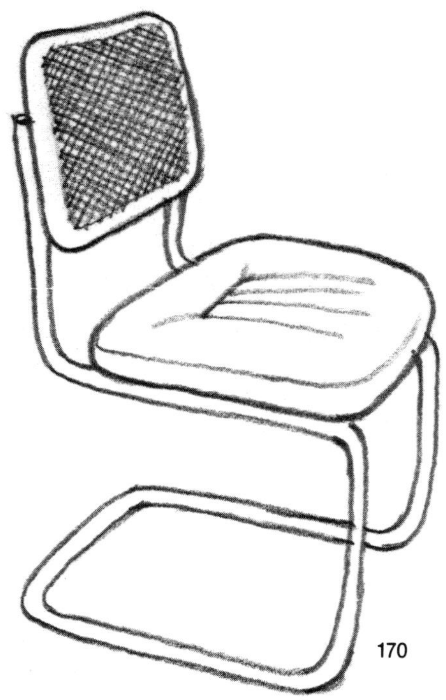

170

170
The act of drawing, by forcing us to concentrate on what we draw, makes us observe things that we otherwise do not pay attention to. When drawing a chair, for example, we begin to uncover the thoughts underlying its design.

the whole, their organization, composition, proportion, etc. Our visual scanning remains at the "looking" level, and we fail to make observations.

OBSERVATION

When we start to draw something, we are forced to make the shift from the mere "looking" level to the "observation" level. The act of drawing makes us concentrate our attention on the object we are drawing. We then begin to discover a whole range of information about the object that we had not thought of or experienced before. We enter a new world of perception, and our visual perception of the object changes. We begin to notice its proportion, material, texture, color, details, and the reasons behind the way it is.

If you are drawing a chair, for example, you notice its performance requirements, how its structural system works, and you slowly begin to realize how its shape and proportion came about. You notice various details, such as how the joints work and why they were made in a specific way. You will also become aware of whether the chair is comfortable, or how it can be improved.

Drawing a building reveals the underlying principles and consideration in its design. We begin to notice the reasoning behind its orientation, details, fenestrations, angles of the roof, or the solar panels, etc. Thus, drawing the building becomes an exercise in understanding the limitations and the possibilities of its design.

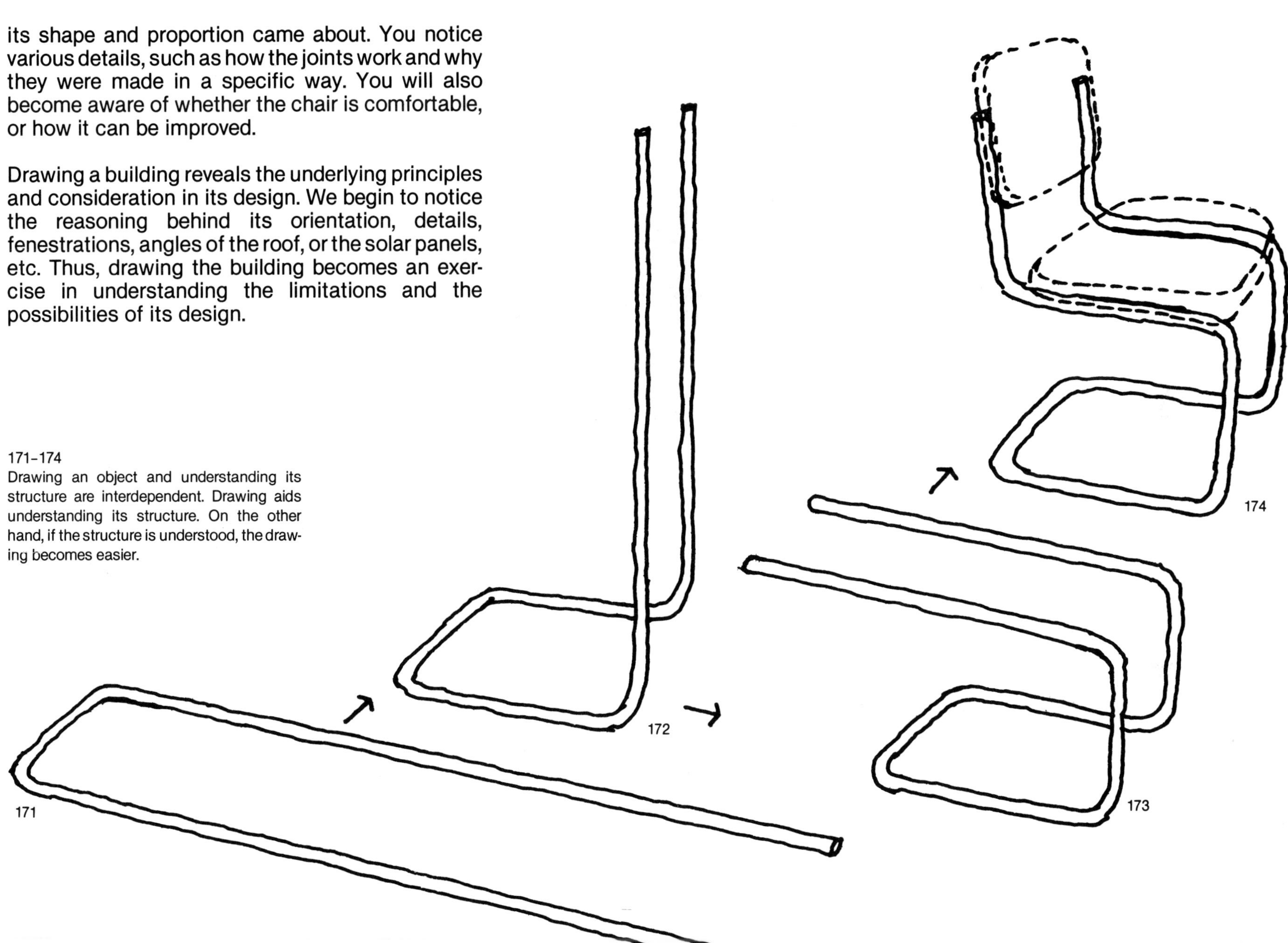

171–174
Drawing an object and understanding its structure are interdependent. Drawing aids understanding its structure. On the other hand, if the structure is understood, the drawing becomes easier.

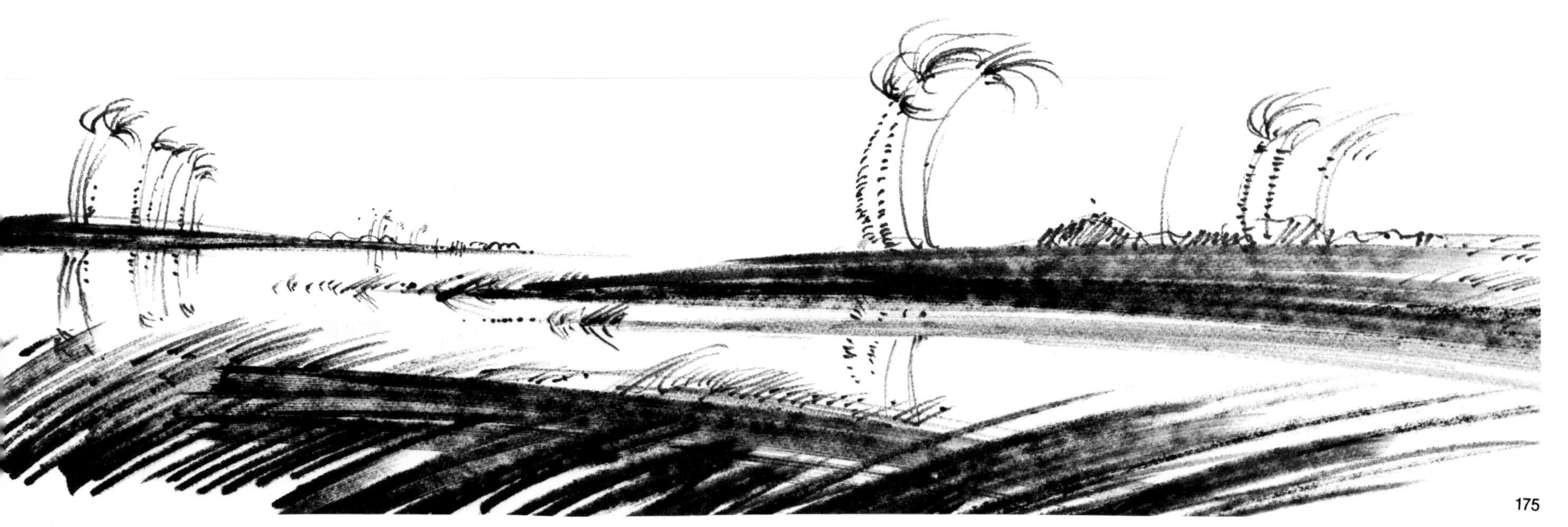

175

175–176
Sketching a landscape will reveal fascinating facts about its climate and regional characteristics. The topography, geology, drainage paths, and the actions of wind, sun, rain, and water together tell a unique story of a given landscape.

176

KNOWING A LANDSCAPE

Normally an open landscape may appear to be a somewhat arbitrary arrangement of irregular landforms, streams or creeks, and plants of various sizes and kinds. But when we start drawing it, we begin to be aware of fascinating natural phenomena. We then begin to notice how the land slopes, its drainage paths, and the reasons behind certain landforms. The story behind why certain trees or plants grew well in certain spots begins to become apparent. We can also begin to see the actions of nature: sun, wind, rain, and snow. We become aware of the local climatic conditions. Any modification or man-made change becomes visible, and the history of the landscape begins to unfold. It tells whether it is loved, cherished, or abandoned. Earth, stone, vegetation, streams, or drainage paths together form its distinct character or personality. Drawing it is feeling it. Drawing it is a process of getting to know its personality.

Drawing a tree is an attempt to understand the nature of the tree. Such an exercise reveals how the trunk and branches hold up as a structural system to protect it against the force of gravitation. It reveals how the tree resists the forces of wind, and how the branches and leaves are arranged to respond to the availability of sunlight.

Drawing human figures is one of the best ways to understand the human body. Such an attempt makes us think in terms of systems rather than of a figure on a landscape. The act of drawing makes us realize that the human body is a harmonious composition of various systems, such as the skeletal system and the muscular system, and understand

177
An environment bears physical marks left by the passage of time. Sketching unfolds its past and present and tells whether it is loved, cherished, or abandoned.

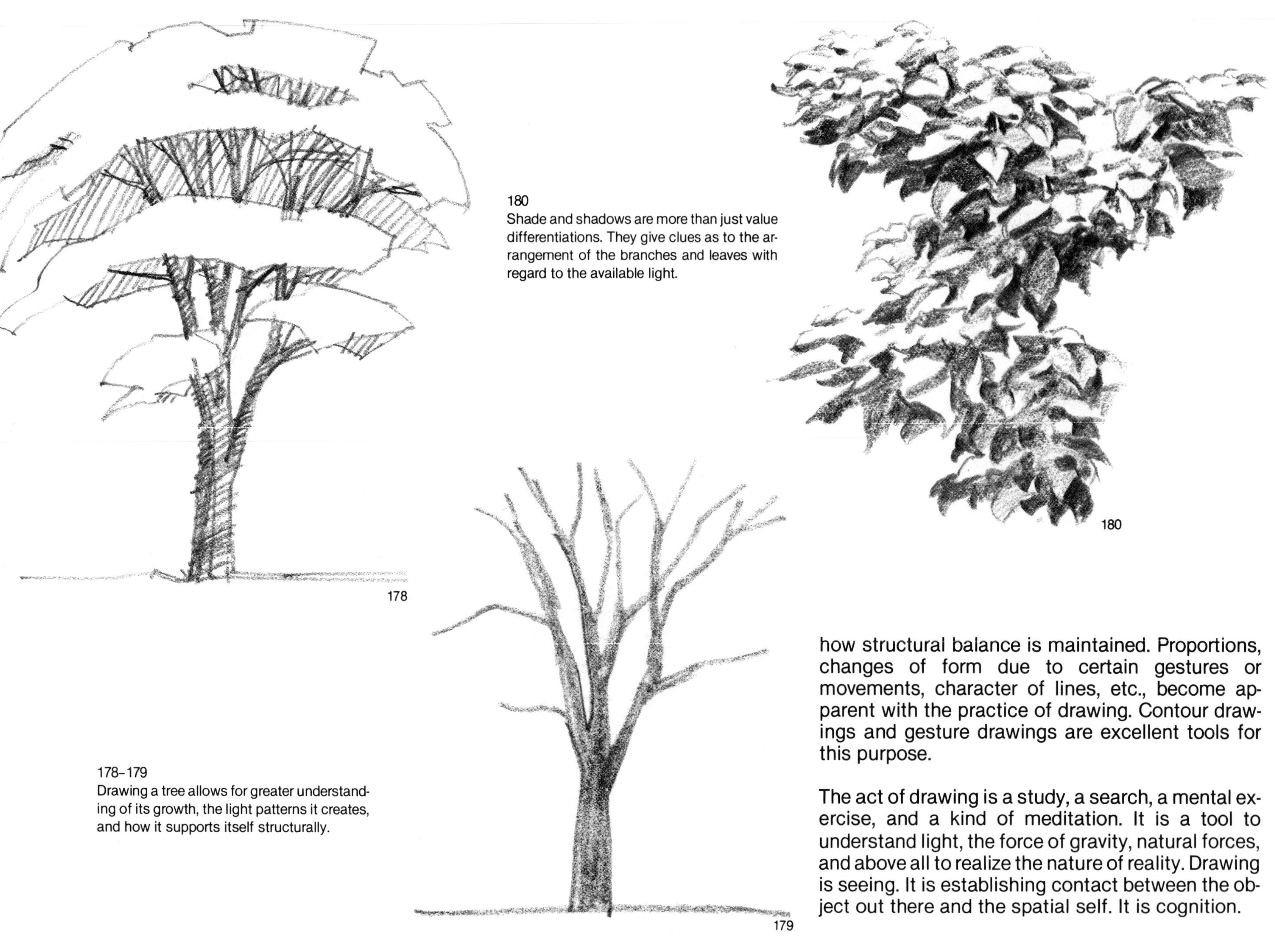

178

179

180

180
Shade and shadows are more than just value differentiations. They give clues as to the arrangement of the branches and leaves with regard to the available light.

178–179
Drawing a tree allows for greater understanding of its growth, the light patterns it creates, and how it supports itself structurally.

how structural balance is maintained. Proportions, changes of form due to certain gestures or movements, character of lines, etc., become apparent with the practice of drawing. Contour drawings and gesture drawings are excellent tools for this purpose.

The act of drawing is a study, a search, a mental exercise, and a kind of meditation. It is a tool to understand light, the force of gravity, natural forces, and above all to realize the nature of reality. Drawing is seeing. It is establishing contact between the object out there and the spatial self. It is cognition.

11

Graphic Analysis

In the history of human civilization, the invention of the telescope, microscope, and their modern versions is of special significance. Until their invention, man's visible world was limited to what was seen with the naked eye. But with the invention of each of these apparatuses, the boundaries of the visible world expanded tremendously. With their use, our vision extends from the details of the heavenly bodies into the inner worlds of cells and molecules. Such increased vision has contributed to many scientific discoveries and technological advances, and thus has dramatically changed our everyday lives.

ANALYTIC PROCESSES

Observing the nature of objects with the naked eye is an art that we have either forgotten or not developed to its greatest potential. We seem to have left this task to scientists and astronomers, who deal with probing apparatuses having astronomical capabilities. Observation is an art. It requires a

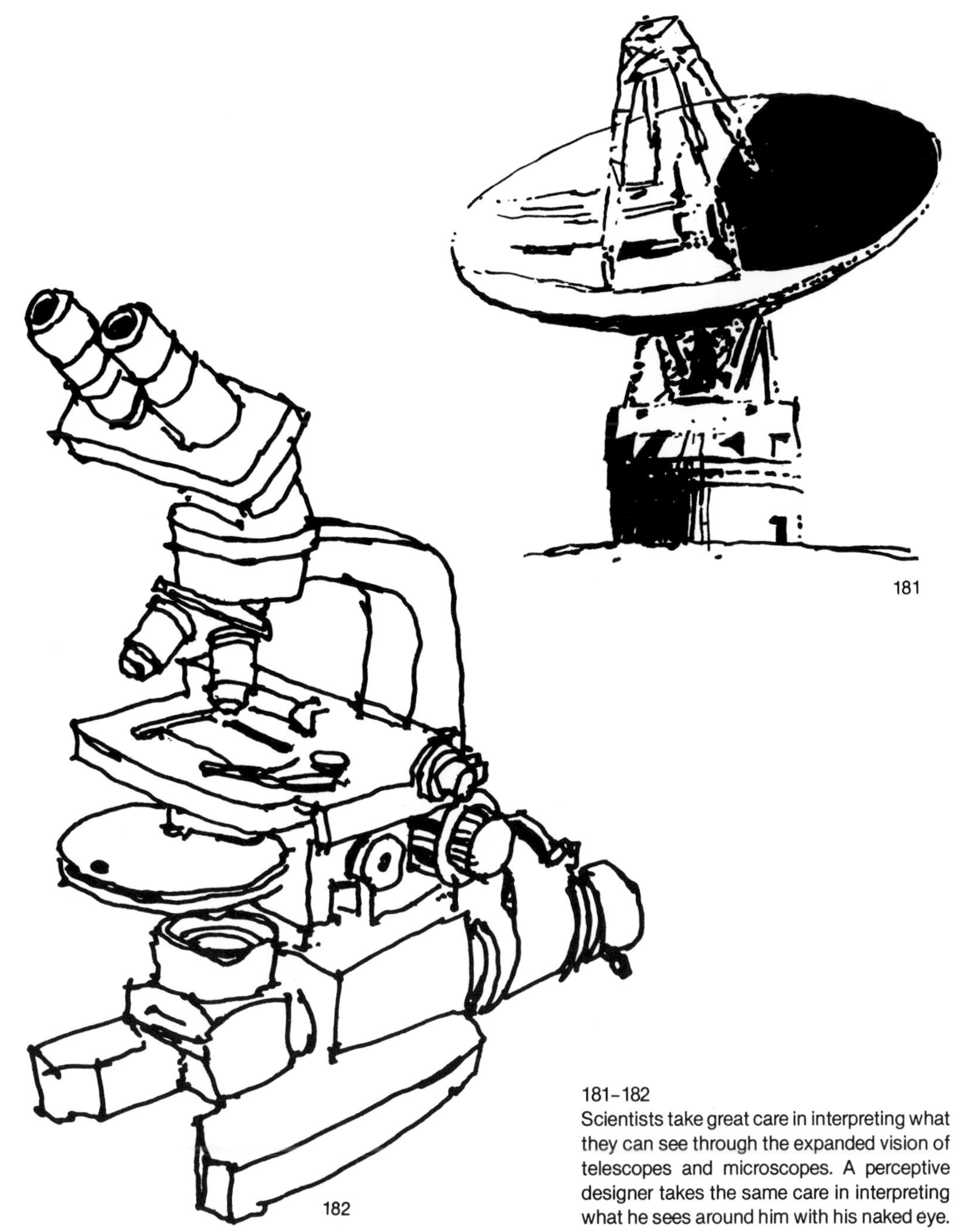

181

182

181–182
Scientists take great care in interpreting what they can see through the expanded vision of telescopes and microscopes. A perceptive designer takes the same care in interpreting what he sees around him with his naked eye.

curious and analytic mind. It is an activity of making cognitive connections. Thus, drawing as a tool for observation is an analytic process. The following few paragraphs discuss how graphic techniques can be used in analyzing and exploring certain aspects that are very important in the design process.

SHAPES AND FORMS

Geometric shapes such as squares, rectangles, circles, and triangles, or forms such as cubes, spheres, cylinders, and cones are abstractions. Our eyes do not readily see them in the object or the landscape unless we focus our attention through sketching. Objects and spaces can be reduced into

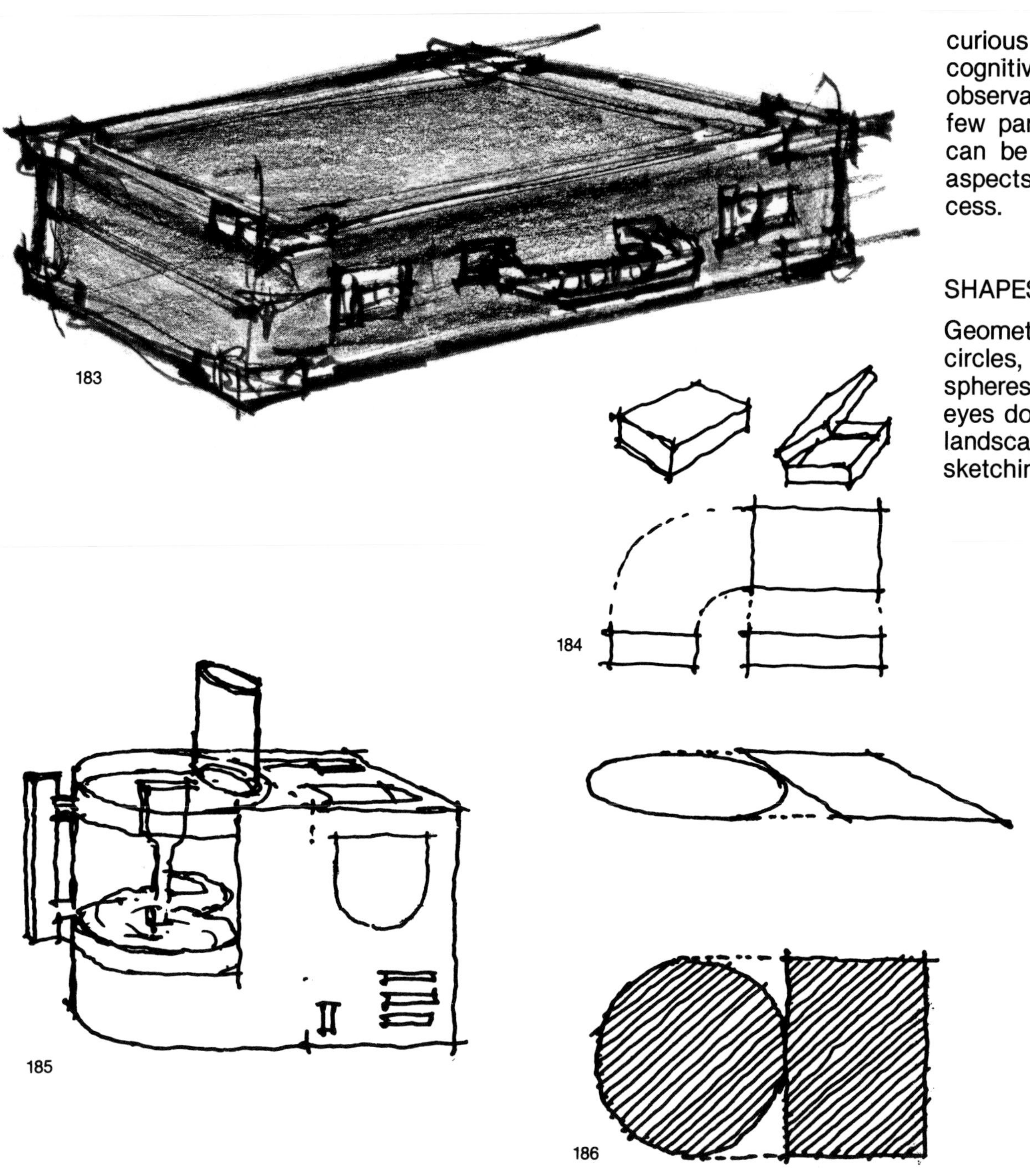

183–186
The act of drawing can uncover basic geometric forms and allow for analysis as to how they are combined to form an object.

187

187–188
A built environment can be reduced to basic geometric shapes and forms and their combinations.

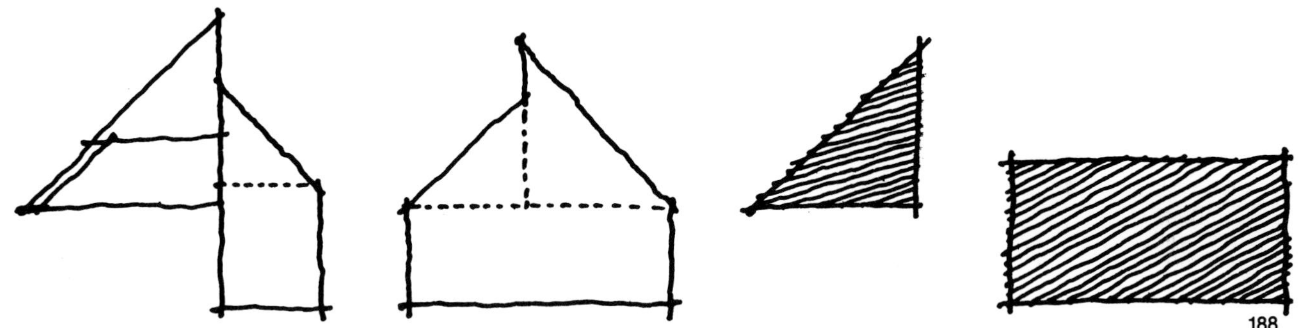

basic geometric shapes, forms, or their various combinations. Similar analysis can be done by exploring the geometric patterns of points, lines, and planes.

Such analysis can also be done in reverse, i.e., the basic geometric shapes and forms can be translated into various objects and spaces. Adding

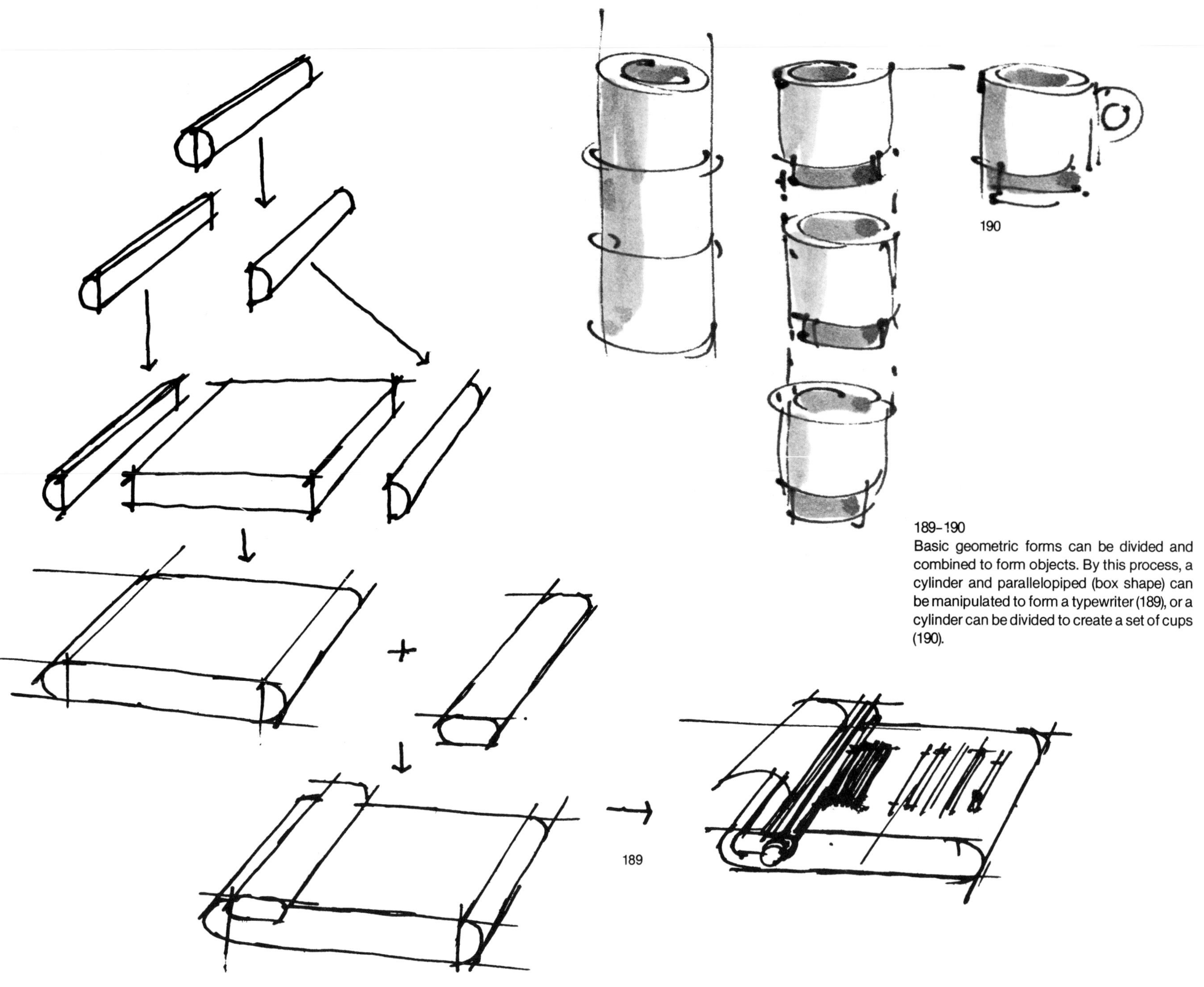

189–190
Basic geometric forms can be divided and combined to form objects. By this process, a cylinder and parallelopiped (box shape) can be manipulated to form a typewriter (189), or a cylinder can be divided to create a set of cups (190).

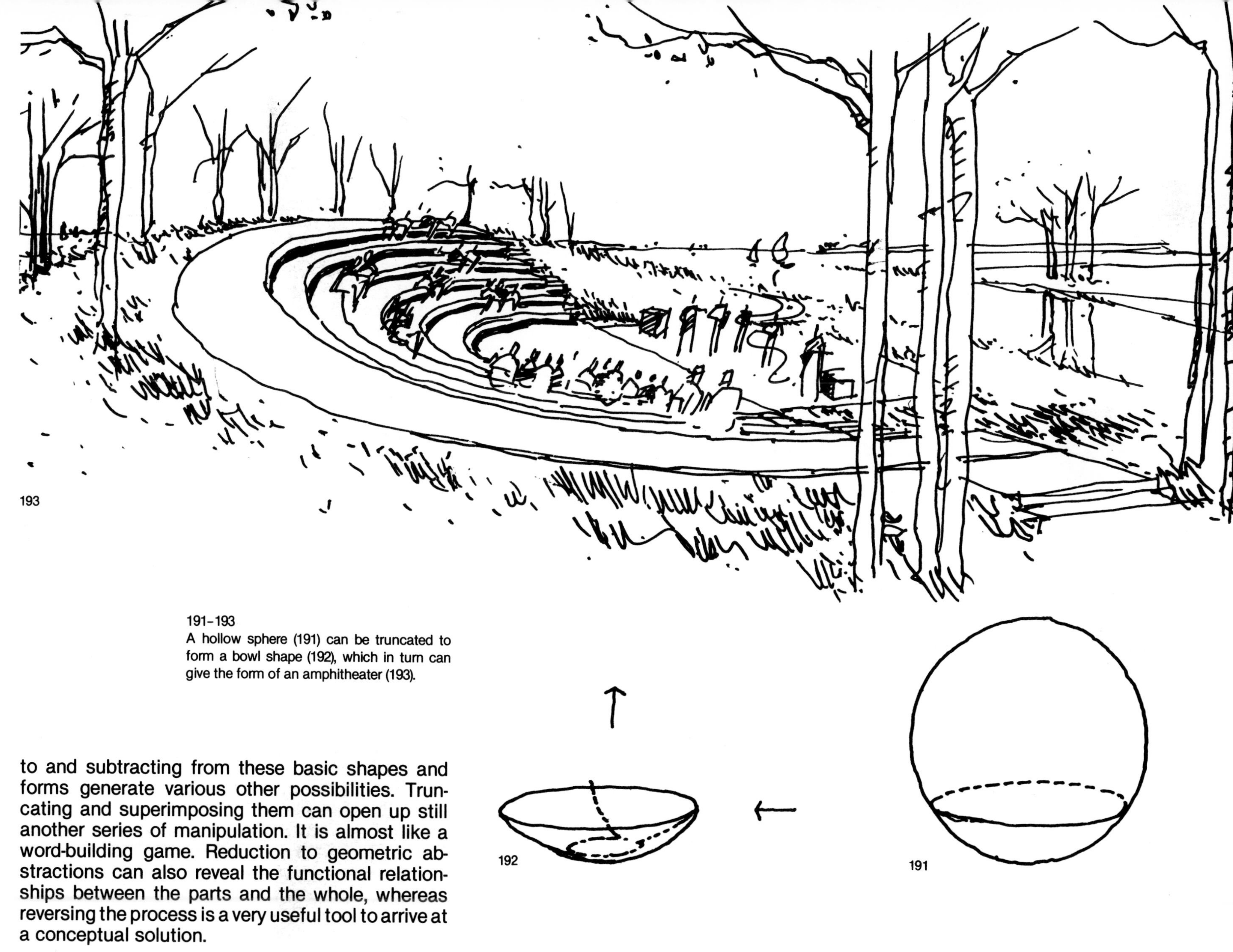

191–193
A hollow sphere (191) can be truncated to form a bowl shape (192), which in turn can give the form of an amphitheater (193).

to and subtracting from these basic shapes and forms generate various other possibilities. Truncating and superimposing them can open up still another series of manipulation. It is almost like a word-building game. Reduction to geometric abstractions can also reveal the functional relationships between the parts and the whole, whereas reversing the process is a very useful tool to arrive at a conceptual solution.

SCALE AND PROPORTION

In design we use two types of scales: absolute and relative. Absolute scale deals with actual size; relative scale is perceptual in nature, as is the case with monumental and intimate scales. Sketching can be effectively used in the analysis and exploration of both relative and absolute scales.

A proportion is the size of one element relative to that of another element. It can describe the ratio of a part to its whole, or of the height of an object or

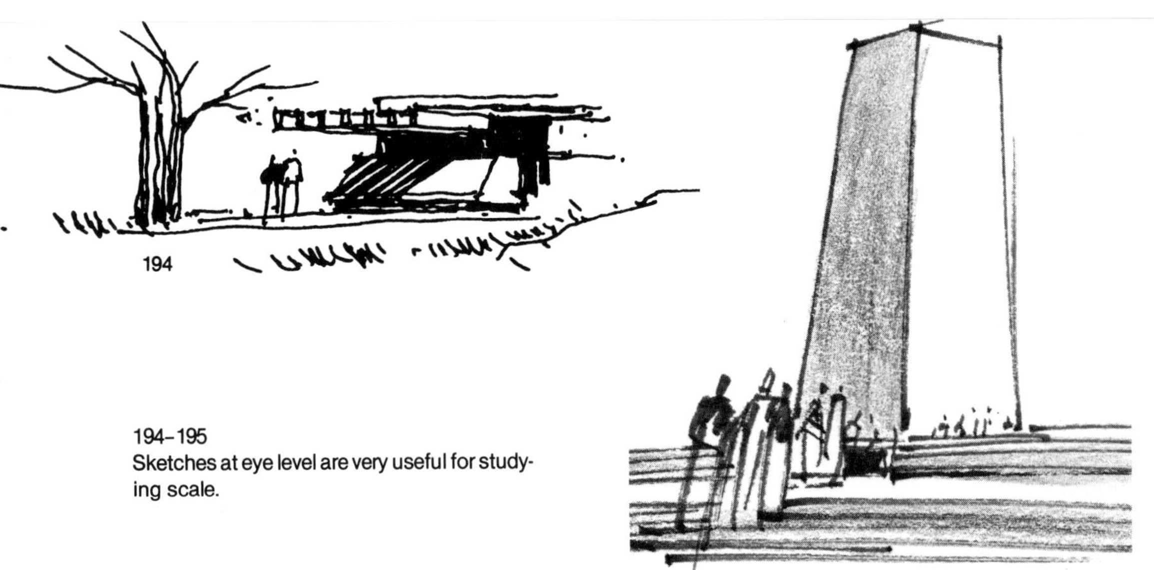

194

195

194–195
Sketches at eye level are very useful for studying scale.

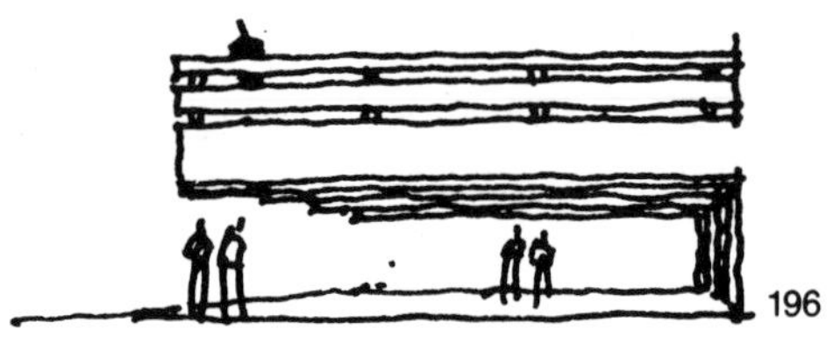

196

196–197
A cantilever may be structurally sound, but visually, its scale may be out of proportion (196). Its visual quality can be improved by modifying its shape; its end may be tapered and its depth may be increased at the connecting side where the moment is high (197).

198
Familiar objects such as steps and benches can define the scale of a building and its components.

197

198

199

200

201

202

space to its width or depth. Proportion can also be applied to a material or structural system. A proportioning system is an aesthetic rationale that the designer may use to establish visual unity and order. Over the centuries, in architectural design, many theories or proportioning systems have been developed, each having its own rationale. The Golden Section, Greek Orders, Modulor, and Japanese "Ken" are only a few of them. Regardless of the theories, the analysis and exploration of proportion through sketches are important exercises for the

199–202
For a given activity, the particular height of a space may be sufficient, but if an area is large the height may be out of proportion (199–200). The space proportion may be improved by increasing the ceiling height to maintain a balance with width and depth (201–202).

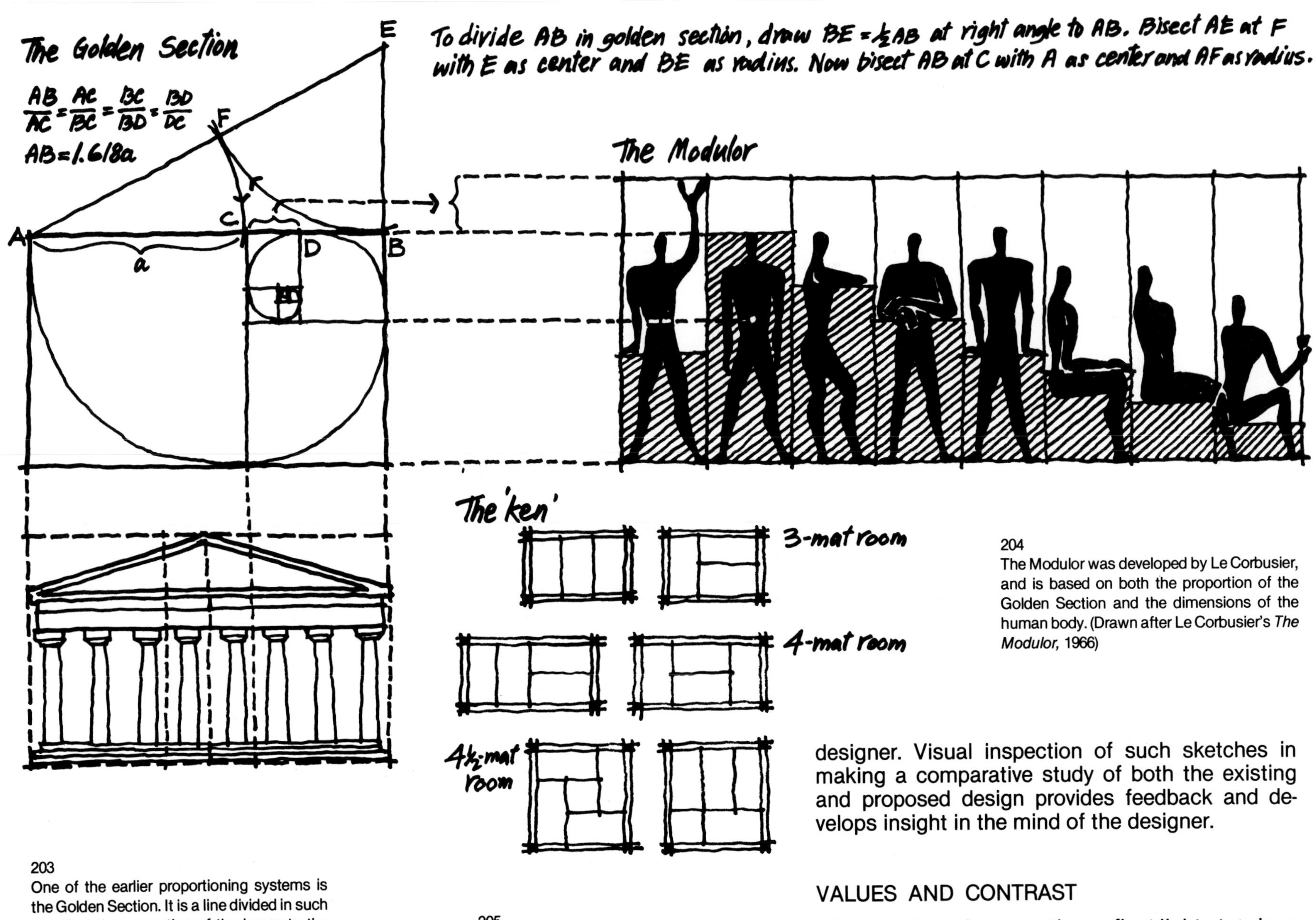

203
One of the earlier proportioning systems is the Golden Section. It is a line divided in such way that the proportion of the lesser to the greater is the same as the greater to the whole. Greeks used it, recognizing that it governs the proportions of the human body.

204
The Modulor was developed by Le Corbusier, and is based on both the proportion of the Golden Section and the dimensions of the human body. (Drawn after Le Corbusier's *The Modulor,* 1966)

205
In the "Ken" proportion system, the number of floor mats and the flexibility in arranging them are the determinants of room size.

designer. Visual inspection of such sketches in making a comparative study of both the existing and proposed design provides feedback and develops insight in the mind of the designer.

VALUES AND CONTRAST

We see objects because they reflect light at various intensities. Values refer to the gradation between black and white. Middle gray is the midpoint in such a gradation. Light gray lies between white and middle gray, whereas dark gray lies between middle gray and black. Of course, various other values occur in between these, depending on how fine the gradation is.

206
We see something because of the contrast of light and dark. The gradation of values adds another dimension to this by showing the differentiation of planes and their orientation.

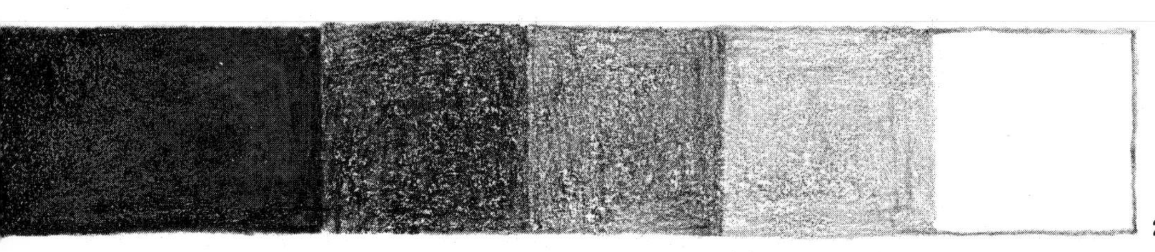

207

208

207–208
A gradation of values can be created by almost any medium. Although drawing with pencils can give fine texture of values (207), pens are equally useful in creating values with scribbles or any pattern (208).

209
Thick lines and scribbles can be used in creating sufficient value differentiation.

210
Use of lines and thick black areas can create high contrasts that emphasize the depth of space.

209

210

Visual experience depends on the phenomenon of contrast. We see objects because of the contrast between light, dark, and various values. A line drawing, printed character, or silhouette is made up of contrasts between black and white, whereas a sketch may contain various contrasts of a number of values including black and white. A contrast between values may define a line or plane. A greater difference between values creates a greater contrast and thus makes such definitions more visible. A change in value is generally associated with a change in plane and thus delineates the volume and depth of an object or space.

211

211
Dots, regardless of how coarse they are, can also be used in creating contrast and value differentiation.

212
High contrast sketches can be very useful in studying spatial quality, for they focus more on variation of planes and overall space rather than on details.

212

Graphic analysis of values and contrasts is an important study tool with regard to spatial quality. Such a study provides clues as to the resulting composition of positive and negative spaces, and its sense of unity. Shades and shadows add another dimension with regard to values and contrasts: abstraction through contrast of *light.*

LIGHT

Light is of magical quality. In the physical sense, it is the source of energy. It is deeply linked with our

213
The lack of contrast or value differentiation makes the sketch a dull one. So is the picture on a cloudy day.

worldly resources, including food. Its presence is a wholesome experience. It is the counterpart of our sense of sight, performing utilitarian functions and aiding cognition. When sunlight falls on a landscape, causing light and dark areas, shade and shadows, and contrasts between highlights and the darkest dark, it presents the landscape to us through abstraction. Compare two pictures of an outdoor place, one taken on a cloudy day and the

other on a bright sunny day. Looking at the first, you would probably say that it is a dull picture. What we really mean by "dull" is the lack of interest due to absence of contrast. In the second picture, the bright sunlight, creating an abstraction through contrast, tends to reduce the landscape into a simple interplay of spaces and forms. Such abstraction or reduction is very helpful in studying spatial quality.

214
The sketch becomes lively if the contrast between the values is increased. This is why a picture becomes interesting on a sunny day.

215
Increasing contrast is a kind of abstraction, for it simplifies or reduces the landscape into its basic shapes and forms by deleting the details from it.

12

Graphic Abstraction and Manipulation

The outside world appears to us in various forms. But our individual mind absorbs such information in its own way and thus creates a world of its own. Such an inner world is very different from the outside world in shape, form, color, texture, sound, and smell. It is different because in our process of absorbing information, we add, subtract, emphasize, discount, and modify the information according to our personal experience and history. It is a kind of personalization process. Our hopes and fears, joys and sorrows, likes and dislikes, aspirations and disappointments are very much a part of it.

PERSONALIZATION

Personalization is a part of the creative process. It is constantly opening up opportunities for new combinations, patterns, and possibilities. Those people among us who cannot internalize the outside world in a personal way are left with no curiosity or inter-

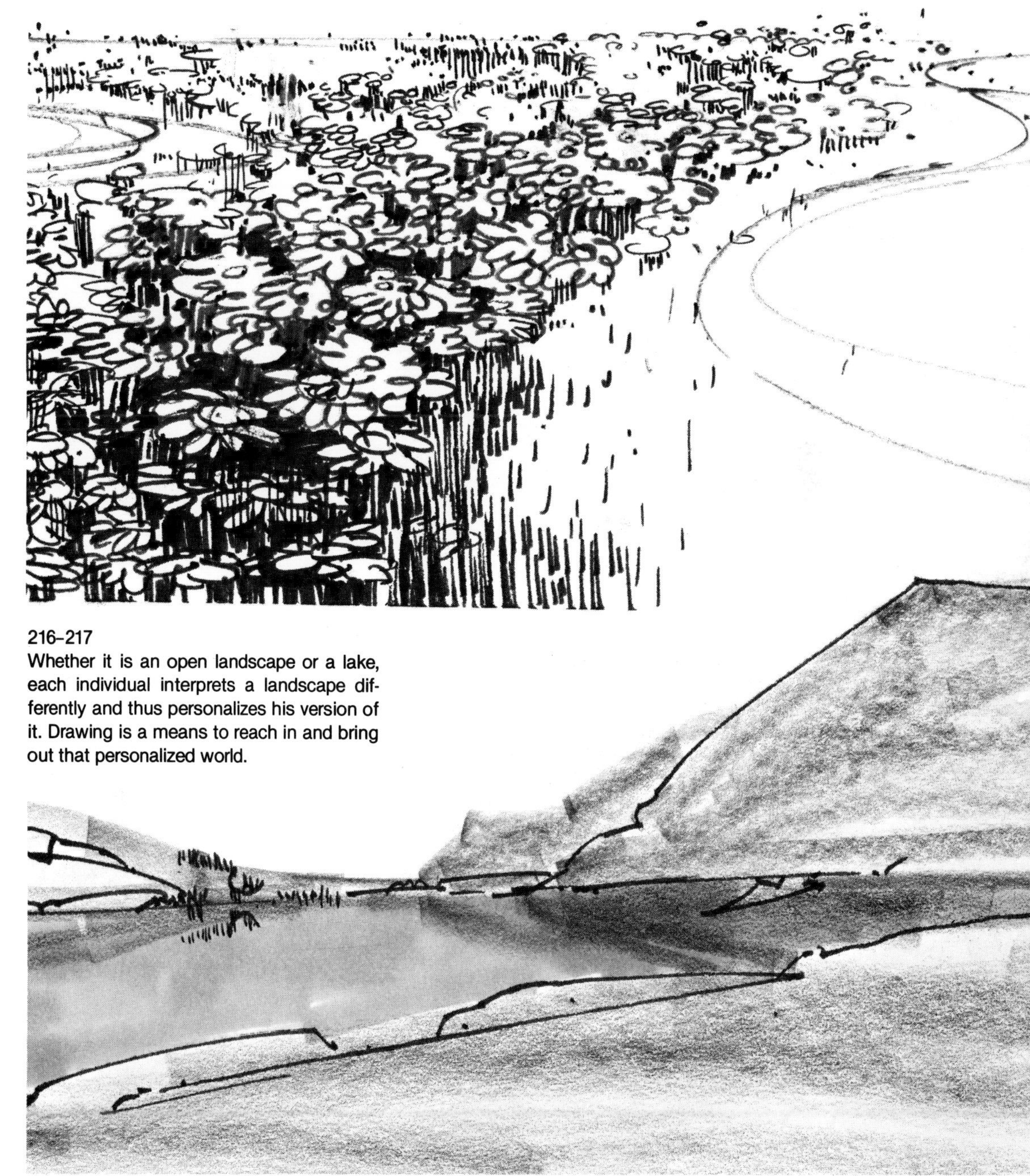

216–217
Whether it is an open landscape or a lake, each individual interprets a landscape differently and thus personalizes his version of it. Drawing is a means to reach in and bring out that personalized world.

pretive capability. To them, the outside world is only a rude conglomeration of lifeless objects, things and entities, and their creative mind is also a narrow one.

Drawing is an attempt to reach into such an inner world. It is a process of bringing out, examining, and exploring the personalized versions of the inner self. It is testing, manipulating, and searching for new possibilities. The following few paragraphs discuss some methods used for such graphic exploration.

ABSTRACTION

Abstraction is a process of reduction or simplification. A building or a park can be reduced to a diagram representing the functional relationships among various activities and circulation patterns. The activities and circulation patterns can be expressed through abstract geometric shapes, lines,

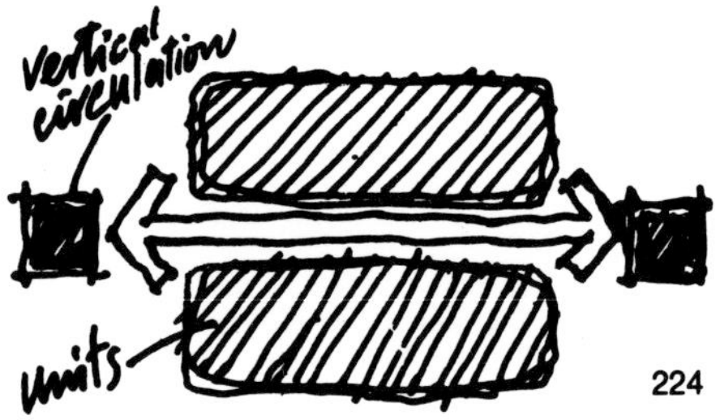

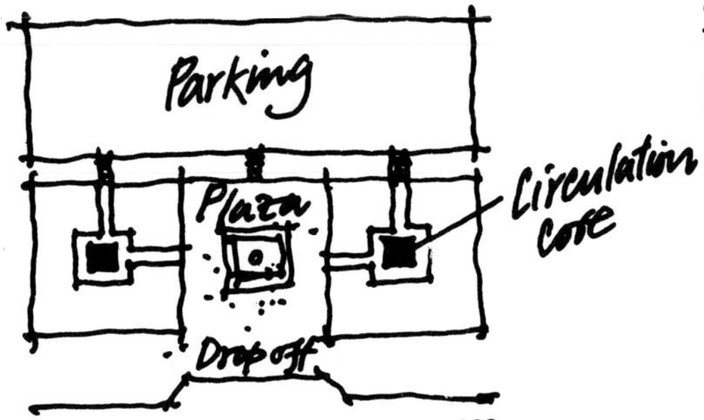

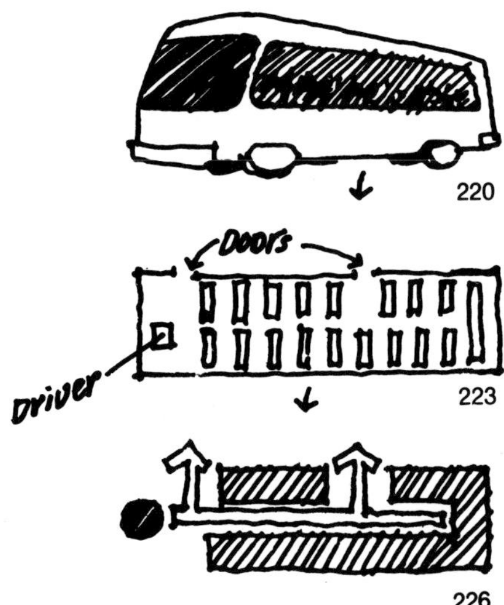

218–226
The world appears to us in three-dimensional forms (218–220). Two-dimensional plans (221–223) reduce three-dimensional spaces. Functional diagrams (224–226) are further abstractions of them.

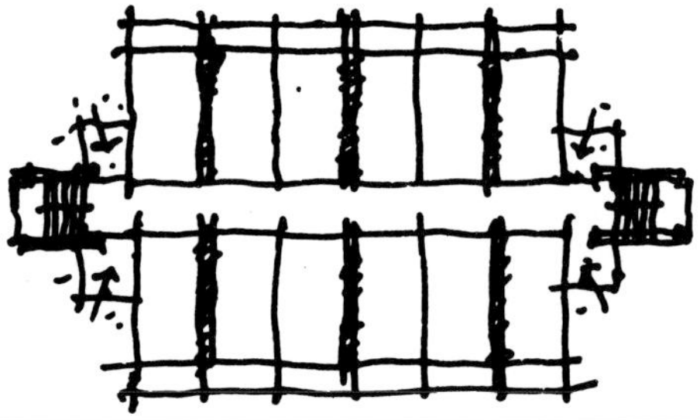

227–232
Using basic geometric shapes, the functional diagrams (from opposite page) can be simplified but retain relative size and importance (227–229). A higher abstraction altogether eliminates the size and weight differentiation (230–232).

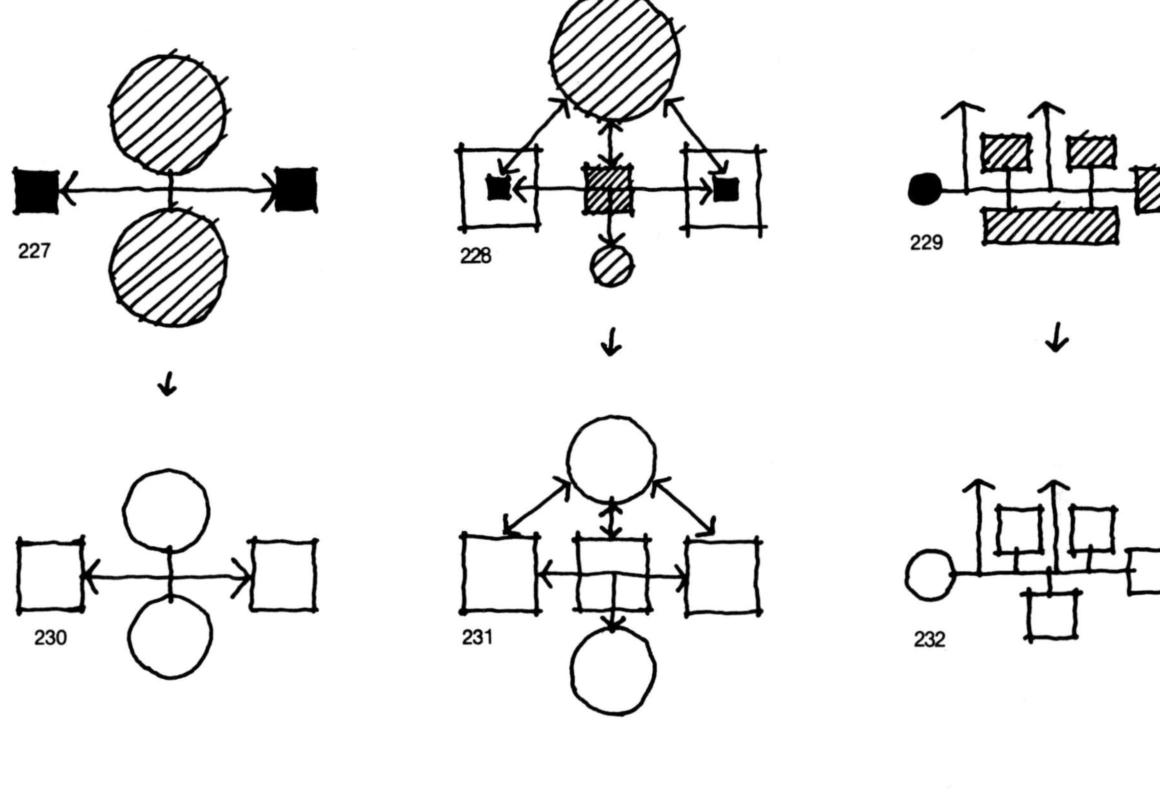

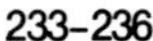

233–236
The relative importance of spaces or entities (233) can be expressed through line weights or values (234), size (235), or relative positions (236).

237–239
Line weight (238) or size (239) differentiation of arrows can be used to describe the relative importance of relationships between entities.

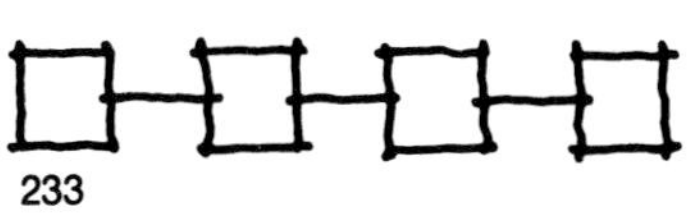
233

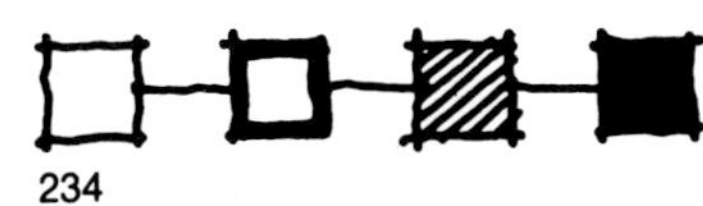
234

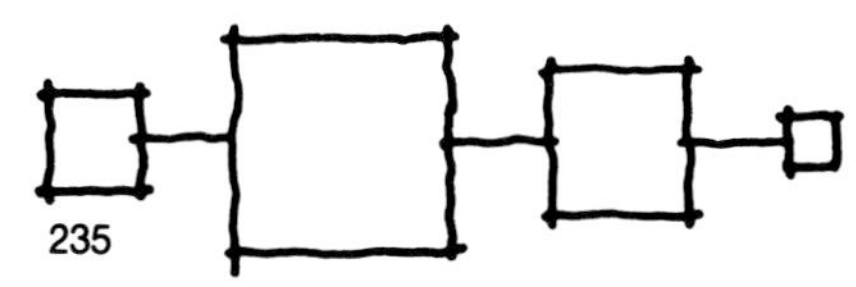
235

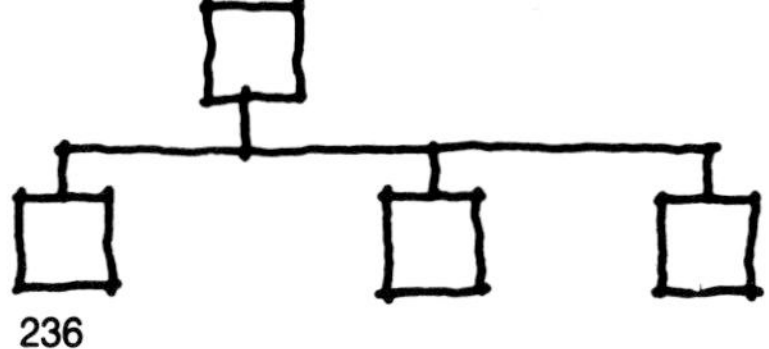
236

planes, or forms. There are various levels of abstraction. At one level, the relative size of spaces may be reflected in terms of the corresponding relative sizes of geometric shapes or forms. A higher level of abstraction may eliminate size differentiation. The relative importance of spaces or intensity of the circulation patterns may be emphasized by line weights, values, size, etc.

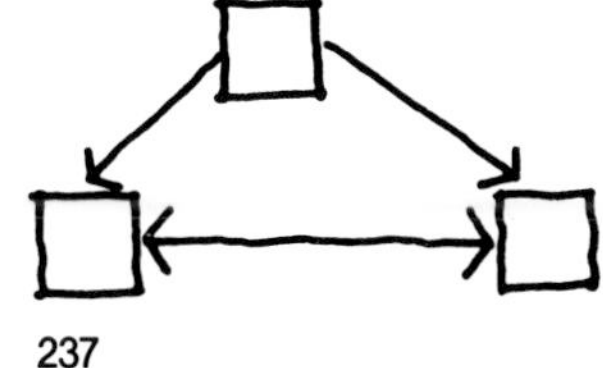
237

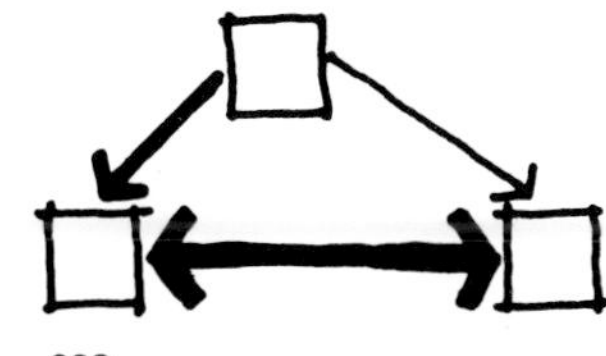
238

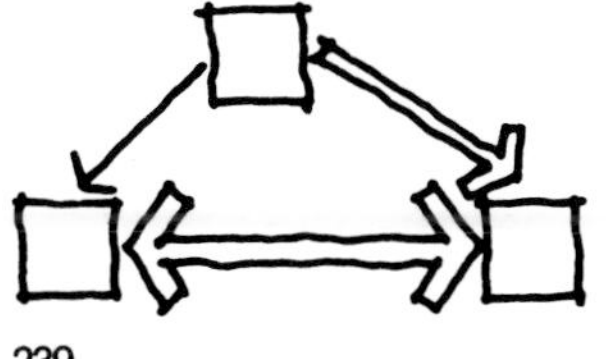
239

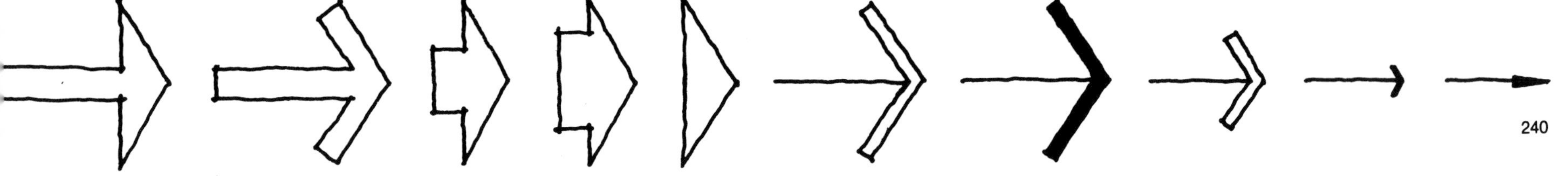
240

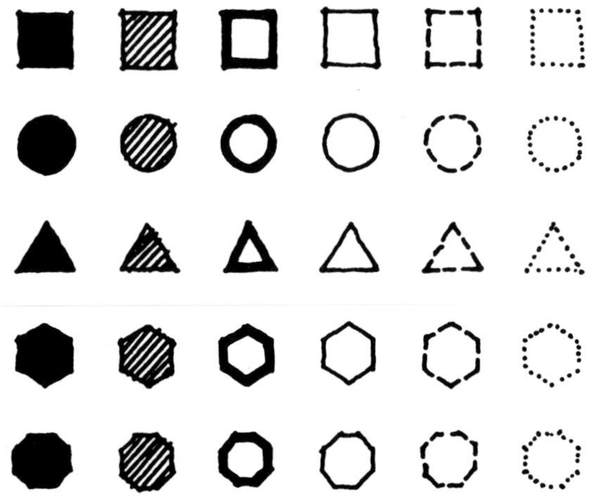
241

240
An arrow is a well understood symbol and can be represented in many ways to convey various ideas.

241
By varying values and line weights, basic geometric shapes can produce many symbols.

242
To represent various types of relationships, arrows can be differentiated by texture, value, and line weight.

243
Basic shapes can be combined to create various symbols.

SYMBOL

A symbol is a very high level of abstraction. We are familiar with and make constant use of many symbols. An arrow is a classic example. It can be modified to represent many ideas or concepts. Circles, squares, and other geometric shapes are used to represent various entities such as an activity, node, or area. William J. Bowman, in his book *Graphic Communication* (1968), considers these kinds of symbols as basic "vocabulary" in graphic language.

Unlike verbal language, the syntax in graphic language is a universal one and is expressed through the type, hierarchy, and arrangement of the symbols. The hierarchy of the symbols can be represented by their relative sizes, line weights, values, etc.

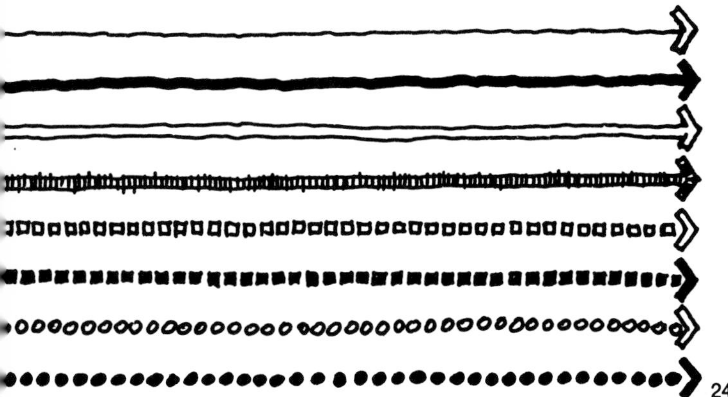
242

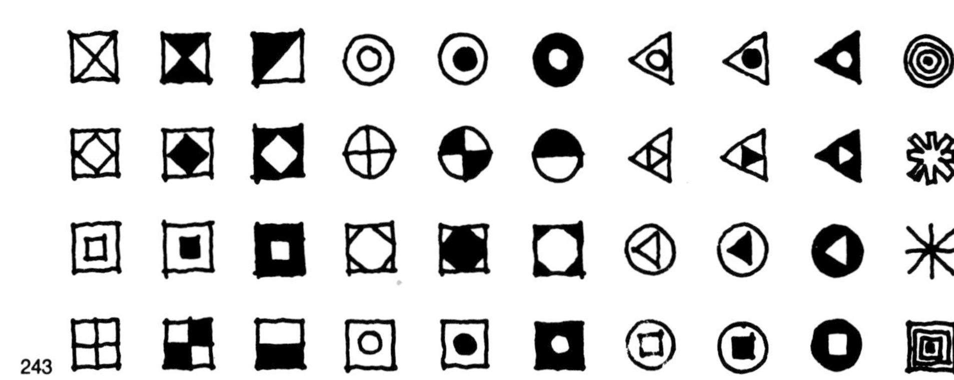
243

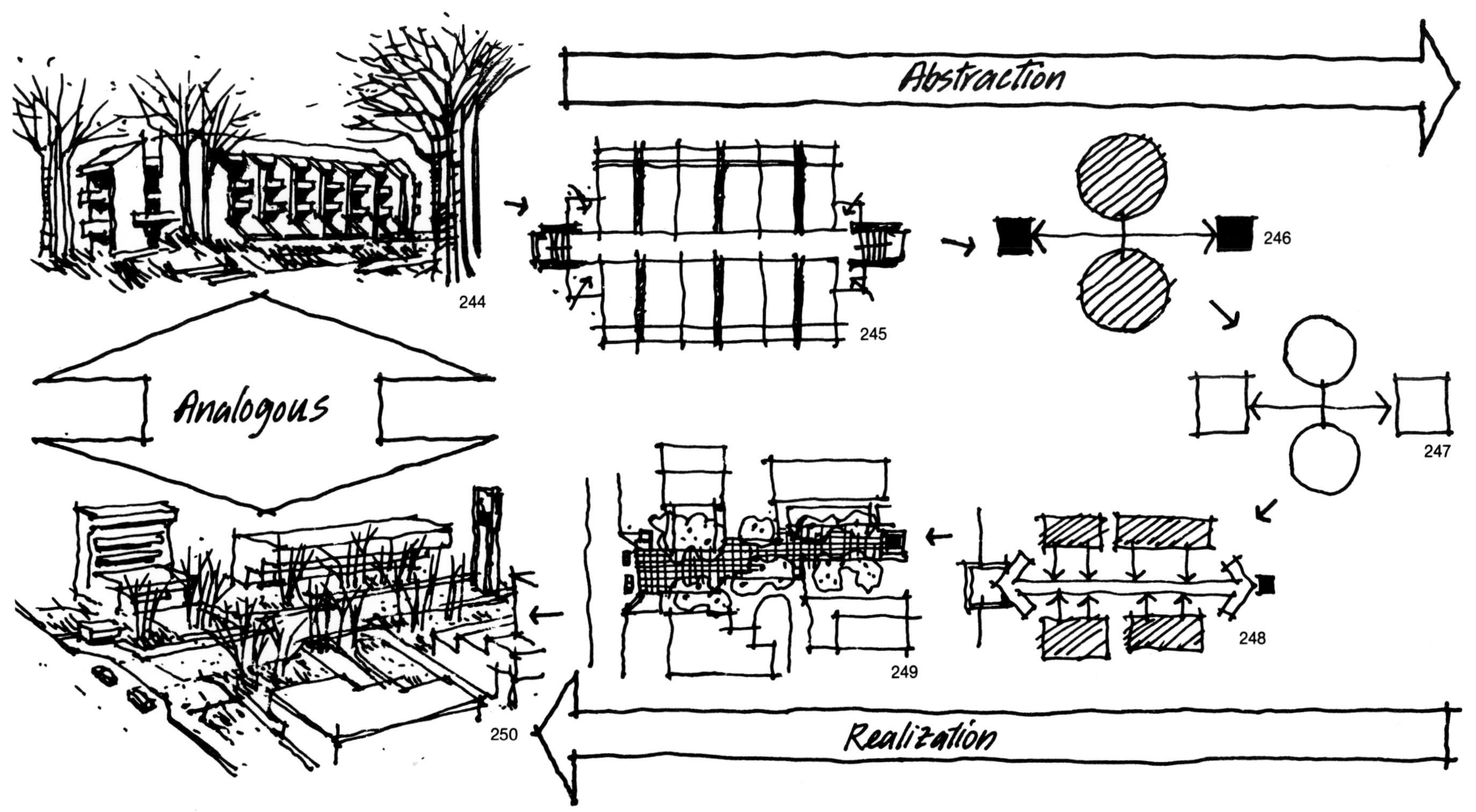

REALIZATION, ANALOGY, AND VISUAL METAPHOR

Realization is the reverse of abstraction. It is the process of taking an abstract concept or diagram and giving it a realistic form through graphic elaboration, i.e., converting it into something that can be easily recognized. An object, building, or space can be reduced to an abstract diagram, and then the diagram can be realized as something else. Such graphic games help us recognize the analogy between two things that are completely remote from

244–250
A building (244) can be reduced to a highly abstract diagram (247) through the steps of abstraction (245–246). The abstract diagram can be realized into an outdoor space (250) through the steps of realization (248–249). Thus, this outdoor space becomes analogous to the building.

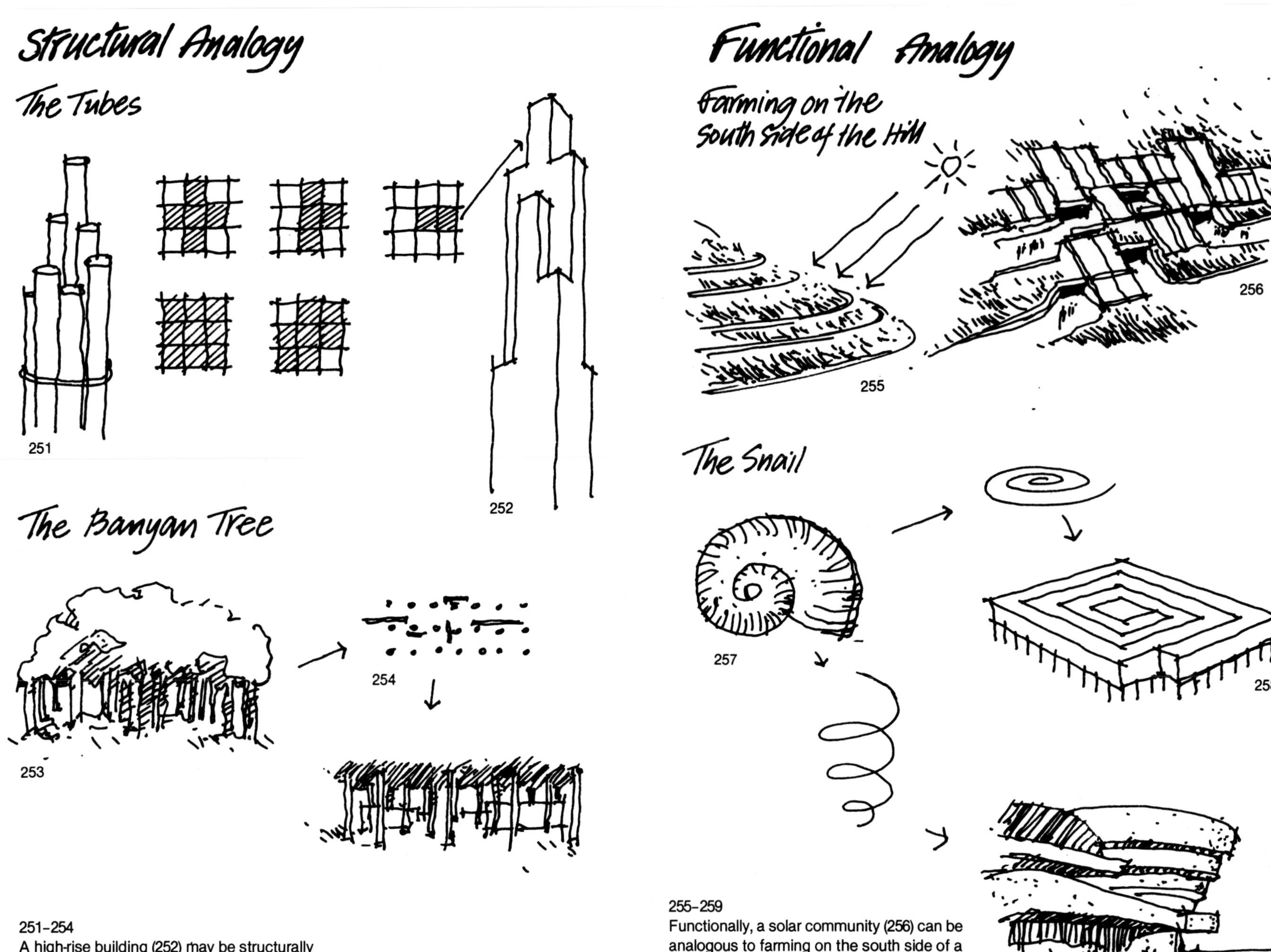

251–254
A high-rise building (252) may be structurally analogous to a bundle of tubes (251), or an interior (254) to a banyan tree (253).

255–259
Functionally, a solar community (256) can be analogous to farming on the south side of a hill (255), or the circulation system of a museum (258–259) to a snail (257).

Visual Metaphor

The Hat

260

261

The Sails

264

265

The Cubes

The Mirror

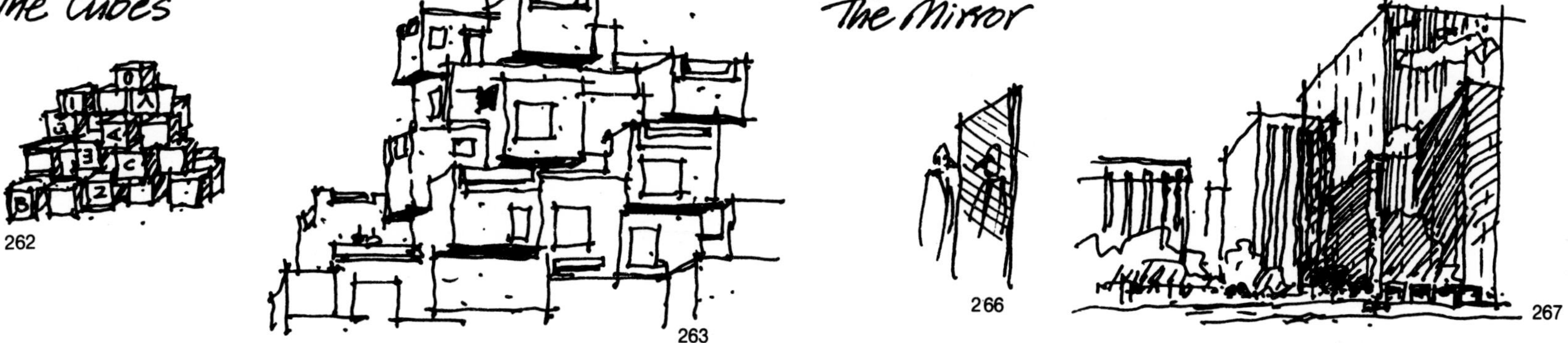

260–267
Visual metaphors are analogies that are direct in nature.

each other. A building may be represented as being analogous to the human body if considered as an assimilation of several systems. For example, the activities or functions of the former are analogous to the muscular system of the latter; the structural system is analogous to the skeletal system; and the plumbing system is analogous to the cardiovascular system. A visual metaphor is a kind of analogy and may be helpful in suggesting form alternatives.

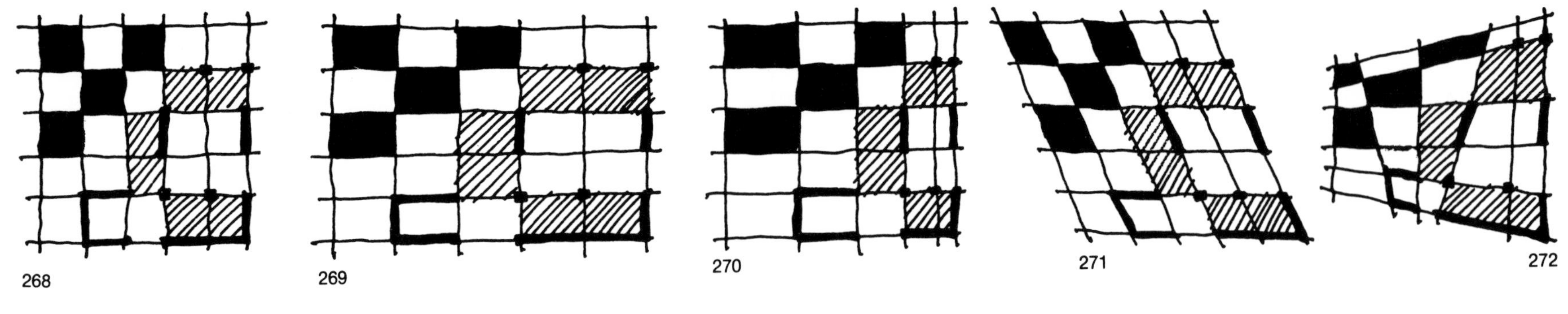

274

273

276

275

278

277

268–272
Distortion can be one-dimensional (269), progressive (270), diagonal (271), or irregular (272).

273–278
A parallelopiped (box shape) can be distorted in scale (273, 275, and 277) and made into an interior (274) or outdoor spaces (276 and 278).

DISTORTION AND PROJECTION

Distorting the drawing or its parts is another method of graphic exploration. It makes us look at things from a different point of view. Distortion can be of various types, among which are distortions of scale, perspective, or proportion. Every one of us sees a drawing from a different point of view. Projecting ourselves into other points of view allows us to see drawings differently. Such projection leads to new graphic analysis and alternatives.

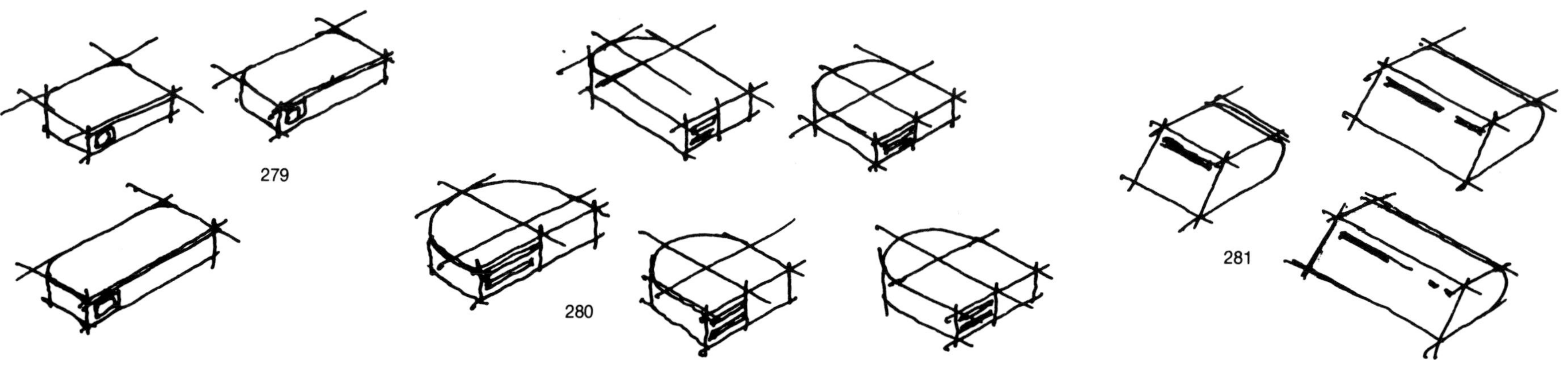

279–281
In product design, distorting any or all of the three dimensions is very helpful in the study of the form.

TOPOLOGICAL TRANSFORMATION

Topological transformation is an excellent example of distortion. While the surface relationship remains the same, the distortion of form produces different objects. For example, a cylinder can be topologically distorted into an annulus (a plane with one hole). A sphere can be transformed into a cup but it will lack the handle since the handle requires a hole.

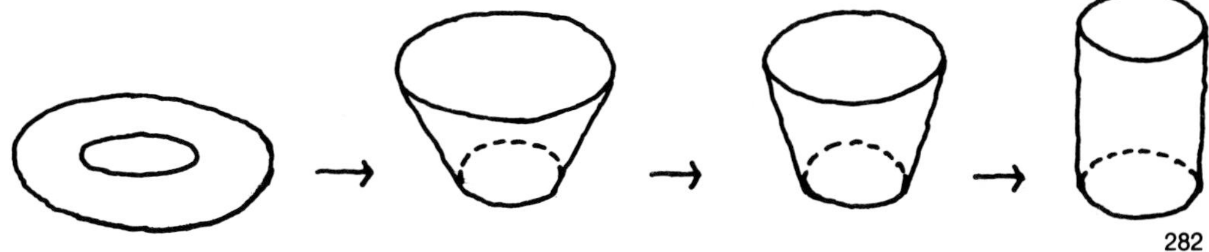

282
Topologically, a hollow cylinder can be distorted into an annulus.

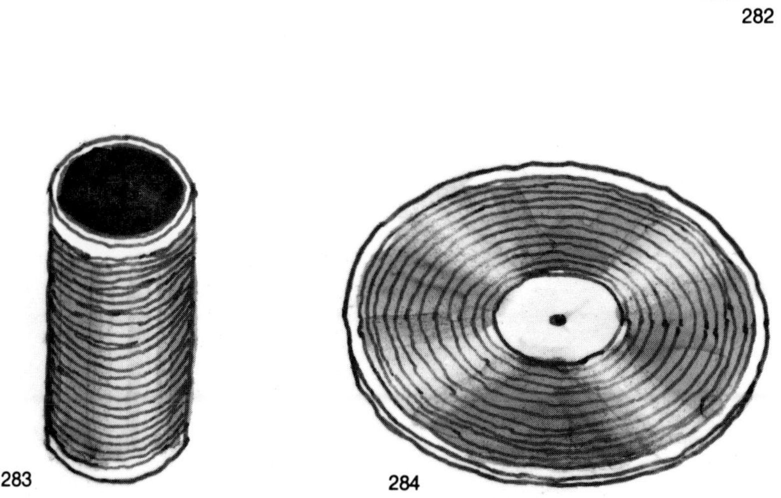

283–284
Early versions of cylindrical gramophone records (283) are homeomorphic to modern discs (284). Since the function of both is the same, the topological transformation was natural.

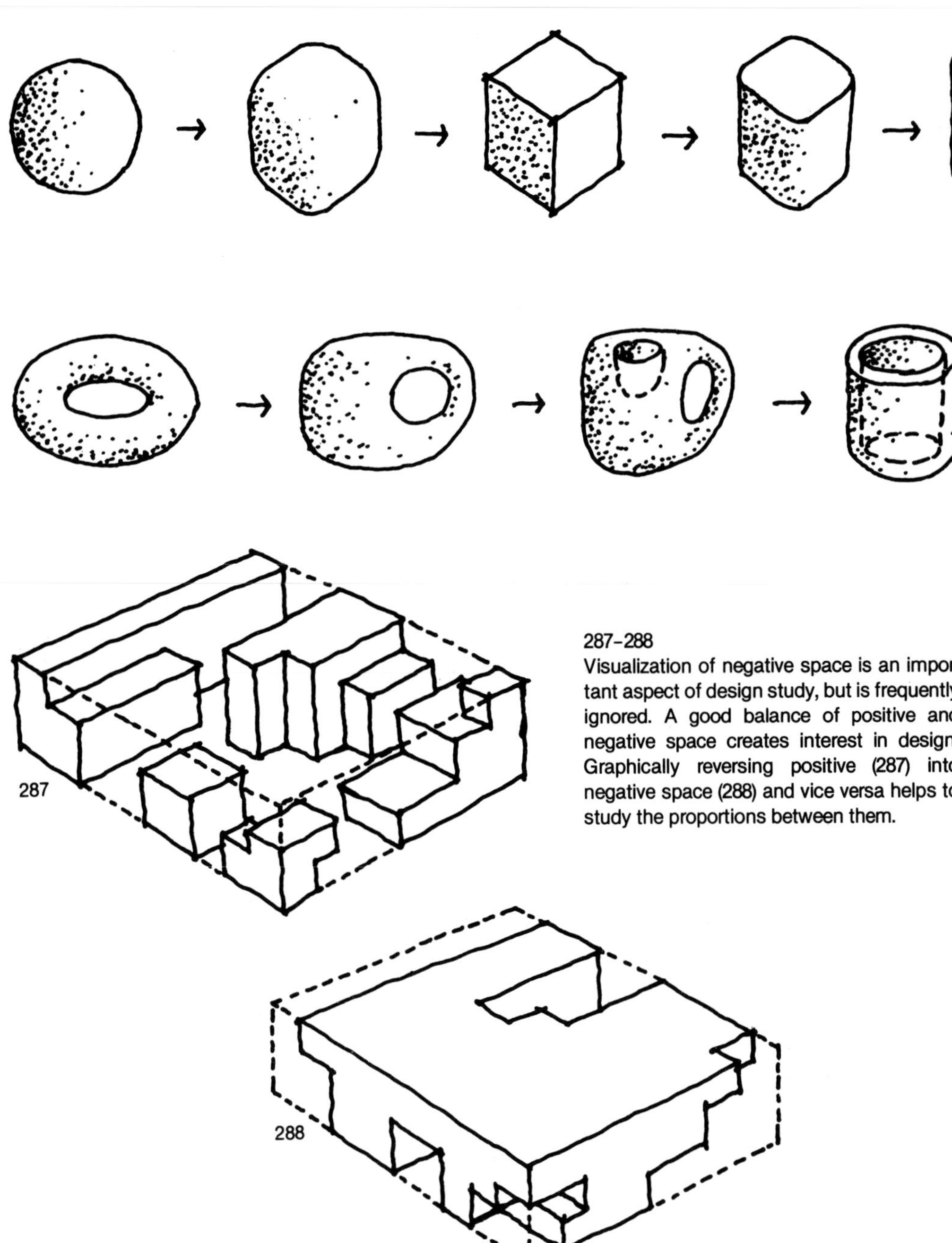

285
Without losing the topological continuity, a sphere can be transformed into a cup, but it will lack a handle.

286
A cup with a handle is a homeomorphic transformation of a doughnut-form. (Drawn after Stephen Barr's *Experiments in Topology,* 1964)

287–288
Visualization of negative space is an important aspect of design study, but is frequently ignored. A good balance of positive and negative space creates interest in design. Graphically reversing positive (287) into negative space (288) and vice versa helps to study the proportions between them.

However, a doughnut-form can be distorted into a cup with a handle without losing the topological continuity. Thus, a doughnut is homeomorphic to a cup, whereas a cylinder is homeomorphic to an annulus. Similar graphic analysis can be made to explore the homeomorphic transformations of a space or object.

NEGATIVE SPACE

Since we (our verbal selves) are in the habit of naming things, in a drawing we look for objects that have names. Thus, we tend to ignore the spaces around the object—negative spaces. As we have seen before, reversing the drawing, i.e., outlining or darkening only the negative spaces by leaving the blank area for the object, can help us see it purely from the standpoint of visual composition. Similar study can also be done for the volumes of spaces, making the solid into void, and the void into solid.

PERMUTATION AND COMBINATION

In algebra, we are familiar with permutations and combinations. Two items can be arranged in 2 different ways and three items can be arranged in 6 different ways. Similarly, four items will give 24 possibilities, whereas five items will produce 120 possibilities. Furthermore, taking five items but considering only two items at the same time results in 20 possibilities, whereas considering only three items at the same time will result in 60 possibilities. These are possibilities only for linear arrangements. But if we take account of all three dimensions in which the items can be arranged, the possibilities increase much more rapidly. Similar permutation and combination games can be played graphically with shapes and forms. With two, three, or four basic shapes and forms, various possibilities can be developed. The derivatives of these shapes or forms

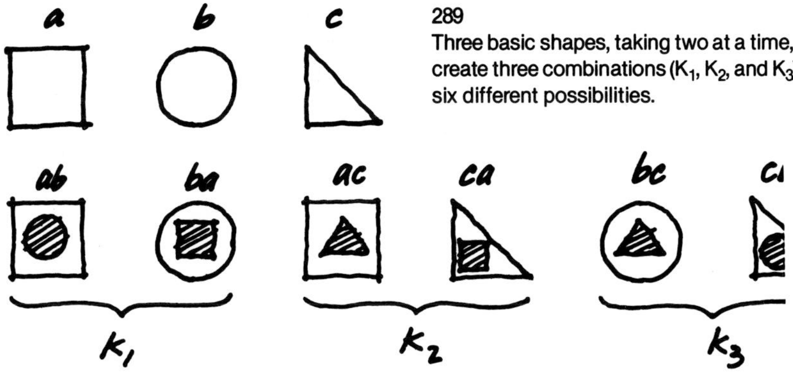

289
Three basic shapes, taking two at a time, can create three combinations (K_1, K_2, and K_3) but six different possibilities.

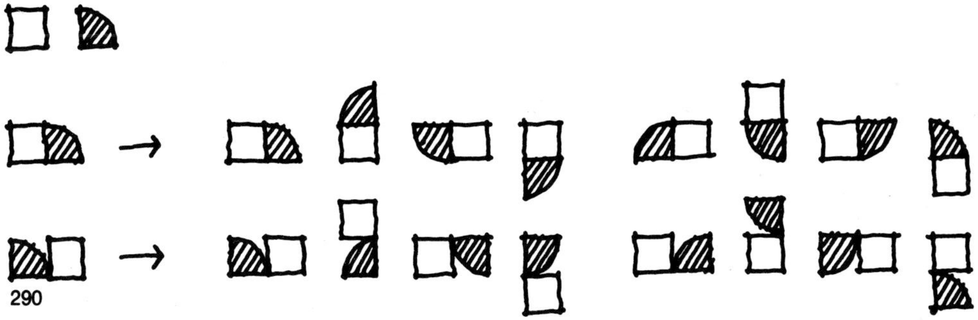

290
A square and pie shape can be arranged in two different ways, each of which can create eight possible arrangements if reversed or rotated in all three dimensions.

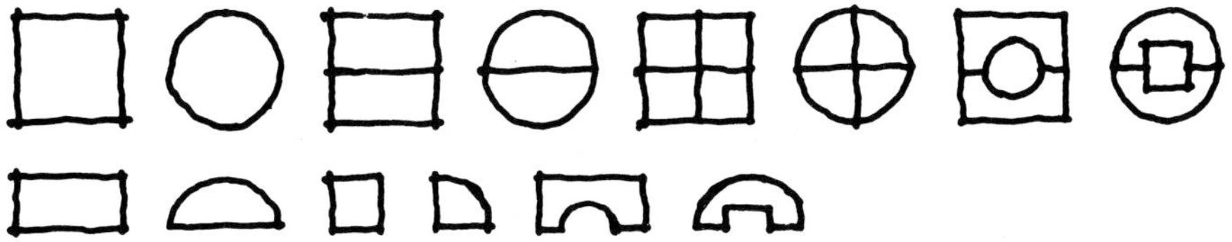

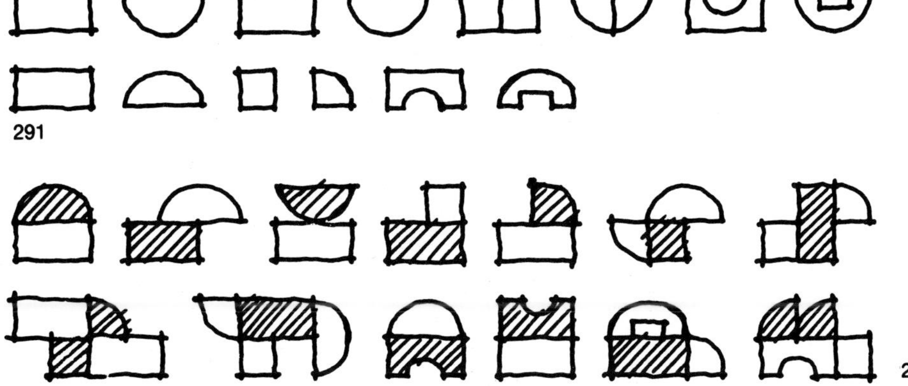

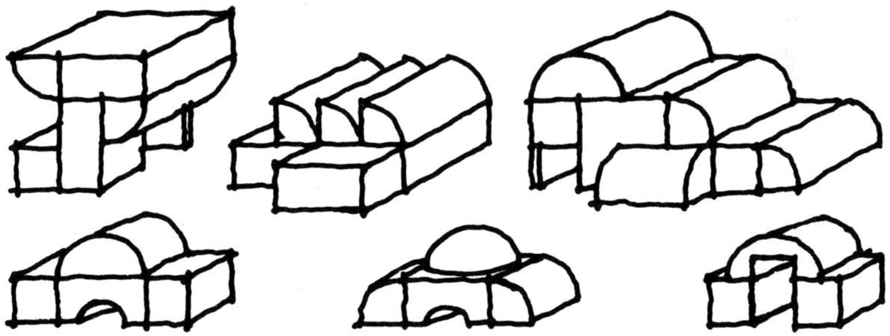

293

291–293
A square and circle can produce a series of derivative shapes (291) that can be combined in numerous ways (292). Similar manipulations can be made in three dimensions and are very useful for design studies (293).

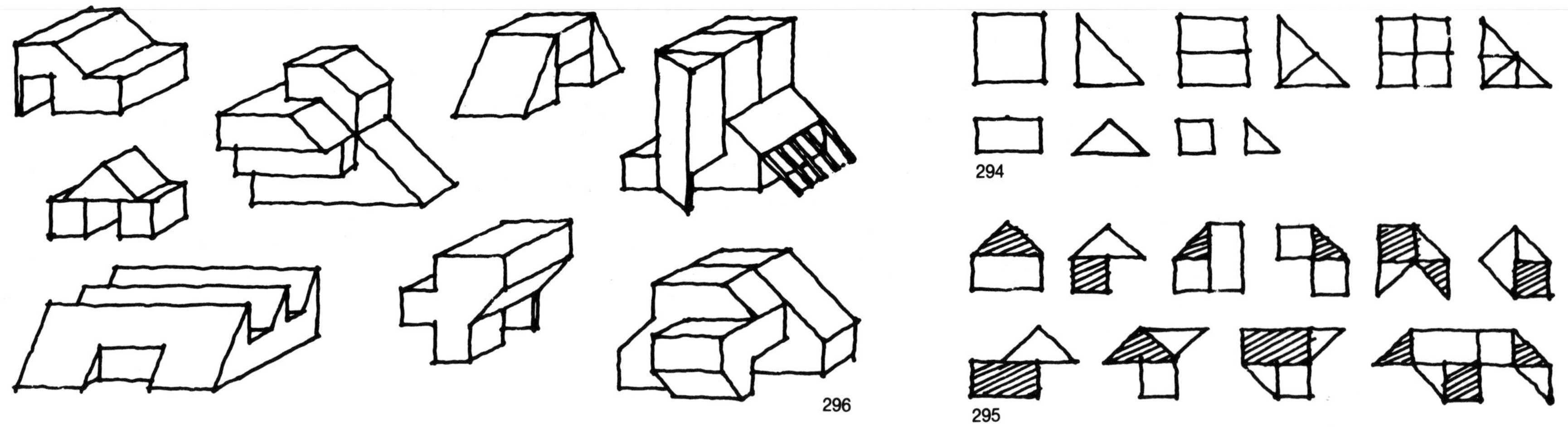

294–296
A square and triangle can produce a series of derivative shapes (294) that can be combined in numerous ways (295). Here, too, three-dimensional manipulation can produce numerous possibilities (296).

297
If three basic shapes—a square, circle and triangle—are combined and manipulated, possibilities in form become still larger.

can become additional items and thus increase the number of possibilities still higher. The square and the pie shape can be arranged into two different ways. Each of these arrangements can create 8 possibilities by rotating or reversing in three dimensions. Such graphic exploration leads to the evolution of new shapes and forms, and thus to new ideas.

Part Five

Graphic Association

13

Organizational Patterns

We saw in the previous chapter that analogies and visual metaphors contribute to the formulation of new concepts and ideas. The reason behind such contributing factors is the fact that there exist certain organizational similarities among objects, spaces, and the biological world. But ordinary eyes fail to see beyond the camouflage of materials, textures, and colors, and thus cannot notice these similarities. It is the ability to see organizational patterns that prompts the development of analogies and visual metaphors. The next few paragraphs will discuss some of these organizational patterns and their graphic expressions.

298–306
Snow crystals occur in hexagonal symmetry which can take various organizational patterns. A crystal takes a shape that can be repeated since atoms in it are stacked in all directions.

307

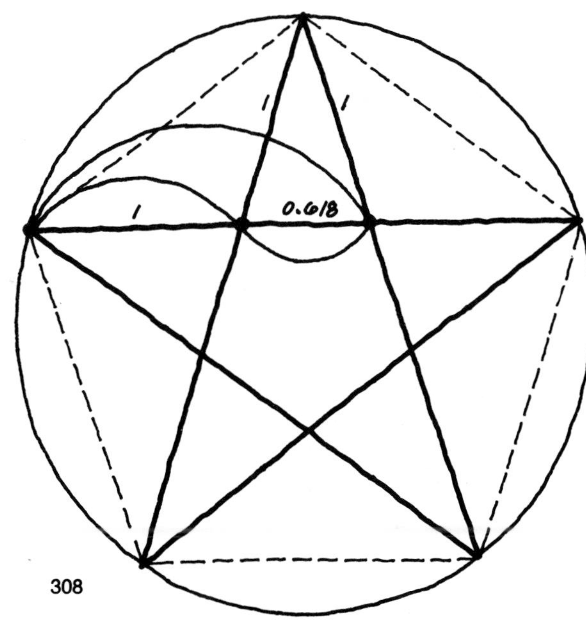

308

307–308
Pentagonal symmetry is absent in the inanimate world of crystals (since structural triangulation is not possible with five at a time) but it is common in living forms of animals and plants (307). Two equal sides of each triangle in the pentagonal star are in the proportion of the Golden Section to the third side (308).

NUCLEAR, MULTINUCLEAR, AND SATELLITE

Both in cell organization and at the subatomic level the nucleus serves as the center of vitality. Thus, a strong central focus is associated with the organization of a *nuclear* model. Graphically, the central entity commands emphasis by virtue of its

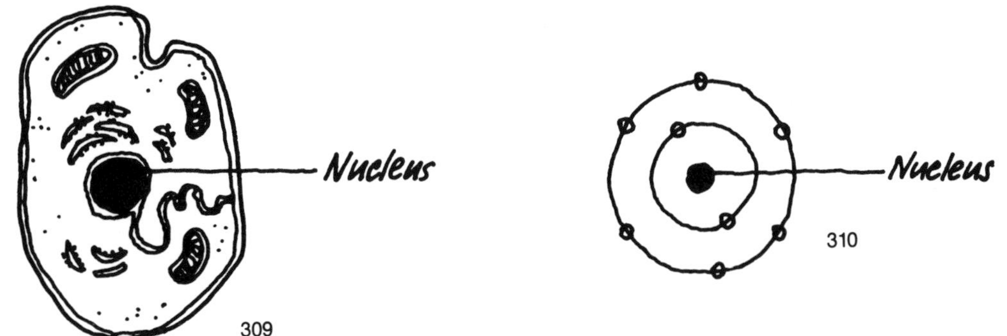

309–310
The nucleus gives unity both to the cell and to the atomic organization.

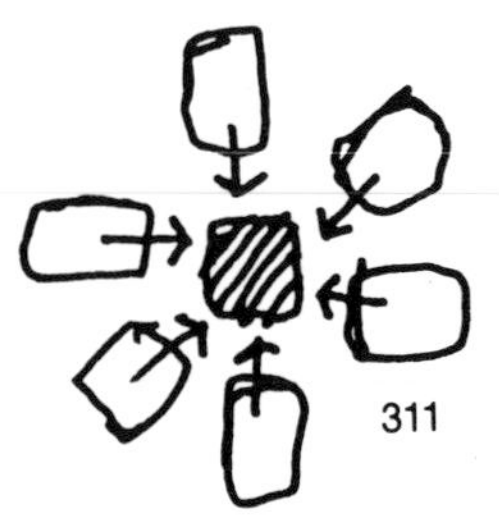

311

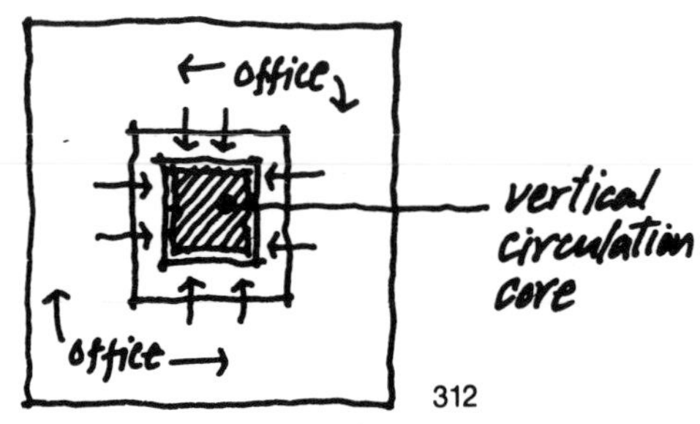

312

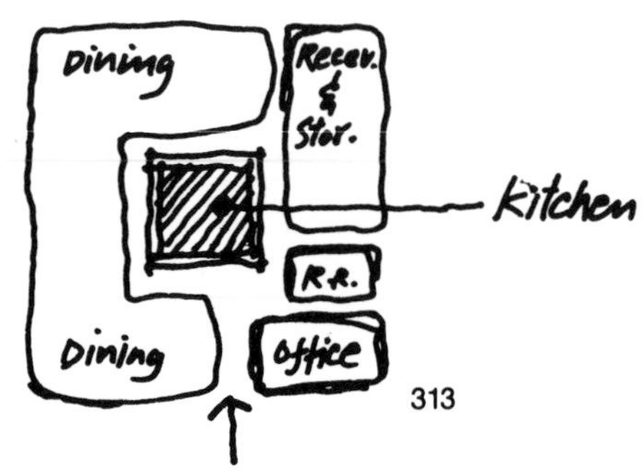

313

311–316
The central entity in a nuclear organization provides a sense of unity.

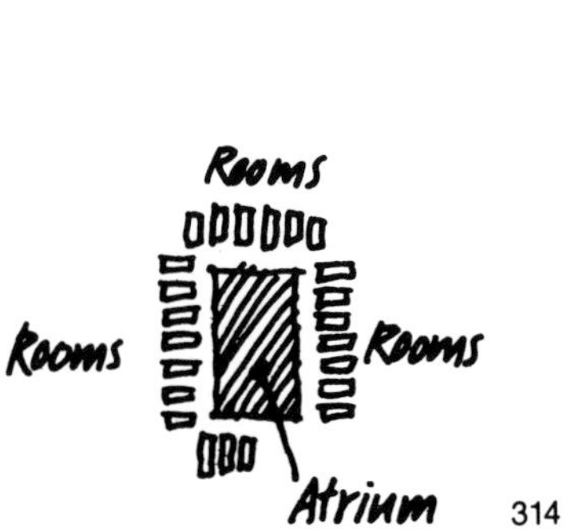

314

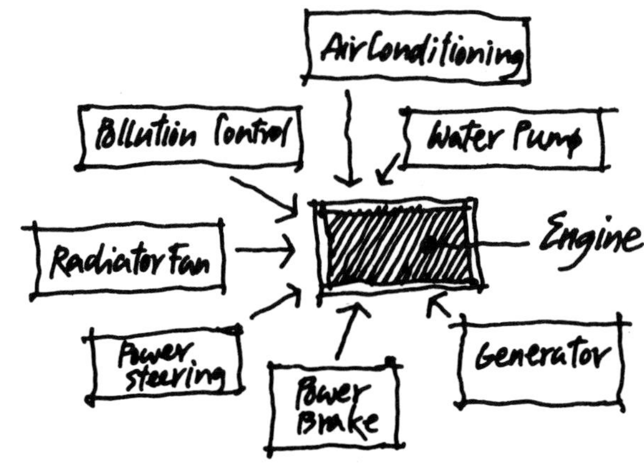

315

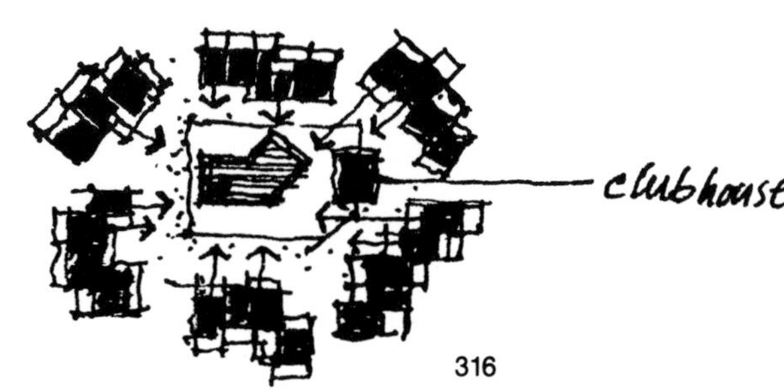

316

317

location and importance vis à vis other entities. This model is also known as *centralized* organization.

A *multinuclear* organization is decentralized, having several nuclei of more or less equal importance. Each nucleus is emphasized and singled out from its surrounding entities while maintaining same hierarchical level with other nuclei.

The organization of the *satellite* model has a large nucleus at the center with smaller nuclei as its extensions. Each of these smaller nuclei, in turn, has

317–318
For an open space, the nucleus can be emphasized by location, scale, or function. In this case, the fountain serves as the nucleus which is emphasized by its size and the sound and movement of water.

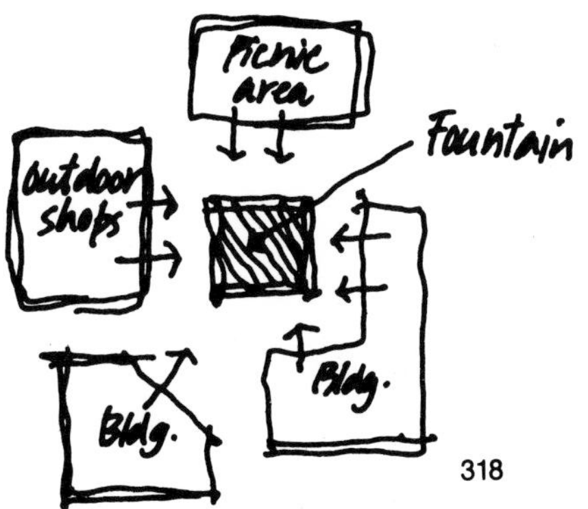

318

319

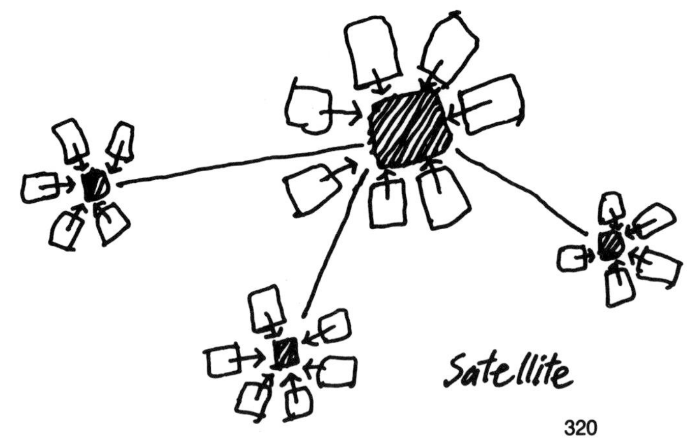

320

319–320
Both multinuclear and satellite organizations have been used for large-scale community development concepts.

subordinate entities that surround it. The large nucleus may also have subordinate entities.

CIRCULAR, INTROVERT, AND EXTROVERT

When entities are arranged in a circle, a sense of participation is generated. Each entity commands equal importance, and thus a sense of common

321–323
A sense of participation, common goal, and orientation are basic elements of circular organization.

321

322

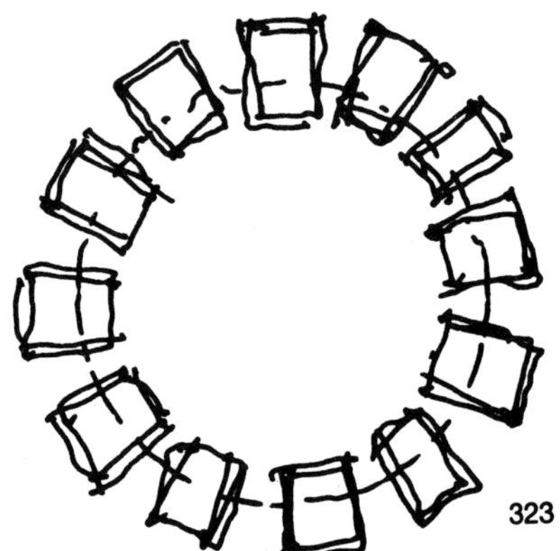

323

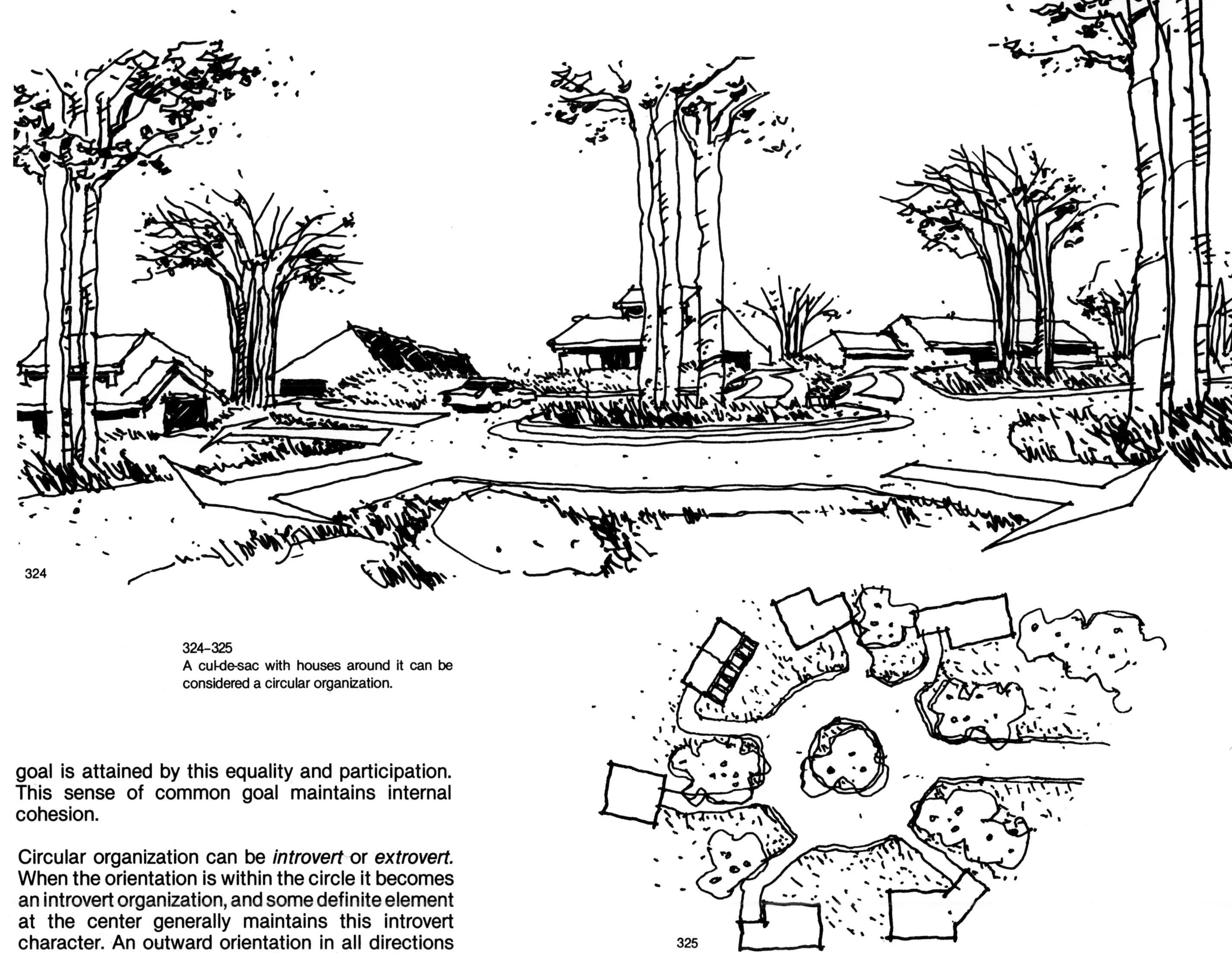

324

325

324–325
A cul-de-sac with houses around it can be considered a circular organization.

goal is attained by this equality and participation. This sense of common goal maintains internal cohesion.

Circular organization can be *introvert* or *extrovert.* When the orientation is within the circle it becomes an introvert organization, and some definite element at the center generally maintains this introvert character. An outward orientation in all directions

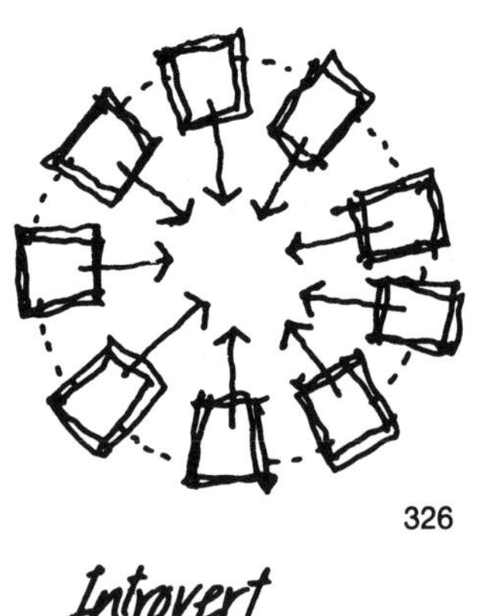

326

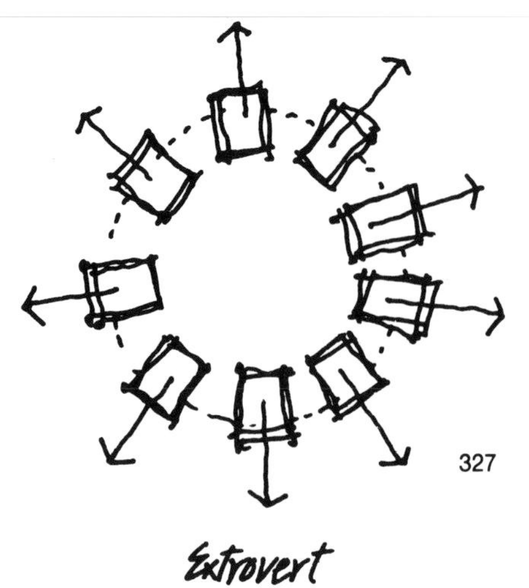

327

326–327
A circular organization can be introvert or extrovert depending on the orientation of the entities.

328–329
A concentric organization can occur with an increasing emphasis toward the center.

makes the organization an extrovert one. Such outward orientation may result from a common cause or interest.

CONCENTRIC

Concentric circles represent hierarchical development with each circle. The emphasis may be associated with the center or periphery. A central emphasis results in increasing importance of the inner circles, whereas peripheral emphasis produces a castling effect, with the outer layers having greater strength and importance.

A concentric organization can have increasing emphasis on both the center and periphery with decreasing emphasis on the middle circles. Such an organization can be reversed, with increasing emphasis on the middle circles and decreasing emphasis on the center and periphery.

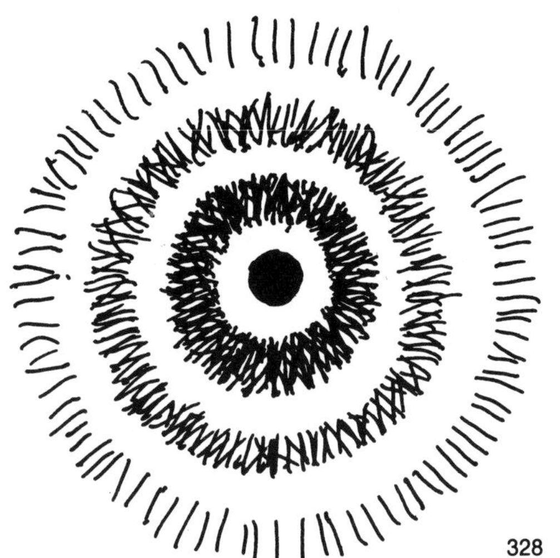
328

329

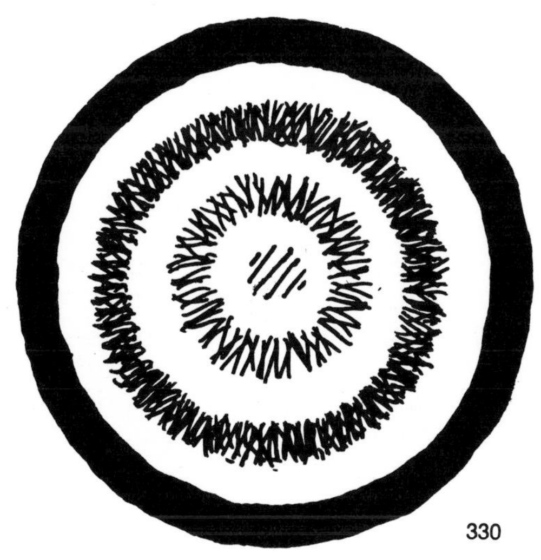
330

331

332

330–333
The emphasis may be reversed by increasing toward the periphery and decreasing toward the center (330). In a single organization, the emphasis may be increasing and then decreasing (331) or vice versa (332–333).

333

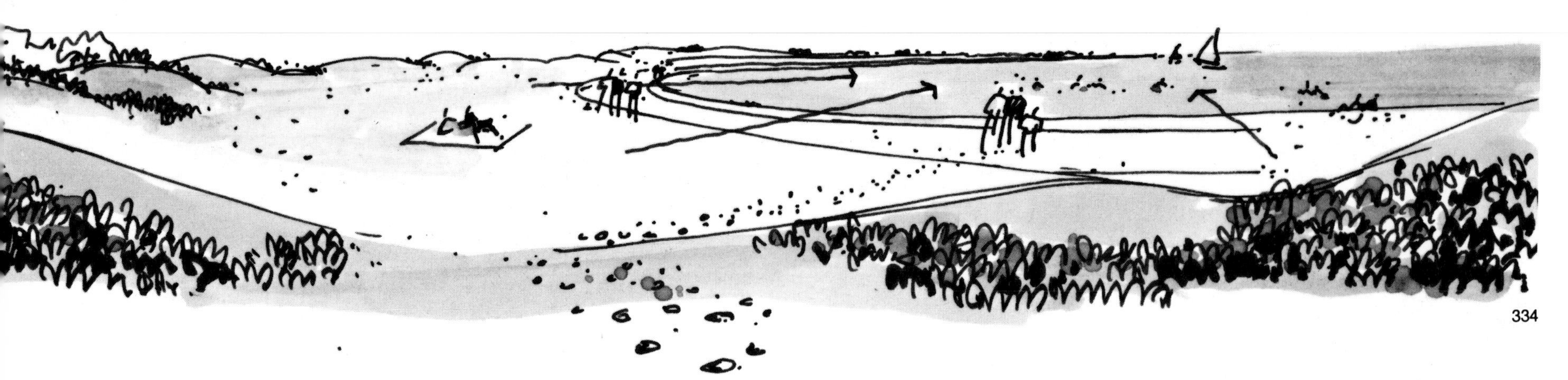

334

AMPHITHEATER AND FAN

The organization of an *amphitheater* model involves a concave arrangement of entities as the spectators and a focal point as the stage. This relationship of spectators and stage serves as a successful graphic concept of spaces for various public places.

334–336
In this case, the body of water serves as the stage and the beach as the spectator.

335

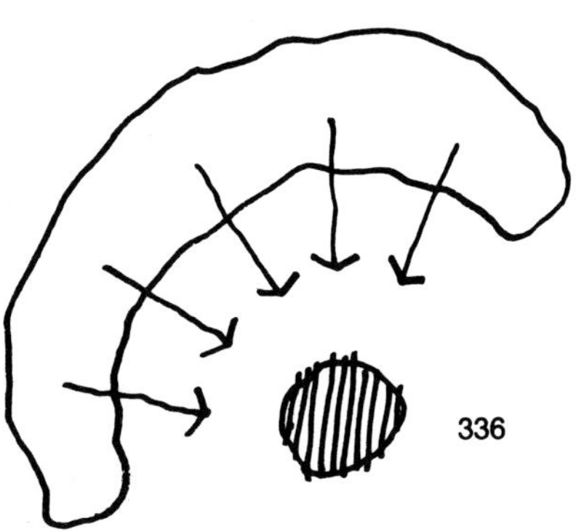

336

Fan arrangement is just the opposite of amphitheater and the emphasis is shifted from the central focal point to the outward direction of the fringe. Here, attention is diverted to a panorama instead of a single element.

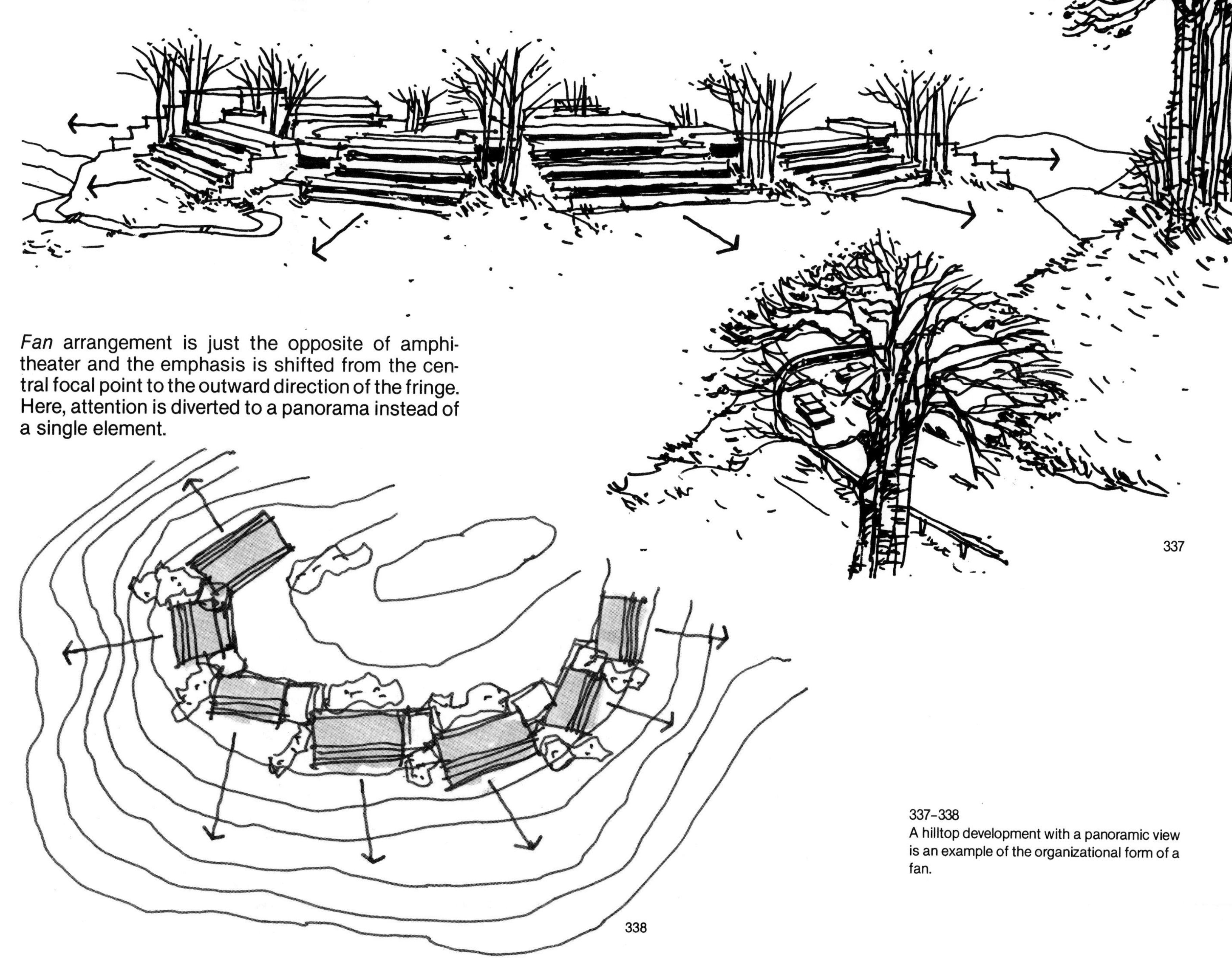

337–338
A hilltop development with a panoramic view is an example of the organizational form of a fan.

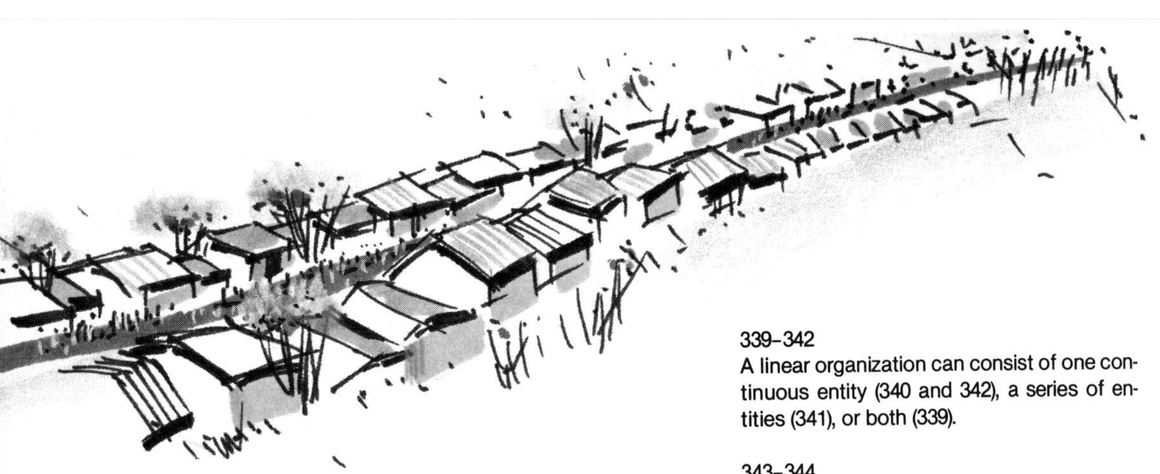

339

340

341

339–342
A linear organization can consist of one continuous entity (340 and 342), a series of entities (341), or both (339).

343–344
A curvilinear organization is dynamic.

LINEAR, CURVILINEAR, AND ANCHOR

Arranging entities along a line or string produces *linear* organization. Such an organization can be *straight* or *curvilinear,* but in either case, it is open ended.

343

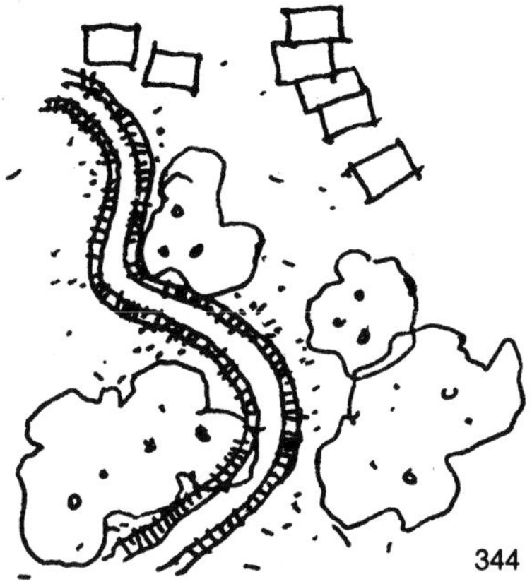

344

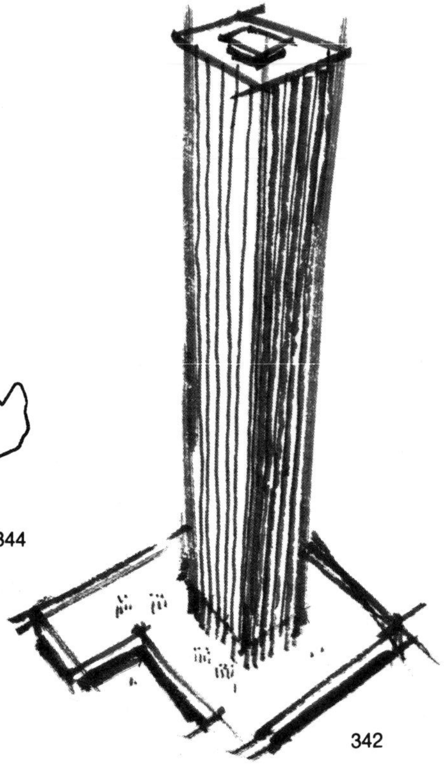

342

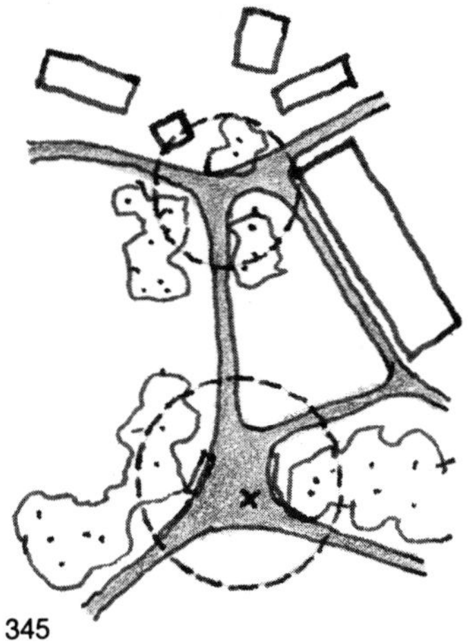

345

346

345–347
In a pedestrian circulation system, the nodes can be thought of as anchors.

The ends of linear organization can be terminated by adding termini or *anchors.* Anchors can also be added at various other points between the ends, especially to emphasize the points of directional

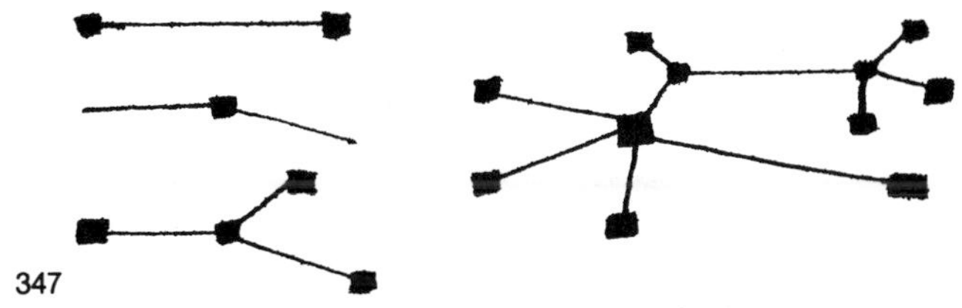

347

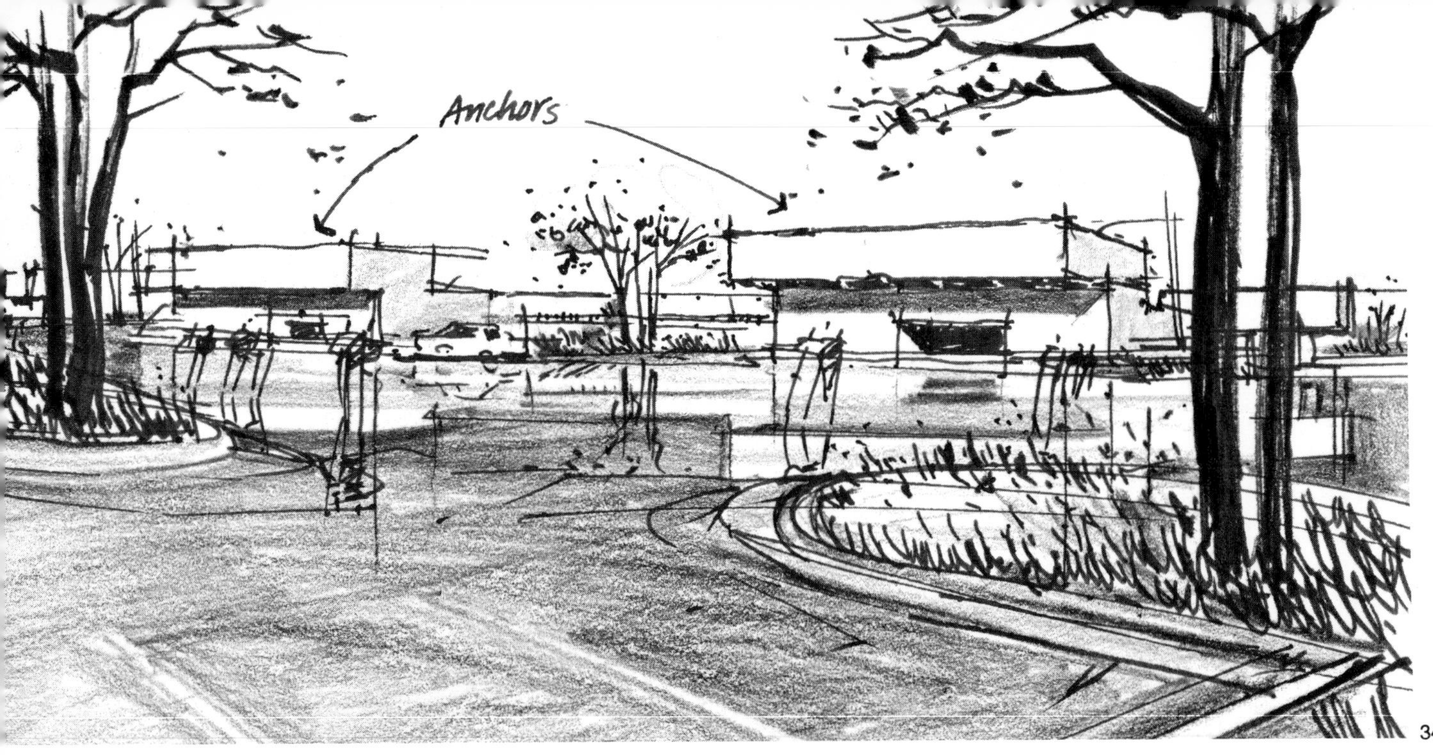

348

348–350
The anchor concept is common in the plan organization of shopping centers (348–349) and airports (350).

change or convergence of lines. This type of graphic concept has been frequently used for airports and shopping centers.

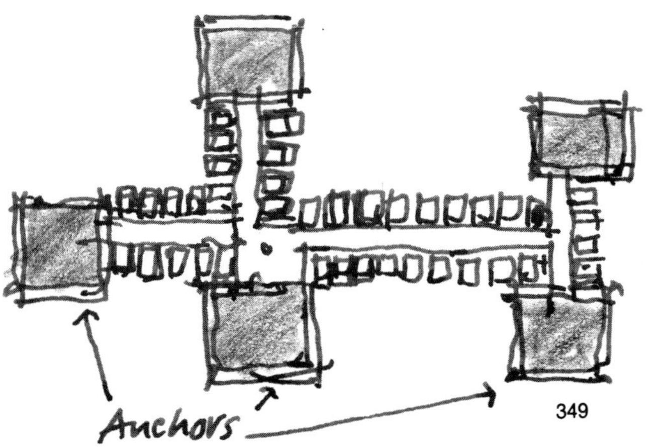

349

350

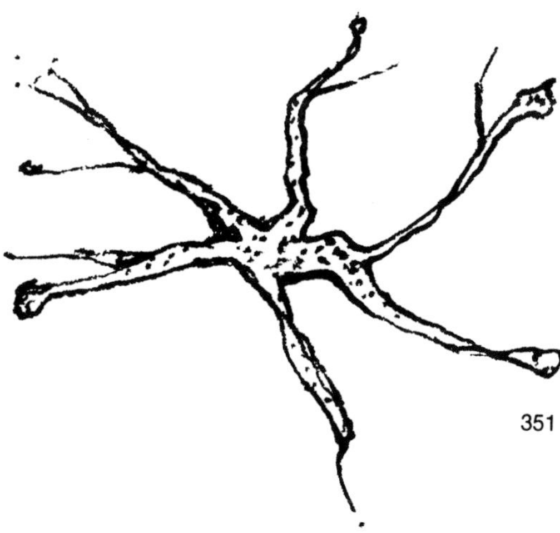

351

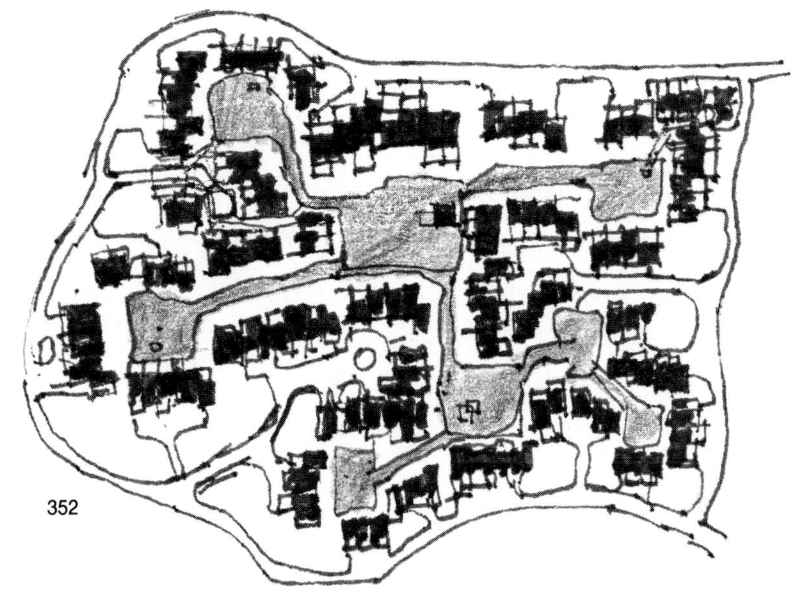

352

BRANCHING

When a system or an entity reaches selectively remote areas, an organization of *branching* or a *finger* model is created. This organizational type is also known as *pipeline.* Pedestrian and vehicular circulations in housing developments or cities represent this type of organization.

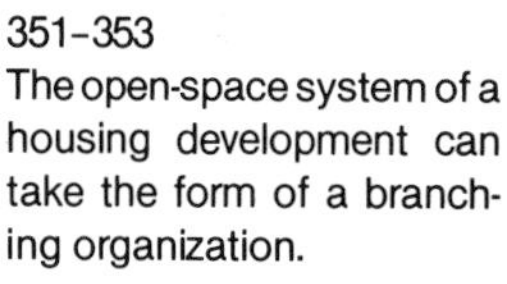

351–353
The open-space system of a housing development can take the form of a branching organization.

353

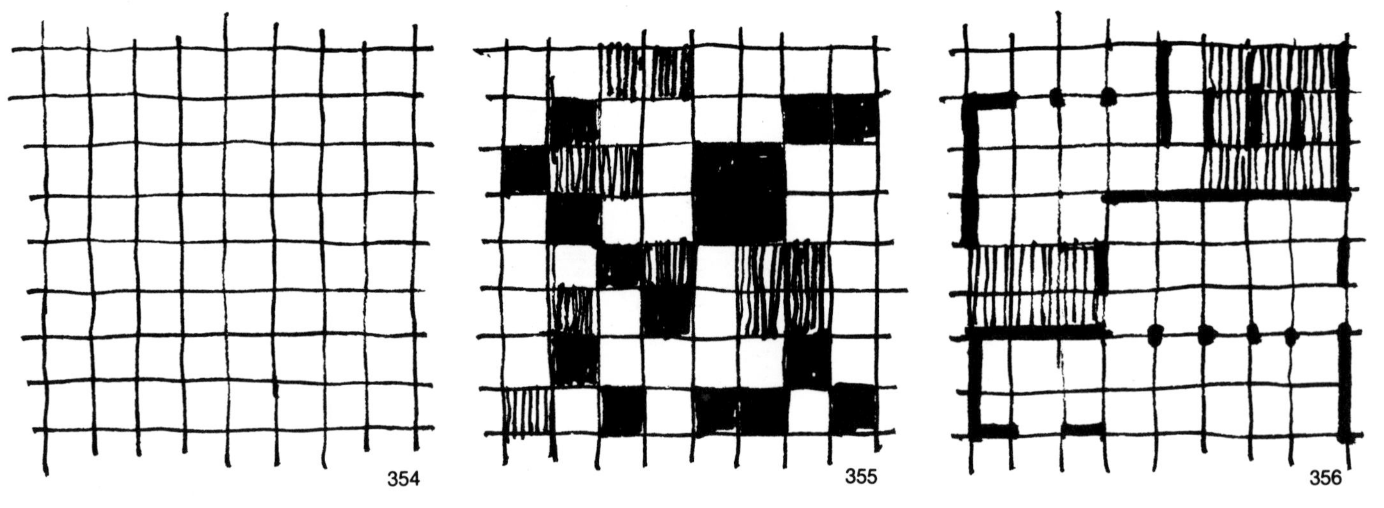

354   355   356

354–362
A checkerboard organization can be developed by using square (354–356), triangular (357–359), or hexagonal (360–362) grids.

CHECKERBOARD, ADDITIVE AND SUBTRACTIVE

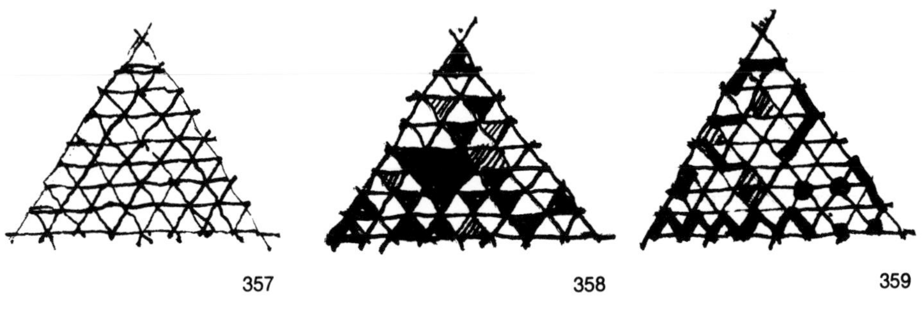

357   358   359

Two-dimensional space can be divided into grids of small squares. An arrangement where the components fill in some of these grids, or every alternative grid, can be called *checkerboard* organization. Grids can also be triangular or hexagonal. This organizational type is very flexible and, depending

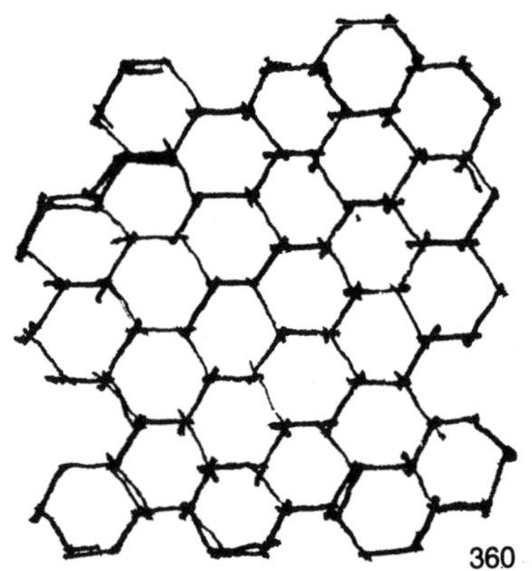

360

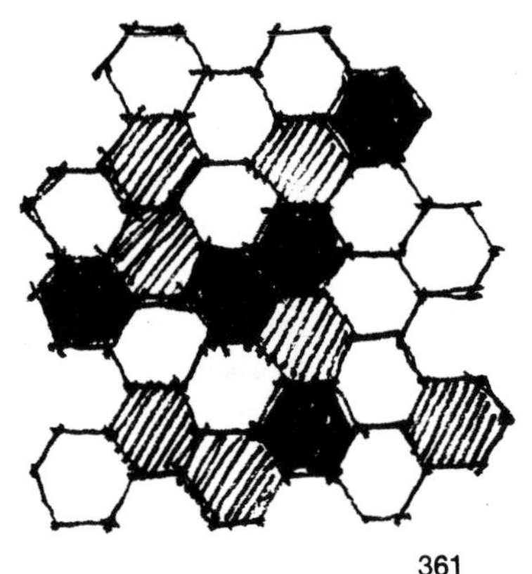

361

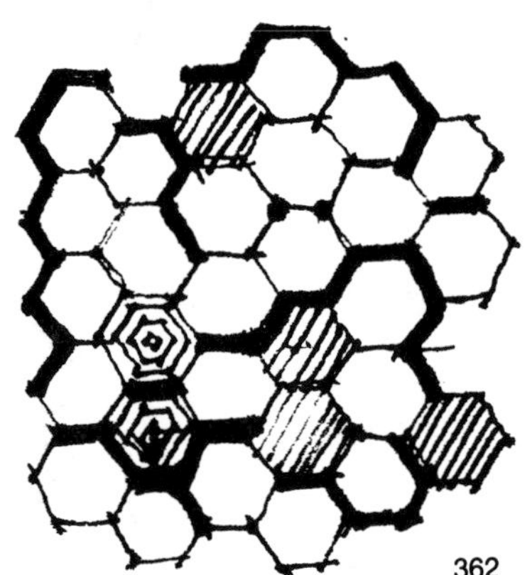

362

363–364
Square and hexagonal grids can be used in three-dimensional spatial studies.

on needs, can be expanded or contracted without losing its very character.

A large space can also be viewed as a compact composition of crystals of small three-dimensional spaces. For example, small cubes can be stacked to form a large cube. Similarly, honeycombs, pyramids, or tetrahedrons can be stacked to form a large space of various configurations. A series of arrangements can be made by filling some of those small crystals of spaces, or alternative ones, thus creating a type of organization that is the three-dimensional counterpart of the checkerboard.

Another series of arrangements can be created by adding to the grids or crystals of space and they may be called *additive* organizations. When a

365–366
A space can be divided into crystals of small cubes and manipulated by adding or subtracting these cubes.

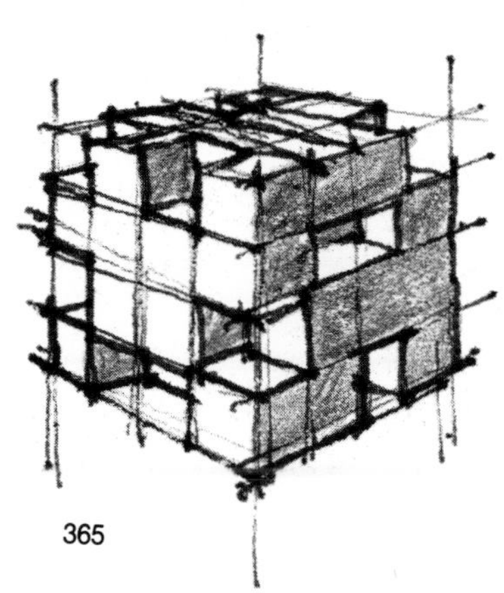

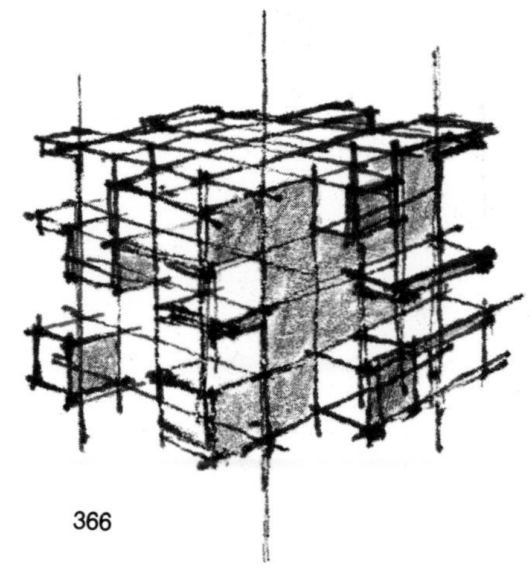

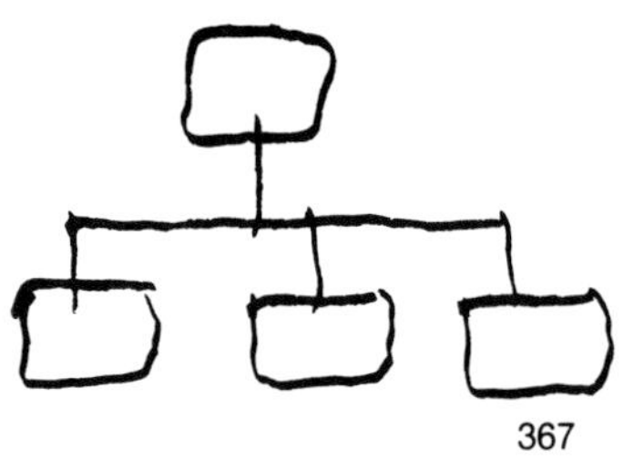

367

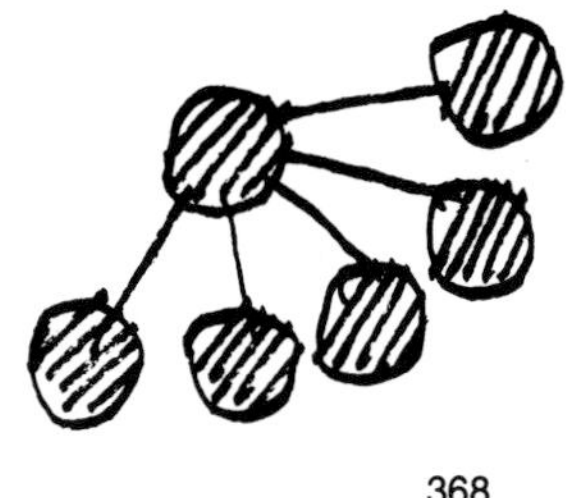

368

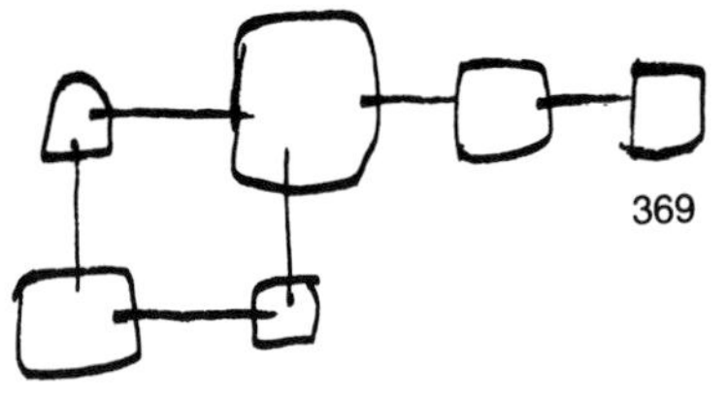

369

370

similar arrangement is made by subtracting from the grids or crystals of space, a *subtractive* organization is created.

HIERARCHICAL

Relative placement can express the importance of certain entities over others and thus create *hierarchy* among them. This kind of organization can be called *positional* hierarchy. The relative importance of specific entities can also be expressed by their relative sizes, which thereby creates the organizational type of *size* hierarchy. Graphically, values and line weights can be added to certain entities to emphasize their relative importance and thus create *qualitative* hierarchy.

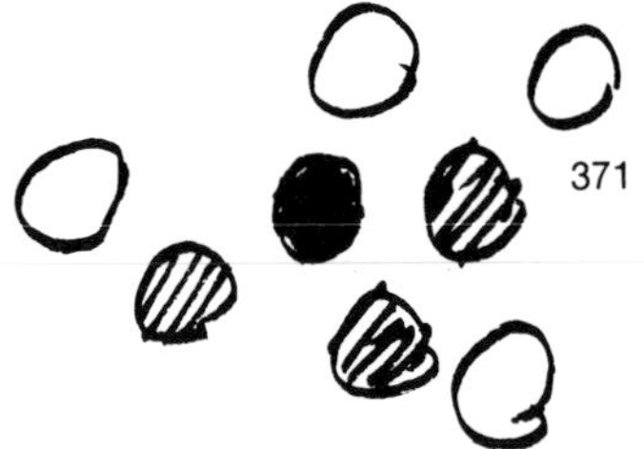

371

372

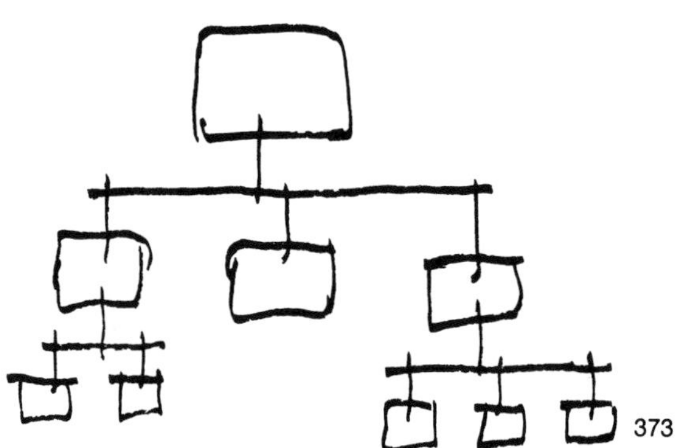

373

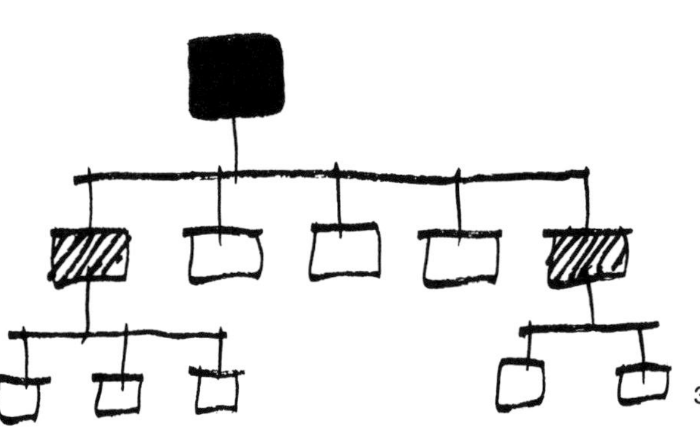

374

367–374
Hierarchy can be created by relative position (367–368) or size (369–370). It can also be created by value differentiation (371–372). Both relative position and size can be used together in expressing a hierarchy (373). All three types of hierarchy can be combined in communicating a single organization (374).

14

Emotional Qualities of Lines

Not all that we see makes the same degree of impact on our emotions. Certain objects, spaces, or events make such deep impressions on our experience that we associate their characteristics with their abstract forms, shapes, and lines. Of the three, lines are the most abstract, and, in design studies, they can be manipulated to evoke desired emotions and feelings. The next few paragraphs will discuss various types of lines, their origins, characteristics, and expressions.

375
The manipulation of lines is an important aspect of fashion design. Pleats, darts, gores, yokes, all involve various considerations of line quality and an understanding of their emotional implications.

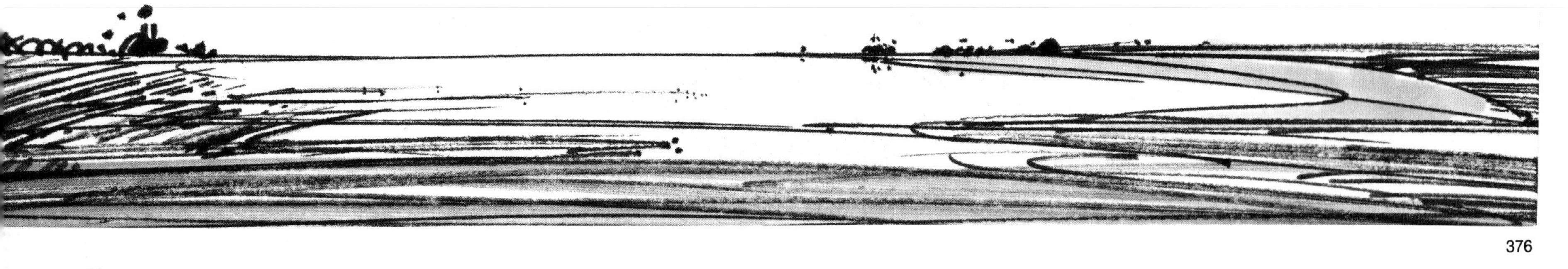

376

377

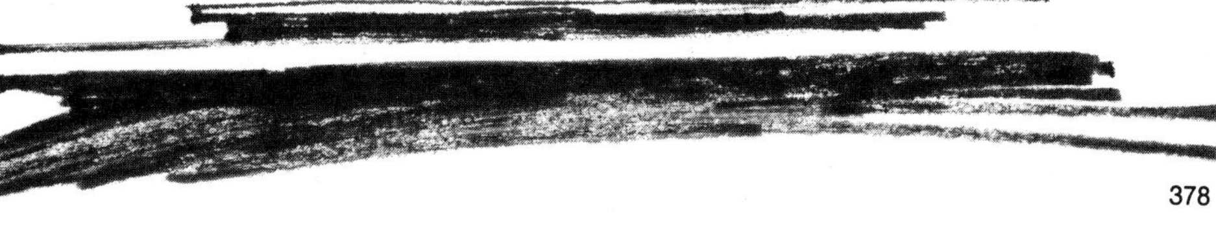

378

379

HORIZONTAL AND VERTICAL

A flat horizon represents a vast space, for in such a situation the visual limit extends over a large area. The horizontality of a large water surface such as a lake or ocean, or that of an open field, gives a feeling of calmness, earthy and satisfying, and thus horizontal lines evoke the same emotions.

376–379
The emotional quality of the horizontal line (377–379) is rooted in the spatial quality of vast open space (376).

Our visual experience is dominated by the force of gravity, the horizon, and the right angle between them. Structural verticality is abundant in nature and in built environments, for it is a natural development in resisting the force of gravity. Thus, lines at right angles, i.e., vertical lines on the horizontal line, represent a sense of stability while a departure from this norm gives a sense of instability.

380

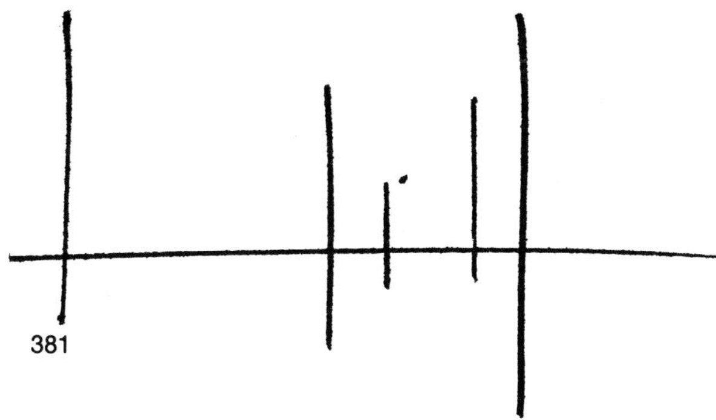

381

380–382
A sense of the stability of vertical lines (381–382) is derived from our common experience of structural resistance against the force of gravity (380).

383

383–384
The right angle created by the horizontal and the vertical line is a powerful expression because this is the most natural and dominating of our visual experiences.

The vertical line alone represents the unresisted force of gravity. It is stately and noble in character. However, two vertical lines next to each other dilute this characteristic, for they tend to oppose each other.

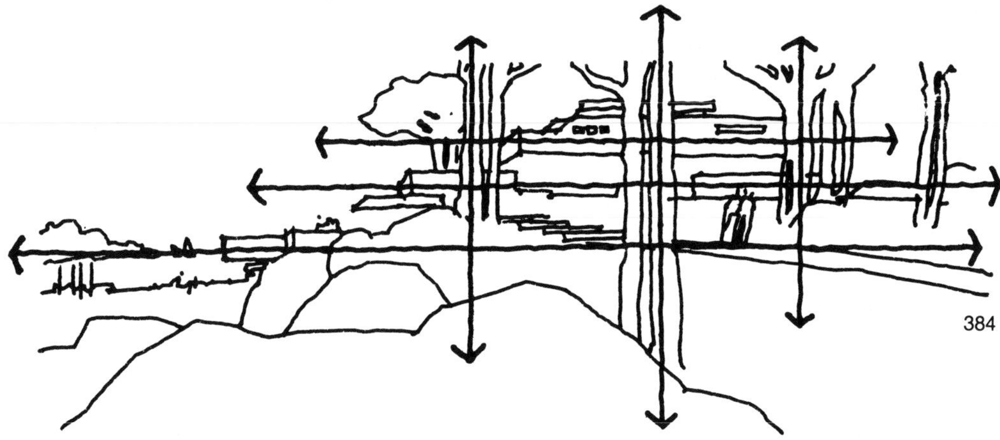
384

385–386
A vertical line by itself is noble and stately but two of them together oppose each other.

385

386

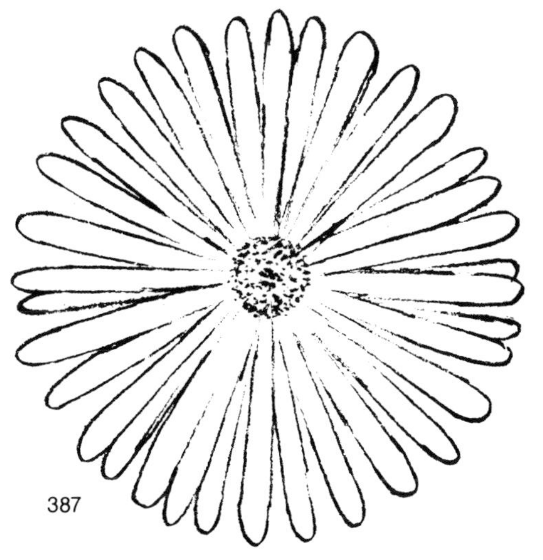

387

388

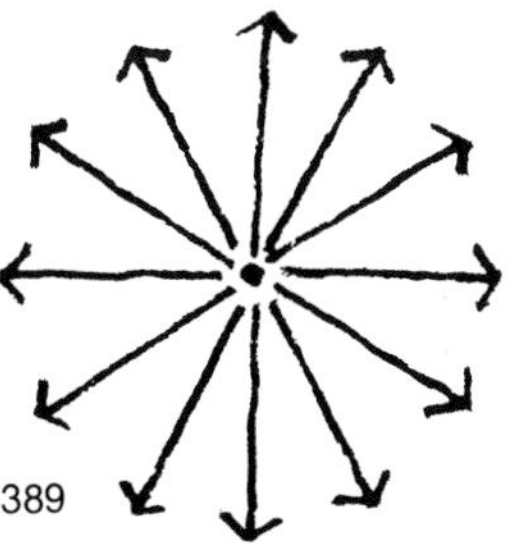

389

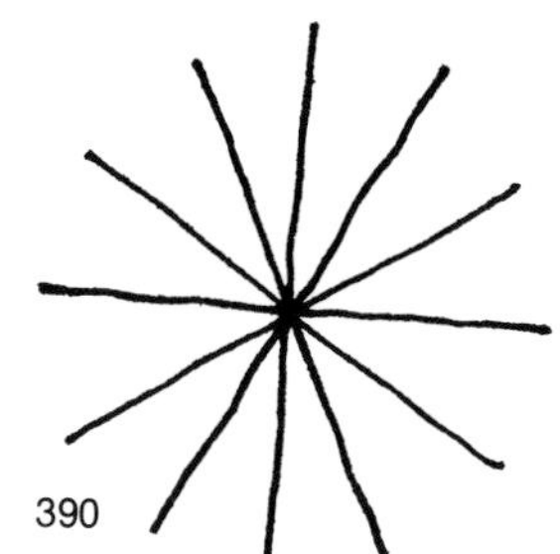

390

RADIAL, DIVERGING, AND CONVERGING

Light, as a form of energy, radiates in all directions from its source. We see the same kind of radiating force in the arrangement of the petals of a flower, in the way living energy flows from the center to the fringe. Thus, radial lines suggest a central concentration of vitality or energy received by the fringe.

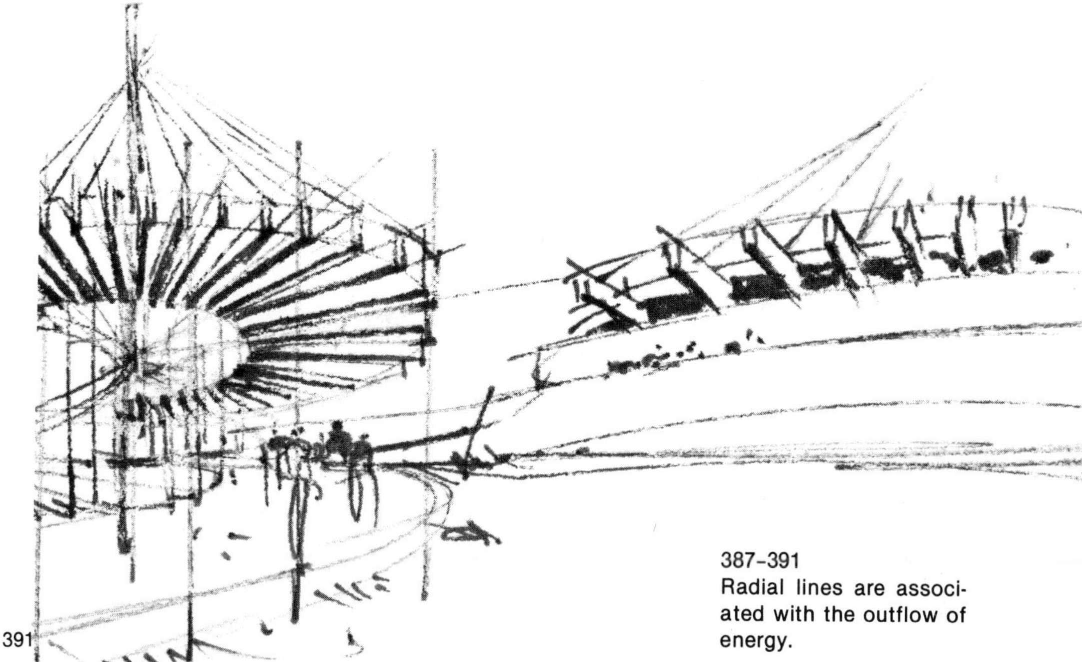

391

387–391
Radial lines are associated with the outflow of energy.

393

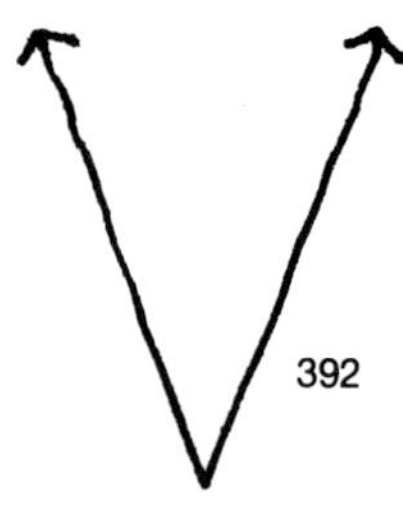
392

392–393
The expanding, increasing, and reaching-out characteristics of divergent lines stem from the sense of progressive separation.

Diverging lines can be viewed as part of a radial configuration and give a sense of expanding, increasing, and reaching out. Converging lines have opposite characteristics, and they generate a feeling of reducing, decreasing, and focusing. In certain situations, they also give spatial depth, creating an illusion of perspective.

394–396
In perspective, parallel lines appear to be converging to the vanishing point, giving an illusion of distance or depth. Thus converging lines have an association with distance and depth.

394

395

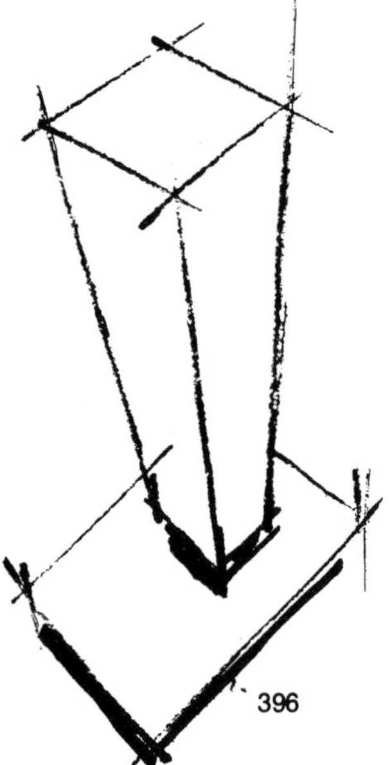
396

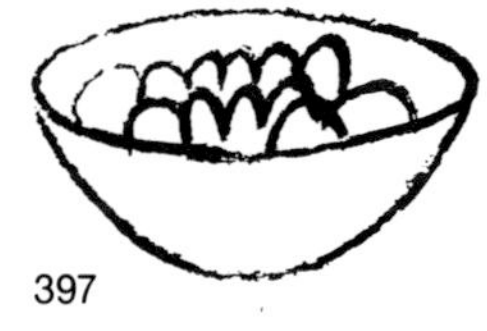
397

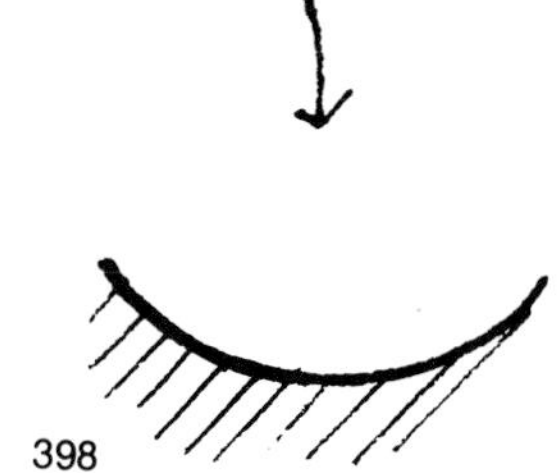
398

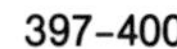

397–400
The concave surface is inviting and protective (398–399) because of its association with a sense of containment (397), whereas the convex surface is repelling (400).

399

CONCAVE AND CONVEX

To provide for space to hold solid or liquid objects, containers must be recessed, cut in, or molded. Thus, most containers come in shapes similar to concave configurations. Consequently, we associate concave lines with a sense of containment. They are inviting, protecting, and shelter-giving. Conversely, convex lines give the feeling of repelling, expanding, and pressing.

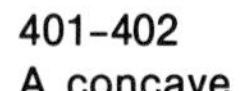

401–402
A concave surface may be emphasized by having two convex surfaces at two of its sides.

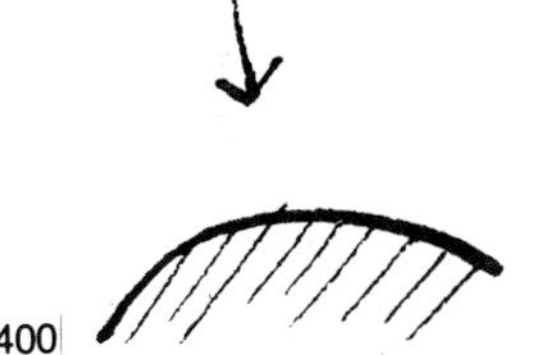
400

401

402

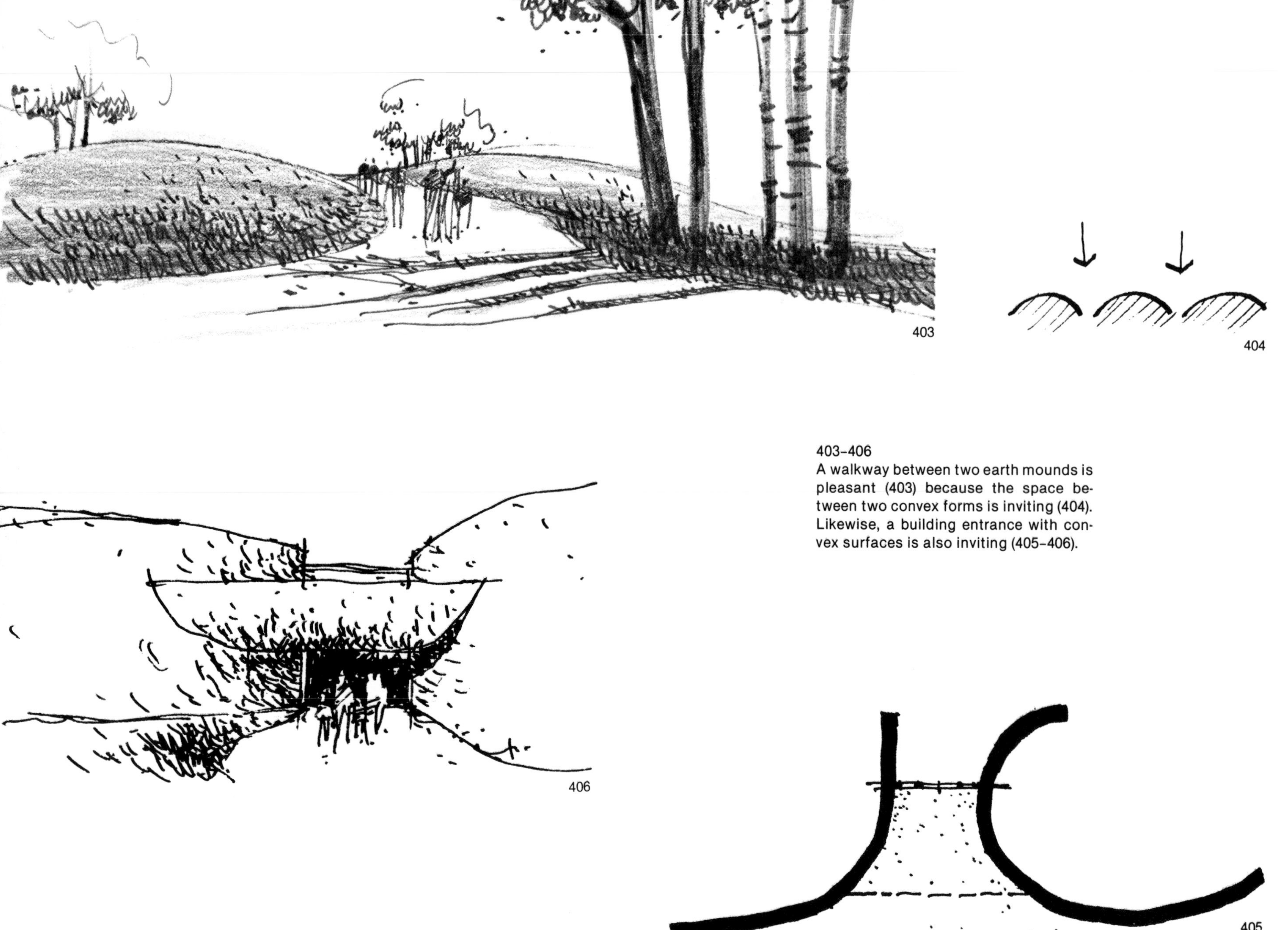

403–406
A walkway between two earth mounds is pleasant (403) because the space between two convex forms is inviting (404). Likewise, a building entrance with convex surfaces is also inviting (405–406).

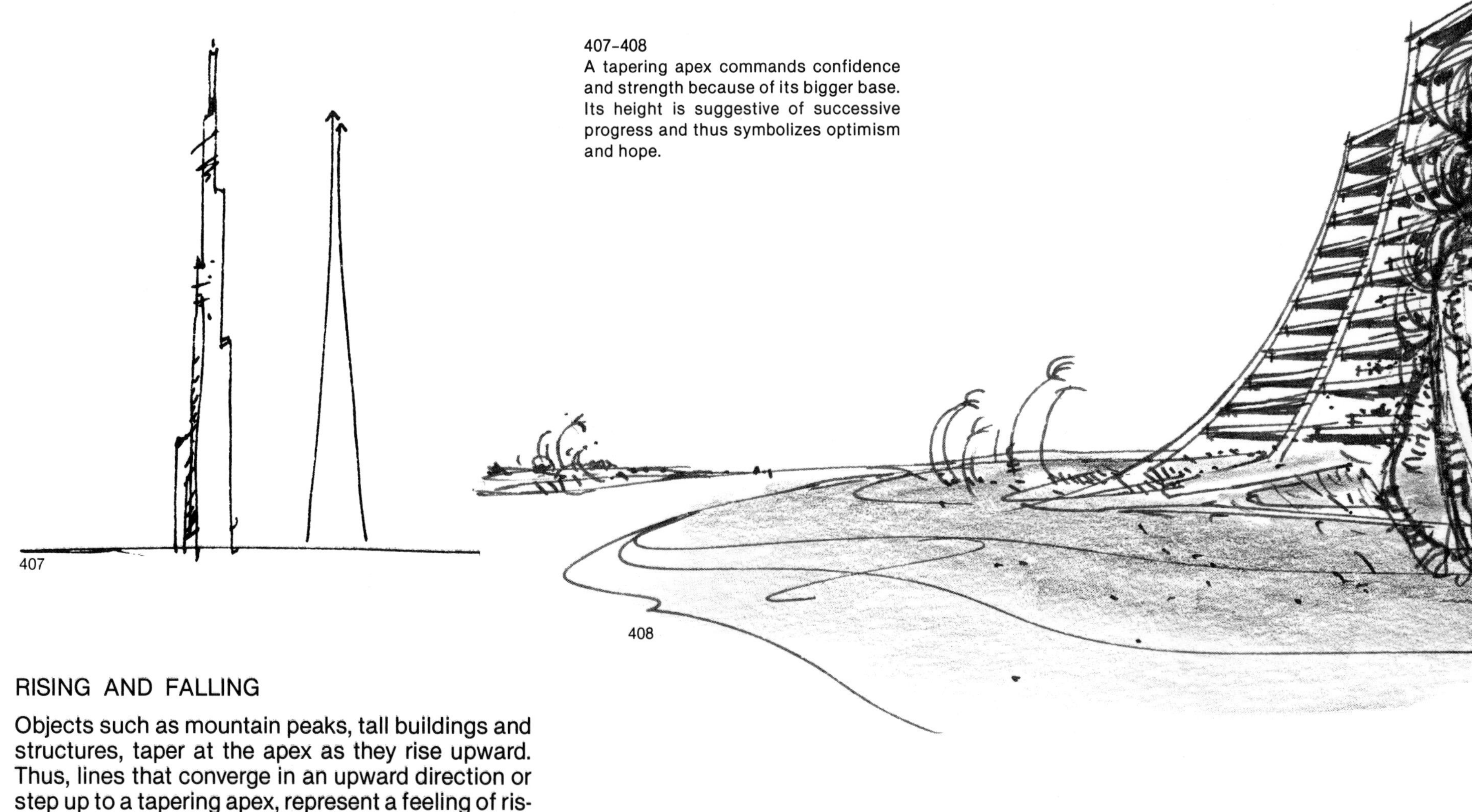

407

408

407–408
A tapering apex commands confidence and strength because of its bigger base. Its height is suggestive of successive progress and thus symbolizes optimism and hope.

RISING AND FALLING

Objects such as mountain peaks, tall buildings and structures, taper at the apex as they rise upward. Thus, lines that converge in an upward direction or step up to a tapering apex, represent a feeling of rising, improvement, attainment, success, and optimism. On the other hand, lines which converge in a downward direction symbolize falling, sinking, degeneration, defeat, and pessimism.

409

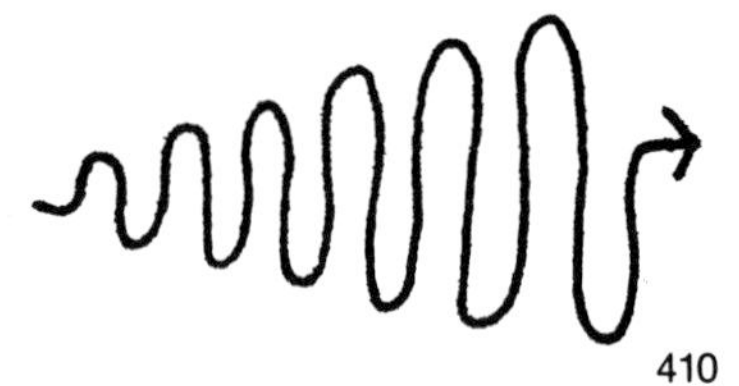

410

411

409–412
Progression can occur in the form of direction (409), volume or size (410), or in steps and height (411–412).

PROGRESSION AND RETREAT

Waves rise, advance, and follow other waves. They break on the shores or beaches and then recede. Their forward movement is a symbol of progression, and that line which represents this motion of waves also gives a feeling of progression. Similarly, successive concave lines that depict receding waves convey a sense of retreat.

412

413–414
A downhill slope with slightly concave surfaces may suggest an emotional quality of retreat.

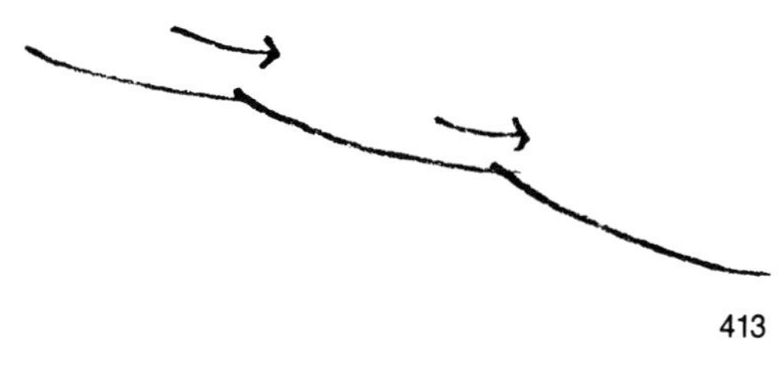
413

414

ACTIVE AND DYNAMIC

Action is associated with motion; quick changes of direction and fast movement are an attribute of the active and the dynamic. Thus, lines that change direction at sharp, acute angles can evoke a feeling of action and dynamic character. This kind of line is used almost universally as a symbol for lightning and electricity since both manifest very fast actions. Action can also be represented by forceful curvilinear movements. This kind of representation is characteristic of gesture drawing.

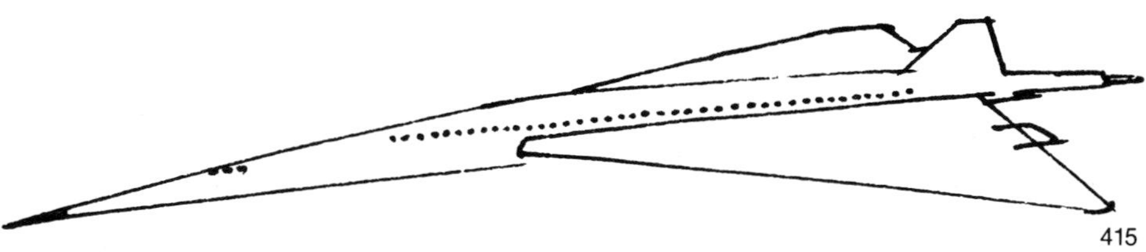
415

415–418
Aerodynamic shapes (415), designed for high speed, are active and have sharp, acute angles (416). This sense of action can also be expressed by smooth and forceful curvilinear lines (417–418).

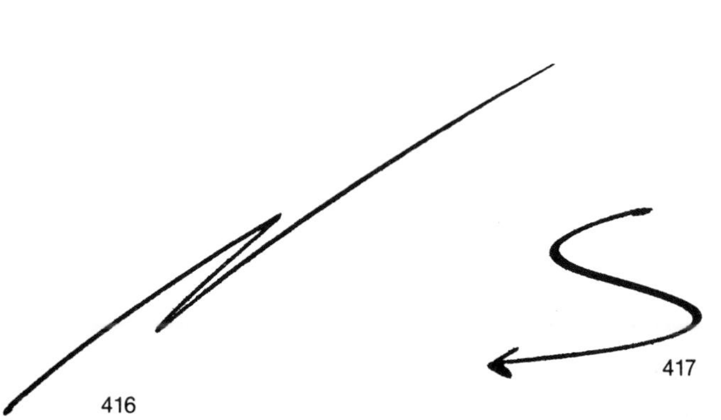
416

417

418

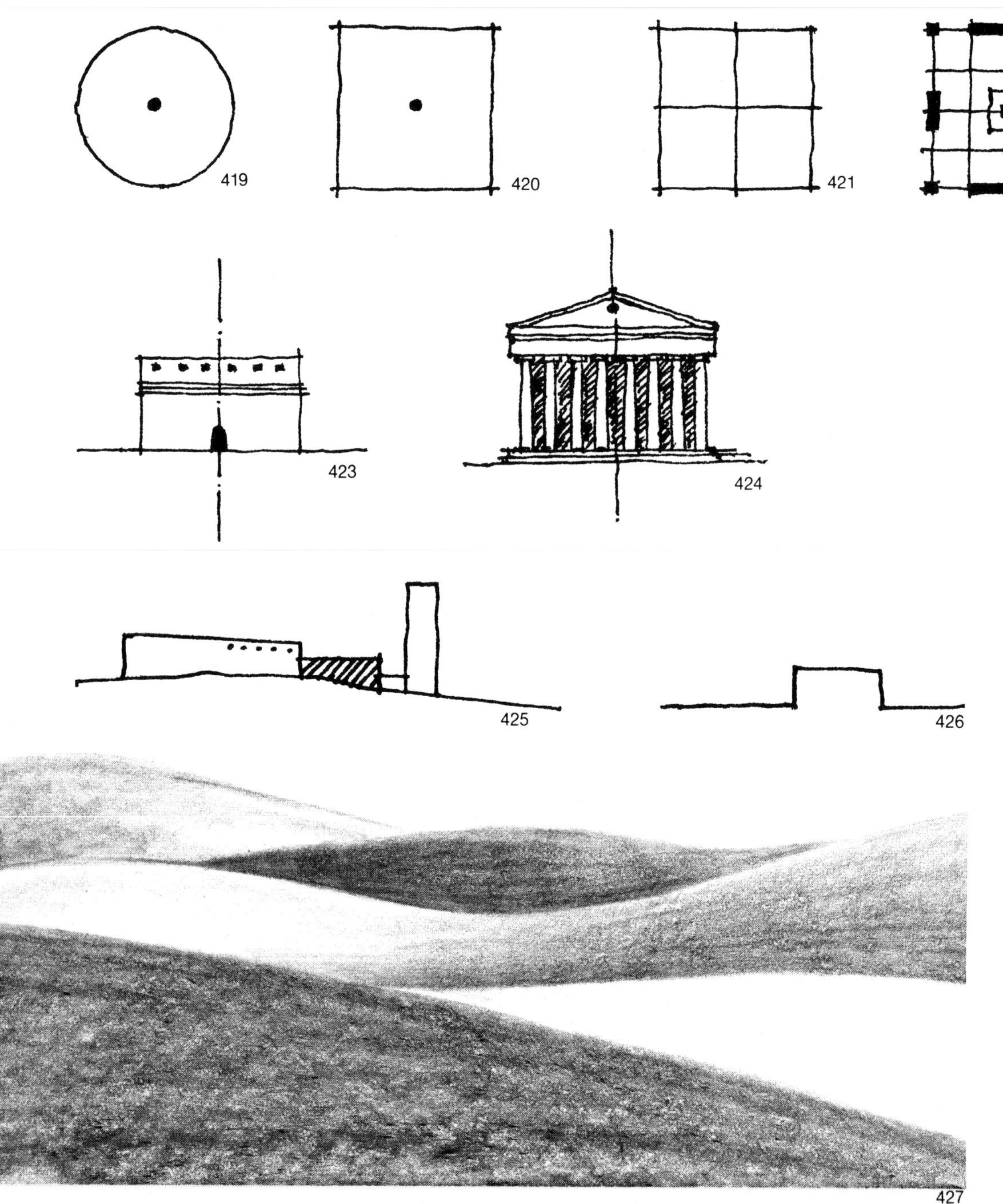

419–424
Symmetries reduce tension and create static compositions.

STATIC AND FIXED

A focal point is associated with centralization. A point at a center of a square or circle, or just a point by itself, leaves uniform space around it, and thus prompts the eye to focus on it; it evokes a static emotion. Perfect stability or bilateral symmetry creates static composition since no tension or imbalance is generated.

425–426
Structural stability is associated with rectangular shapes of conventional built form.

STRUCTURAL STABILITY

Simple buildings of overall conventional shapes represent structural stability and strength. Thus, the configuration of lines that gives the illusion of their form against the horizontal ground plane creates a sense of solidity and strength.

ROLLING, WAVERING, AND MEANDERING

The action of wind, air, water, and snow creates natural forms with sweeping and rolling curves. Thus, continuous lines with gradual changes of

427–428
The fluidity of a rolling landform (427) can be captured by the curvilinear shapes of a pool or the earth mounds around it (428).

428

curves represent feelings of flowing, rolling, swelling, sliding, and fluidity. On the other hand, an irregular wavering line symbolizes uncertainty and weakness, but a line that is meandering imparts a casual and relaxed feeling.

429

SMOOTH AND REFINED

Undisturbed dunes and seascapes convey a very delicate mood. Their spotless and smooth quality is reinforced when tiny details on them become ap-

429–430
A wavering line lacks confidence (429), whereas a meandering line can be relaxed and interesting (430).

430

431

431
Tiny details on an undisturbed seascape create contrast with its smooth sweeping lines and reinforce its delicate and refined quality.

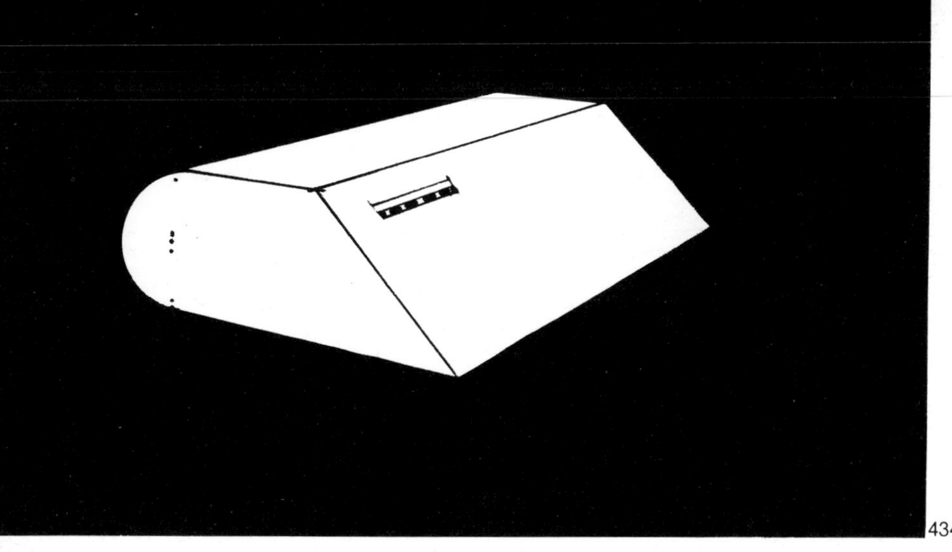
434

parent. These details provide contrast to continuous refined lines. Thus, when details are carefully placed on sweeping lines, a feeling of refinement is evoked.

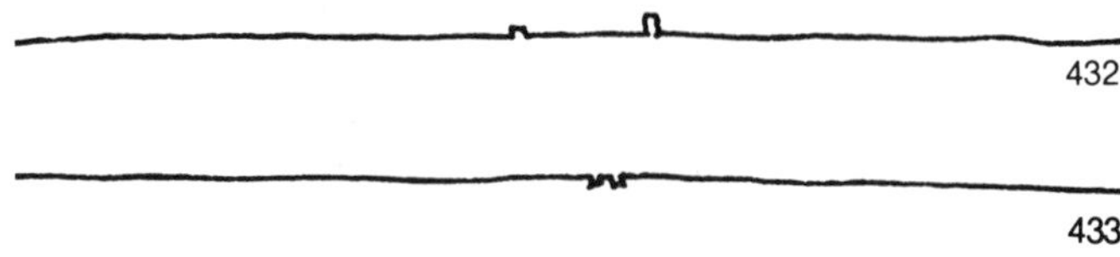
432

433

432–434
A suggestion of tiny details against simple forms or lines can add a refined look.

435–436
The roughness of irregular lines is associated with broken edges.

437–438
The brutal qualities of jagged lines are associated with the sharp points of animal teeth.

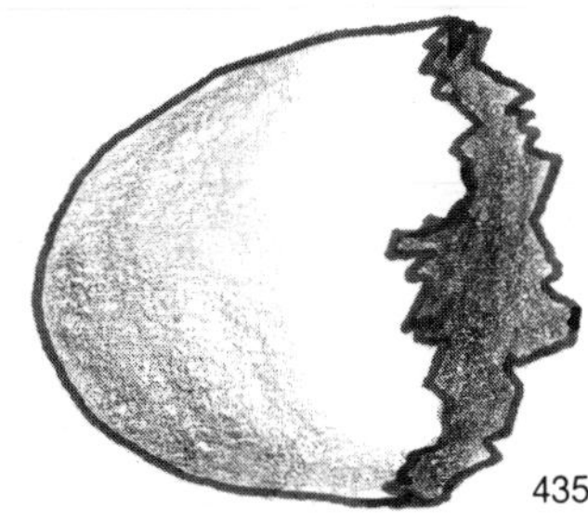
435

ROUGH AND BRUTAL

Irregular lines with sharp points express roughness since similar rough edges are created when something cracks or breaks. Like the points of animal teeth, the sharpness of angles is hard and brutal. Thus, jagged lines with continuous directional changes, creating angles and sharp points, will generate an emotional quality of hardness and brutality.

436

437

438

Part Six

Creativity and Graphic Thinking

439

440

15

Nature of Creative Behavior

Philosopher Arthur Schopenhauer once said, "Genius is closer to madness than to ordinary intelligence." The literature is filled with descriptive evidence of mental disturbances and abnormalities of many highly creative artists, scientists, musicians, novelists, and poets. Newton was a paranoid schizophrenic; Darwin, a hypochondriac; and van Gogh, a neurotic-hysteric. Pascal and Swift seemed to have suffered from paralytic dementia, while both Michelangelo and Raphael were believed to be melancholic. Beethoven's eccentricity bordered on insanity, while Byron appeared to have a schizophrenic personality. The author of this book is not

439–440
Although psychological abnormality is not a precondition for high creativity, many highly creative people seem to have had eccentric behavior. The eccentricity of Beethoven (439) was close to insanity and van Gogh (440) was believed to be a neurotic-hysteric.

441
Arthur Schopenhauer, who believed that genius is closer to madness than to ordinary intelligence, himself suffered from psychological abnormality.

441

442

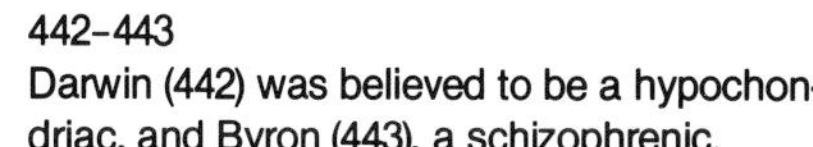

442–443
Darwin (442) was believed to be a hypochondriac, and Byron (443), a schizophrenic.

443

444
Philosopher Friedrich Nietzsche spent a life of loneliness, misogyny, and physical pain from lifelong illness. In his later life he was convinced that these miseries were a necessary condition of his creative work.

suggesting that mental abnormality is a precondition for high creativity. Such a suggestion would be invalid simply on statistical grounds. However, there are certain behavioral aspects of creativity that may appear to be abnormal but that are very relevant to our discussion and must not escape the scope of this book.

WHAT IS CREATIVITY?

The word *creativity* is an overused word and thus tends to have various meanings. But for our purposes, creativity has to do with an original and better solution to a problem, and the proposal, development, and implementation of such a solution. The key words are *original* and *better.* Creativity is also different from high intelligence. It has been found that there is a very low correlation between creativity and IQ (intelligence quotient). Although there seems to be some minimum IQ associated with creativity, an increase in IQ does not correlate with higher creativity.

"Original"
+
"Better"

High IQ ≠ High Creativity

CONCEPTUAL FLUENCY AND FLEXIBILITY

One of the intellectual characteristics of creative individuals is *conceptual fluency,* the ability to come up with a large number of concepts or ideas quickly. One example is how rapidly one can respond when asked to name art supplies and equipment beginning with a vowel or list categories into which 500 slides from a trip can be stored. Greater ease in such response provides one with greater choices and consequently increases the probability of coming up with creative solutions. *Picture fluency* is a kind of conceptual fluency in pictorial form and can be regarded as its visual counterpart. It is a predominant characteristic of creativity in design and visual arts. Picture fluency will be discussed further in 17th chapter.

Conceptual flexibility is the ability to change a frame of reference. Creative individuals are able to "shift gears" with regard to approaching a problem. The graphic equivalent of such behavior is the ability to make graphic manipulations such as projection, distortion, topological transformation, and visual metaphor, which were discussed in 12th chapter.

INDEPENDENCE

Creative individuals tend to give uncommon and atypical answers to questions and make remote connections that are original and intriguing. In their minds, they perceive themselves as different, and their sense of mission tends to isolate them from average people, thus causing them to feel lonely sometimes. They tend to arrive at independent judgements on issues, rely more on the evidence of their senses rather than on the group consensus. They allow and express impulses, whims, and "inner voices" regardless of whether they are realistic or not. They view authority as conventional, arbitrary, and temporary rather than final or absolute. They separate information from the source and evaluate it on the basis of the information itself rather than on the basis of the source.

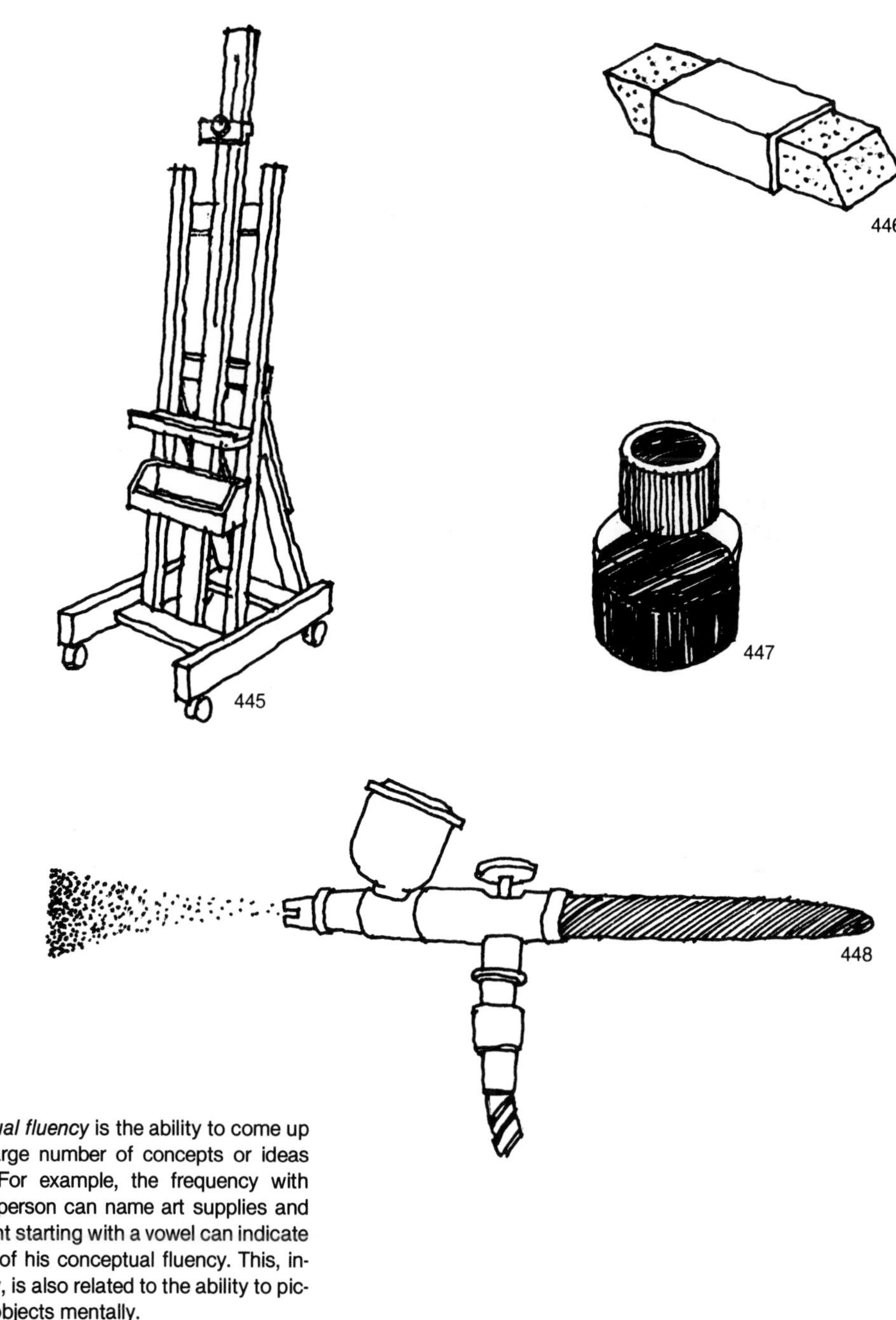

445–448
Conceptual fluency is the ability to come up with a large number of concepts or ideas quickly. For example, the frequency with which a person can name art supplies and equipment starting with a vowel can indicate the level of his conceptual fluency. This, incidentally, is also related to the ability to picture the objects mentally.

449
The *t'ai-chi tu,* depicting the simultaneous but opposing forces of yin and yang, is a Janusian proposition.

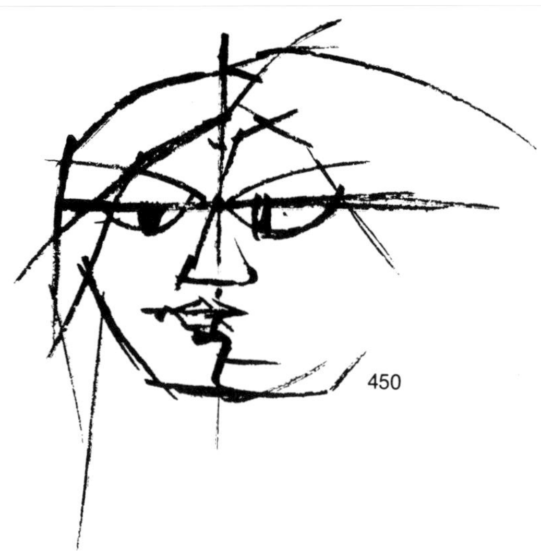

450

451

JANUSIAN THINKING

Albert Rothenberg, in his book *The Emerging Goddess* (1979), discusses about two interesting concepts in characterizing creative behavior. They are: *Janusian Thinking* (named after the Roman god Janus who has two opposite faces) and *Homospatial thinking.*

Janusian thinking is characterized by simultaneous consideration of two or more opposing concepts, images, principles, or forces side by side. In such thinking, the mental conception of each of these opposing ideas or principles is not separated by temporal sequence. Recent experimental evidence shows that Janusian thinking is linked with creativity in general, particularly in the fields of design and visual arts.

The concept of yin and yang in Taoism is an obvious Janusian proposition. The "t'ai-chi tu," or the symbol of the Supreme Ultimate of Taoism, visually depicts the simultaneous but opposing forces of yin and yang. The Buddhist concept of nirvana, which is simultaneously nonlife and nondeath, is another Janusian formulation.

Janusian thinking is predominant among visual artists. What separates the creative artist, architect, or designer from the general public is his perception of space. He views empty space simultaneously with full space, i.e., space that is filled with some object. To him, empty space has a content and shape of its

450–451
Simultaneous perception of two views (450) or events has to do with Janusian thinking. In this preliminary sketch (451) for a painting, views at different points in time have been compressed to depict their simultaneity, the same line sometimes expressing two views. How many faces do you see?

own. Such concurrent perception of full and empty space makes the experience a unified one and enables him to uncover the real nature of form, light, and color. In dada and surrealist paintings, we also see the simultaneous depiction of rest and motion, dream and reality, or events at different points in time.

HOMOSPATIAL THINKING

Janusian constructs are abstract. Homospatial thinking is needed to translate Janusian constructs into concrete and comprehensible concepts. In the development of the general theory of relativity, Einstein's simultaneous consideration of falling and being at rest, or his concept of gravitational field both in terms of inertia and acceleration in space, suggests the process of homospatial thinking.

Homospatial thinking is the simultaneous or conjunctive consideration of two or more aspects of the same spatial condition. In this process, considerations are made in spatial terms. Thus, in architecture and other design fields, this is of particular importance, for creative spatial conceptualization entails concurrent deliberations on various facets of a given space. For example, consideration of positive and negative spaces in a facade also requires the contemporaneous visualization of interior spaces behind the facade, or a multiuse space

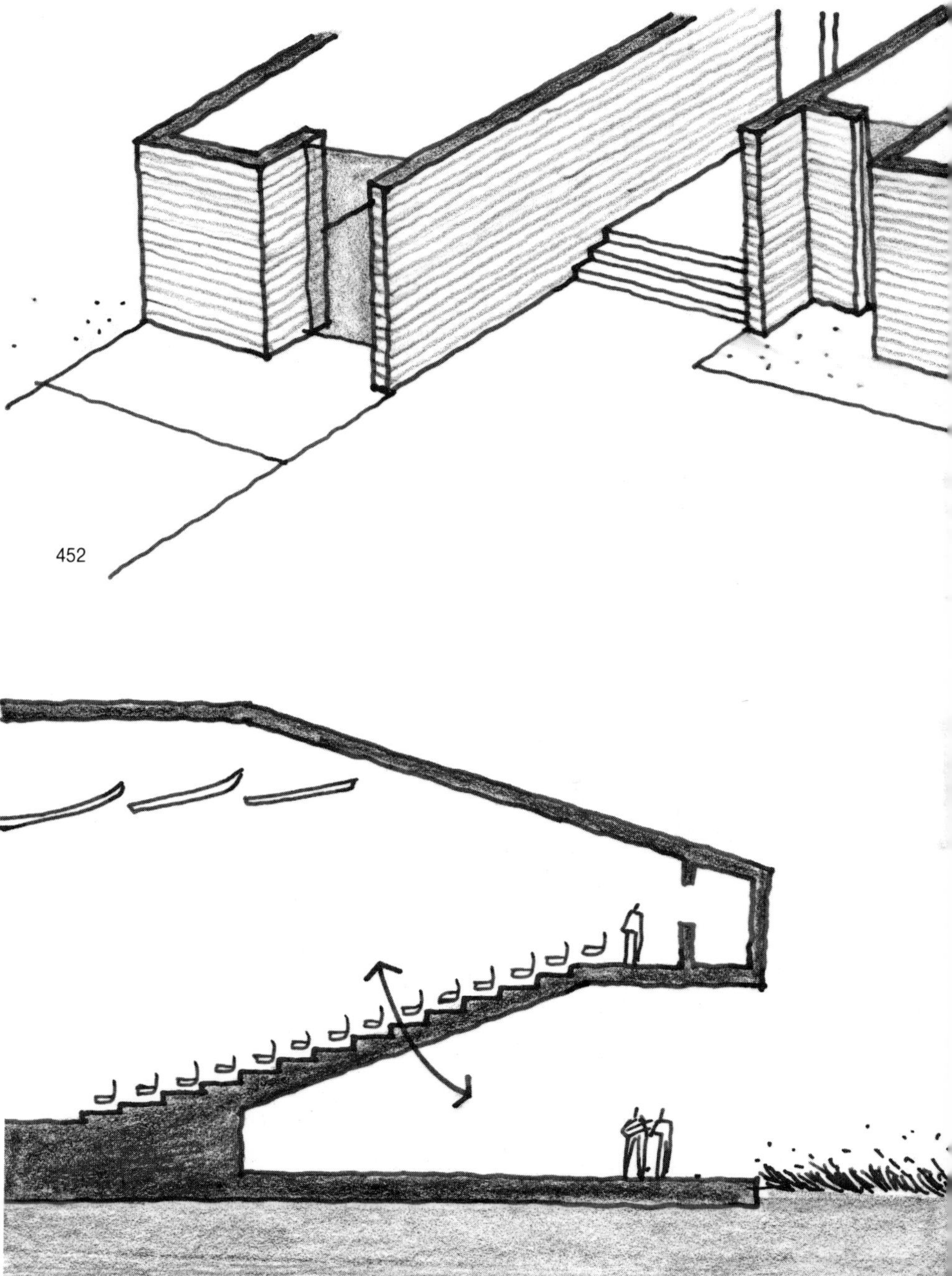

452–453
Homospatial thinking entails simultaneous consideration of two or more spatial aspects of the same object. Consideration of the positive and negative space in a facade requires simultaneous consideration of the spatial configuration of the interior.

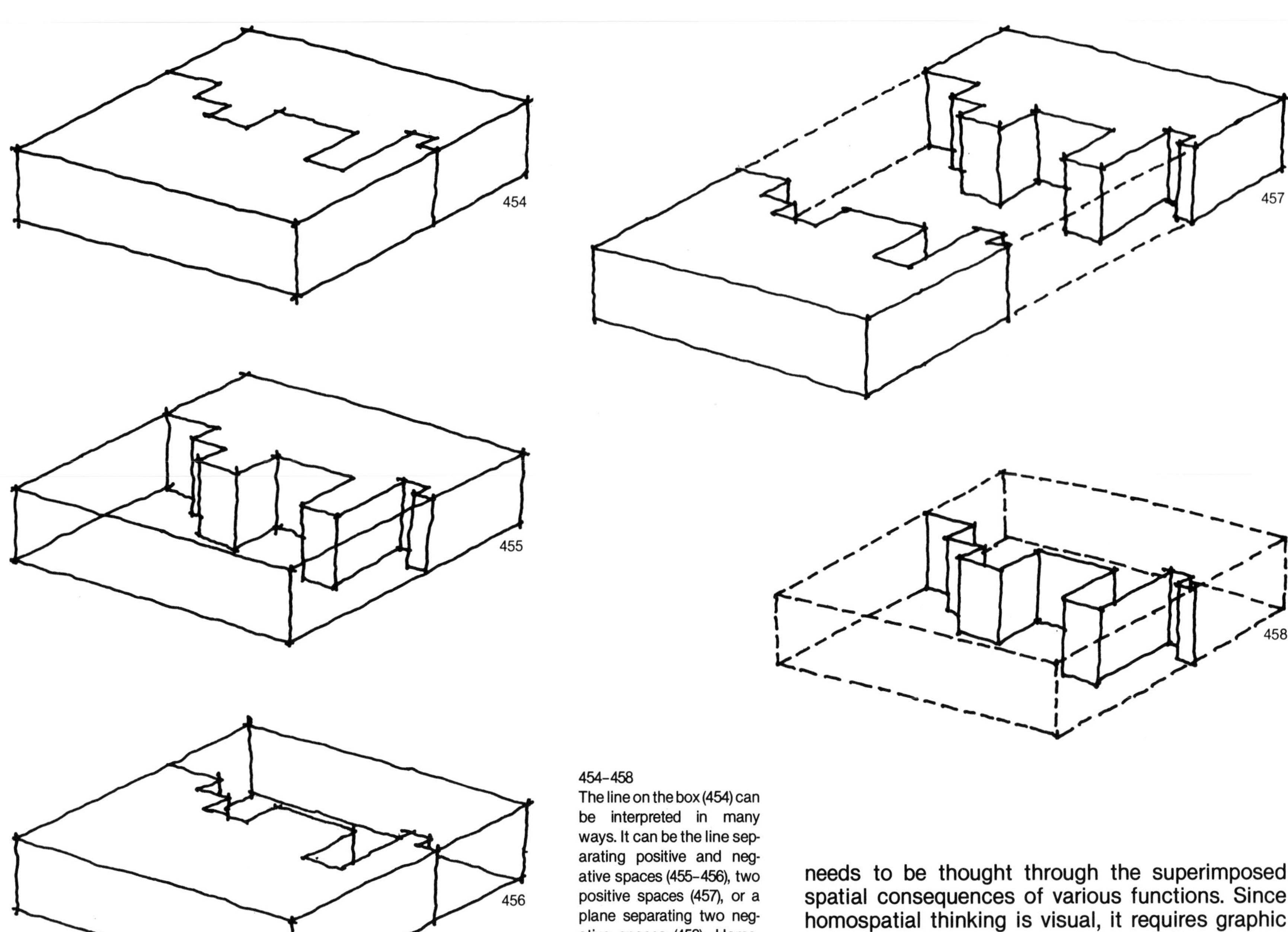

454–458
The line on the box (454) can be interpreted in many ways. It can be the line separating positive and negative spaces (455–456), two positive spaces (457), or a plane separating two negative spaces (458). Homospatial thinking gives simultaneous consideration to all of these possibilities.

needs to be thought through the superimposed spatial consequences of various functions. Since homospatial thinking is visual, it requires graphic tools to explore the full potential of this process, while graphic exploration itself improves homospatial thinking.

16

Fantasy and Graphic Exploration

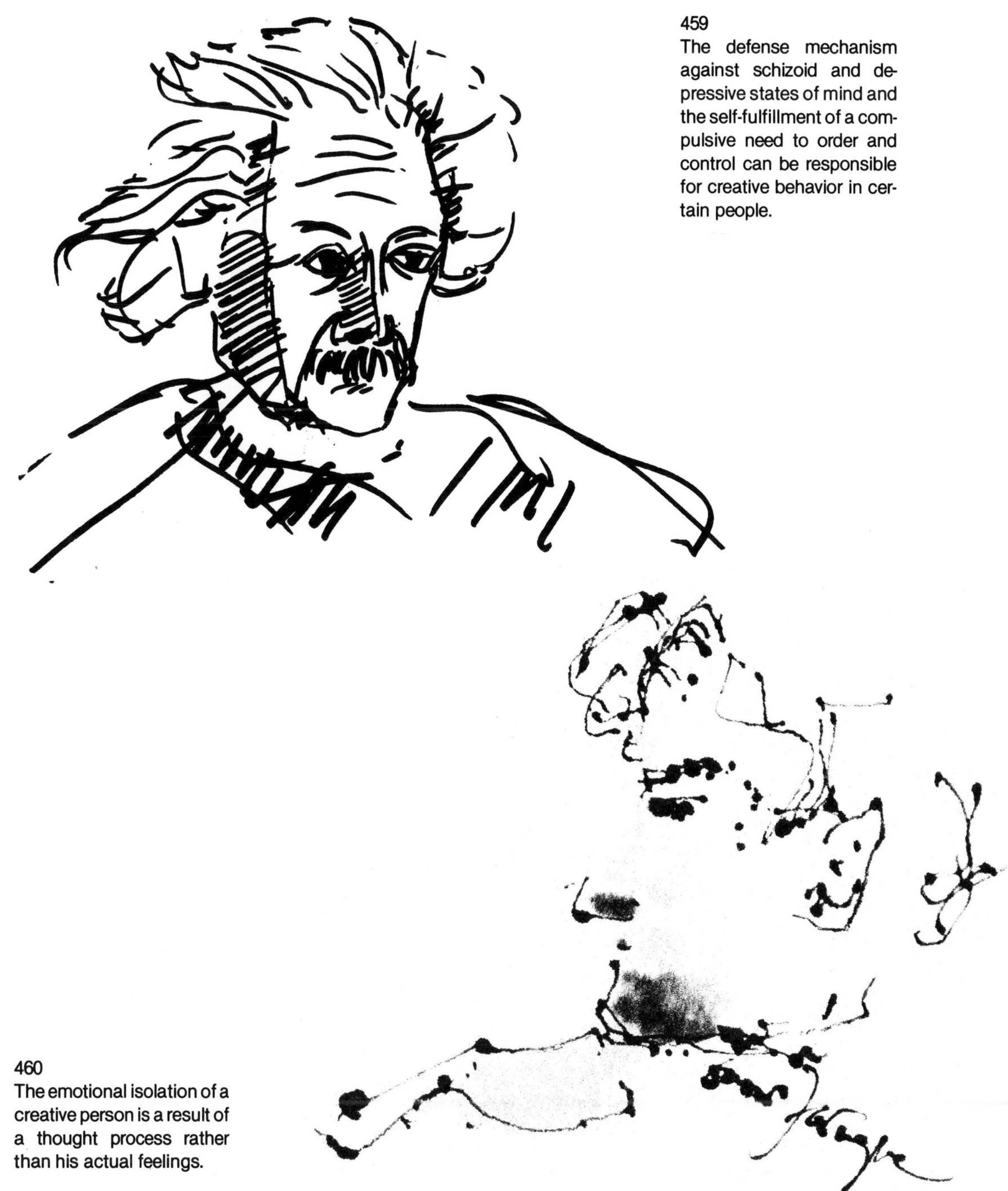

459
The defense mechanism against schizoid and depressive states of mind and the self-fulfillment of a compulsive need to order and control can be responsible for creative behavior in certain people.

It has been suggested that creativity can be viewed as giving expression to the wish-fulfilling fantasies of those who are dissatisfied for some reason or other. For example, creativity can be regarded as a defense mechanism against schizoid and depressive states of mind. It can also be thought of as the self-fulfillment of a compulsive need for order and control.

Detachment or lack of ordinary human contact characterizes the behavior of a schizoid person. He appears to be on a wave length different from the people around him and displays a cold personality, giving an impression of superiority. However, these characteristics do not reflect his actual feelings. Rather, his behavior is guided by intellectual decisions to meet the needs of particular situations. Thus, his emotional isolation is a result of a thought process instead of true feelings. What is deep-seated in his behavior is a basic mistrust at the emotional level. Consequently, he attempts to refrain from emotional involvement to avoid risk and the

460
The emotional isolation of a creative person is a result of a thought process rather than his actual feelings.

anxiety of potential rejection. Instead of interacting with people, he remains preoccupied with his inner world of fantasy. This also explains why he has a tendency to make independent judgements and remote connections, and to come up with unusual solutions.

On the other hand, a manic-depressive temperament stems from the attempt to protect oneself from the loss of self-esteem. Unlike the schizoid, the depressive is dependent upon emotional involvement and maintaining good relations with the people from whom he receives love and approval. This dependency makes him vulnerable. Thus, the withdrawal of love and approval creates great anxiety for him and, driven by the search for self-esteem elsewhere, he seeks greater recognition of his merits through creative acts.

There is another type of behavior that is deeply linked with creativity although it is very much a part of normal life and can hardly be called pathological. It is the act of play. Play serves as an outlet for emotions characteristically very similar to the fantasy of the schizoid, the search for self-esteem of the depressive, and the obsessive's need for control and order. Yet it is sharply different from any of these pathological states in the sense that it is a deliberate simulation. Because of this same distinction, it enjoys a different kind of freedom and spontaneity.

PLAY AND FANTASY

Freud compares the artist's act with that of a child at play. Each, in essence, does the same thing,

461
A creative person is often preoccupied with his inner world of fantasy.

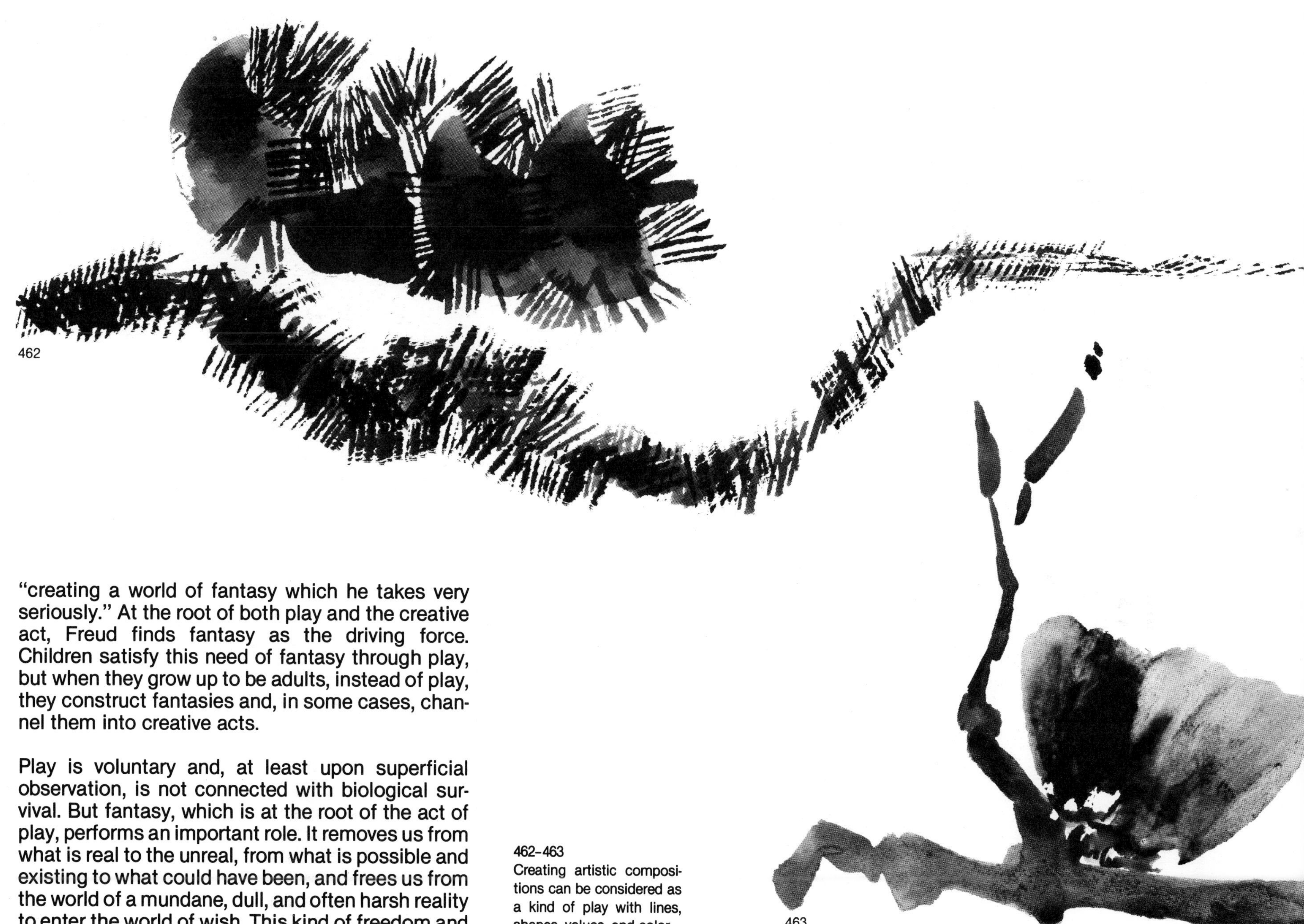

462

463

"creating a world of fantasy which he takes very seriously." At the root of both play and the creative act, Freud finds fantasy as the driving force. Children satisfy this need of fantasy through play, but when they grow up to be adults, instead of play, they construct fantasies and, in some cases, channel them into creative acts.

Play is voluntary and, at least upon superficial observation, is not connected with biological survival. But fantasy, which is at the root of the act of play, performs an important role. It removes us from what is real to the unreal, from what is possible and existing to what could have been, and frees us from the world of a mundane, dull, and often harsh reality to enter the world of wish. This kind of freedom and

462–463
Creating artistic compositions can be considered as a kind of play with lines, shapes, values, and color.

464

464
It is playfulness that makes the artistic creation a discovery process.

465

465
In exploring new possibilities in form, fantasy serves as the driving force.

exploration, regardless of how wishful it is, is deeply connected with the development of new ideas and imaginative alternatives, both at individual and societal levels. Thus, in the making of a new or better world, fantasy and, consequently, play serve as the driving force.

GRAPHIC EXPLORATION AS PLAY

Graphic exploration such as doodling and making thumbnail sketches is a kind of play where both fantasy and curiosity are at work. Doing this requires a temporary departure from the real world that crowds the mind with conventional and mediocre concepts. Studies of this type are essential to the formulation of new design ideas and possibilities.

466

Unfortunately, many designers do not take sufficient time to make such graphic exploration with an all-out effort. The reason is simple. We are afraid to express our fantasies because they may disappoint others or break with tradition.

467

468

466–470
Doodling on notepads (466) and making thumbnail sketches (467–470) are a kind of play driven by fantasy.

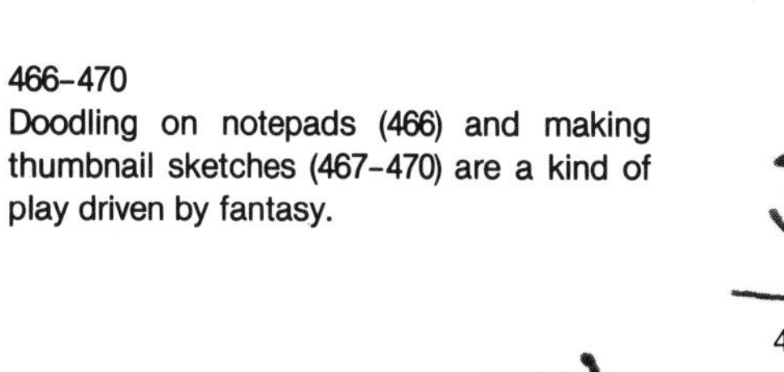
469

Most of us doodle on note pads, especially when we are bored in a class, lecture, or meeting. In such situations where a pen or pencil and a pad lie within reach, we play with them in the form of doodling. We doodle because to draw is a natural instinct. Even at the age of three we drew as if it were the most natural thing to do. But as adults, we do not share this doodling with our friends or colleagues because it belongs to the inner world, the world of fantasy. The seriousness of the real world makes us hide them. Every line, every stroke, regardless of how nonsensical it is, enjoys a spontaneity that only the playfulness of a child can match. The designer's graphic studies should have the same kind of playfulness where he lets his inner self participate in the process.

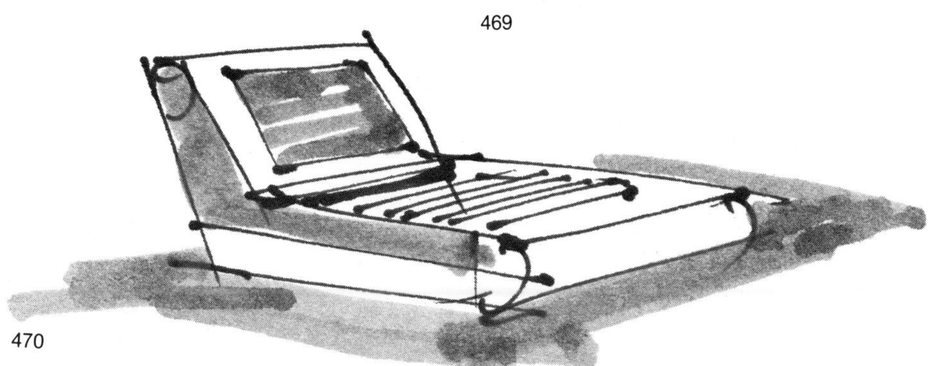
470

471

471–472
The distance separating a given space and the person who draws it leads to objective realization, which increases his grasp and mastery of it. Such grasp and confidence is important for him to make creative manipulations of that space.

472

There is another dimension to the act of drawing. A certain distance must be maintained between the object and the person who depicts it. While such a distance is necessary in order for him to portray the object, the same distance also leads him toward objective realization. Thus, drawing serves as a symbol or an abstraction of the object. This capacity for abstraction increases a person's grasp and mastery of the object from which he detaches himself by depicting it. This sense of mastery and confidence enables him to manipulate images or symbols through addition, deletion, distortion, or modification.

17

Picture Fluency, Images, and Ideas

We have discussed conceptual fluency as an attribute of creative behavior. The examples we provided were of a verbal nature, such as naming drafting supplies beginning with a vowel or listing categories for storing 500 slides from a trip. To generate such verbal concepts we also had to make a visual search through the mind's eye since our primary information processing occurs at the pictorial level. Thus, the abundance of images at the pictorial level increases the possibilities of new ideas and this provides a higher conceptual fluency. Rapid conception of such visual images can be called *picture fluency* and the ability to directly transfer those images on to paper is highly critical in

473–477
Picture fluency is the visual counterpart of conceptual fluency. It is the ability to make rapid mental conceptions of pictorial images and transfer them on to the paper in front of us.

473

474

475

476

477

478

481

484

479

482

480

483

478–484
Fantasy and daydreaming play an important role in the development of picture fluency. It also requires the ability to manipulate what we have in the picture catalog of our minds.

coming up with graphic choices. Picture fluency, being the visual counterpart of conceptual fluency, maintains a strong association with the visual perception of objects and spaces around us. An element of fantasy and daydreaming plays an important role in its development.

IMAGES AND IDEAS

The mind is fast. It is constantly receiving new images and ideas, changing them, and forming new ones. This process goes on even when we are engaged in everyday chores. You may be shopping in a department store for something; although you are trying to focus your attention on the particular item you want to buy, from time to time your mind may roam around in various directions. It is also receiving various other stimuli from a number of sources—items in the store, displays, decorations, people and their clothes, the floor, the ceiling, etc. These stimuli are going to your appropriate memory banks and triggering new images and ideas or changing old ones. Picture fluency is associated with the frequency with which we engage in this kind of expansion of our visual memory banks.

The mind is like a river where ideas are flowing through it like currents of water. People with fixed ideas are like a river with stagnant water where there is no current, no flow or change of water, and thus, they have nothing to contribute in terms of new ideas. On the other hand, creative people with new ideas are like forceful rivers with vigorous currents of water. They are dynamic, and they change their views because the current of ideas flows at full strength in them.

TENTATIVE IDEAS

While the creative person is full of ideas, such ideas are tentative and changing. Ideas, like water, change continuously and soon disappear unless they are captured by some means. Since new ideas are tentative, the mind seeks modifications and improvements. Documenting these ideas graphically constitutes a commitment about what they are, and there is a natural resistance to do so since the mind hopes for still further improvement. There is also a

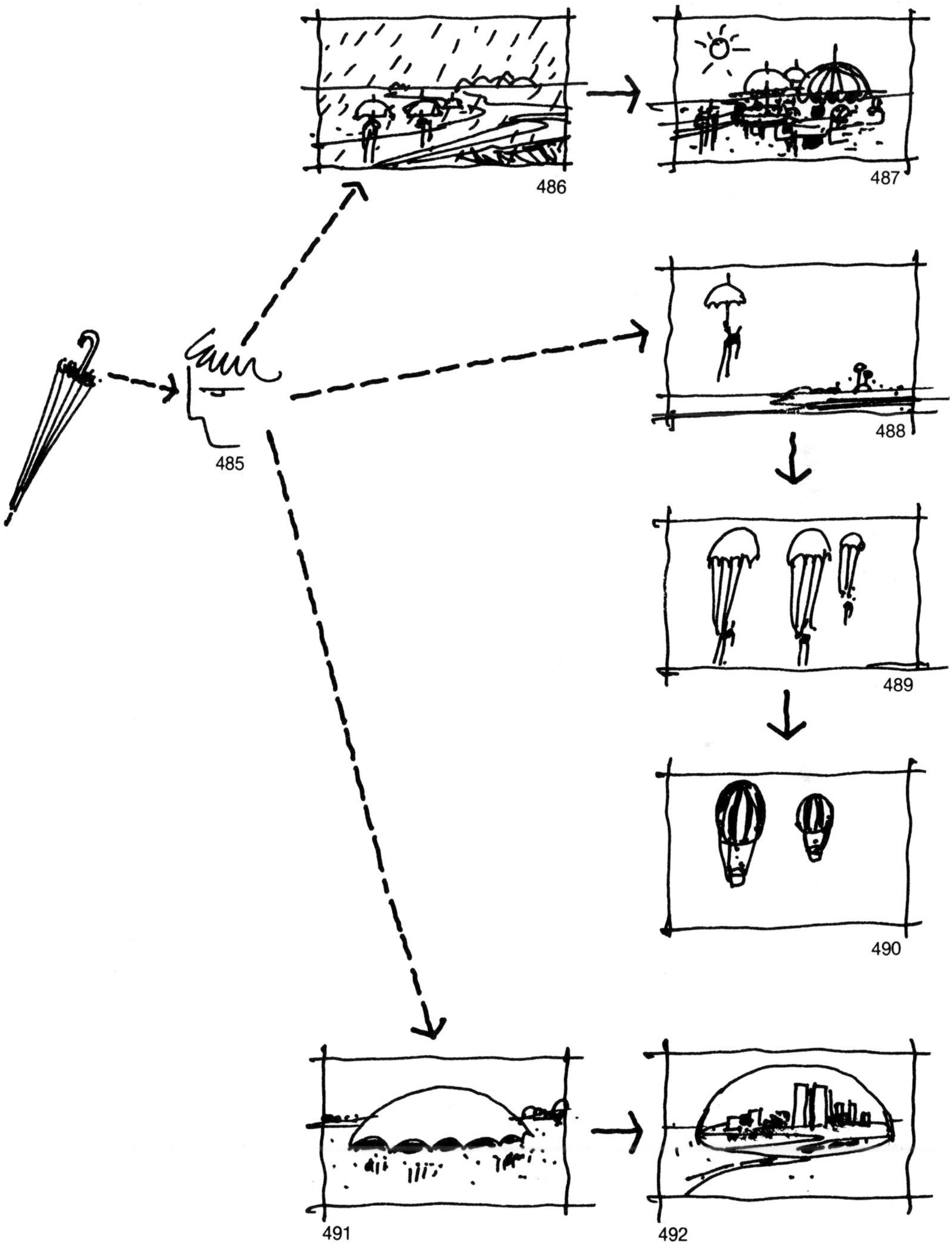

485–492
The image of an umbrella may trigger chains of other images.

493

493–495
Documenting ideas through sketches is a commitment about what they are, and unless they are documented it is hard to evaluate or improve them.

494

495

fear that documentation or commitment may disturb tradition and the rational self. (Creative ideas are generally disturbing.) Students of design frequently suffer from such noncommitment. This is natural and indicates that the mind is functioning at the conceptual level and seeking improvement of the idea. But without graphic documentation or commitment, it is difficult to see and examine the idea. Thus, sketching takes the idea from its tentative state and displays it on paper for visual scrutiny.

VISUAL SCRUTINY

Tentative ideas are like rough guesses. They are not solutions or answers by themselves. They are only attempts at reaching the goal of a new solution or answer. They are generated out of will, tension, or simply out of mental games. They originate in a hurry. They are glimpses of the mind. Thus, they are only approximations, possibly containing inconsistencies or conflicts. At the initial stage, the mind tends to ignore such conflicts since it only seeks to find the general idea in a new frontier. Sketching makes inconsistencies and conflicts visible by graphically freezing them on paper. It also displays the organizational relationship between parts and

496–497
Tentative ideas are only approximations suggesting an attempt toward the goal of new solutions. The process of documenting them graphically forces us to think about the problems we have not thought about before.

the whole, and thus helps scrutinize the organizational plausibility of a system or object.

When you have an idea and you are having difficulty in drawing it, what is really happening is that your idea is either incomplete or contains conflicts, and you are too rational to let yourself draw it; you are afraid to draw something that exposes your daydreams or that will not make sense. But the problem is this: Unless you draw it, it is hard to do something about its incompleteness or conflicts. The resolution to this dilemma is to boldly start drawing anyway, and soon you will find that your idea goes through changes and evolves into a new one.

The act of drawing forces us to think. It is a corrective process. It prompts decision making. As designers, we like and conceive new ideas. But it is the process of drawing that pressures us to examine and decide on them, evaluate, develop, and use them. Otherwise, the ideas remain at the level of our wish list.

Before concluding this chapter, a special point should be made. We have seen that both Janusian and homospatial constructs are deeply rooted in

496

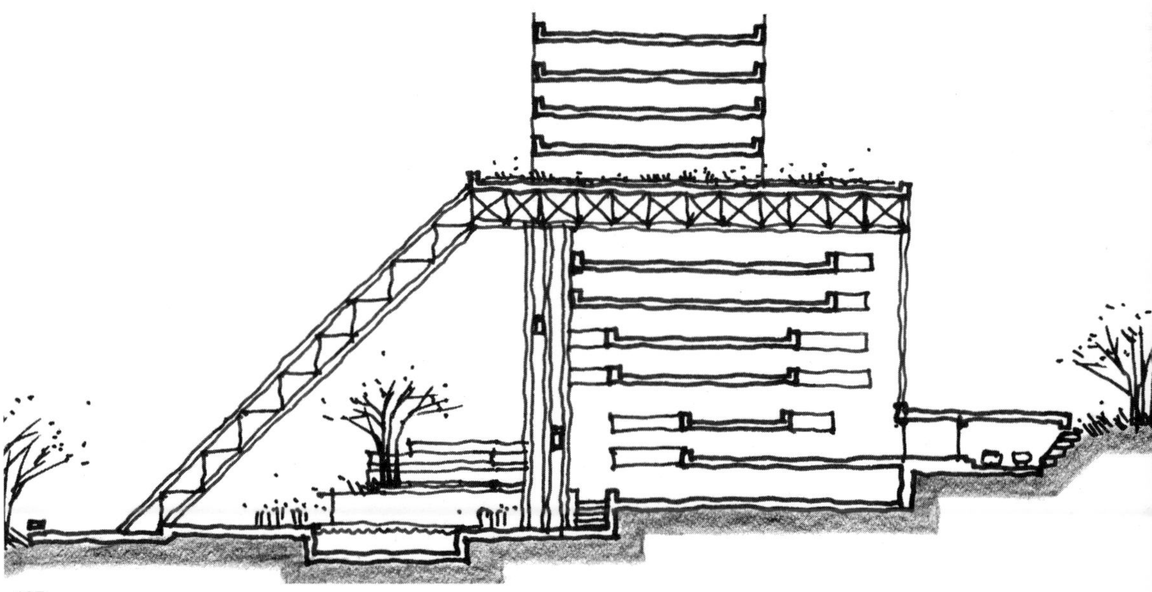

497

498
The interpretation and creative manipulation of space involves simultaneous perception of the composition of lines, shapes, and values, as well as their symbolic aspects. We may attribute such dual perception to the two modes of thinking characterized by the right and left brain hemispheres.

paradoxical thinking. We have also seen that picture fluency and playfulness in graphic exploration have their roots in the world of fantasy. Both paradoxical thinking and fantasy belong to a world different from the logical and rational world. And yet it requires plunging into both of these worlds to come up with an innovative and practical solution to a problem. This is why a highly creative mind makes quick departures from the rational plane to the irrational and intuitive plane, and vice versa. Or, we may say that the creative mind is simply using both sides of the brain.

Part Seven

Design Through Sketching

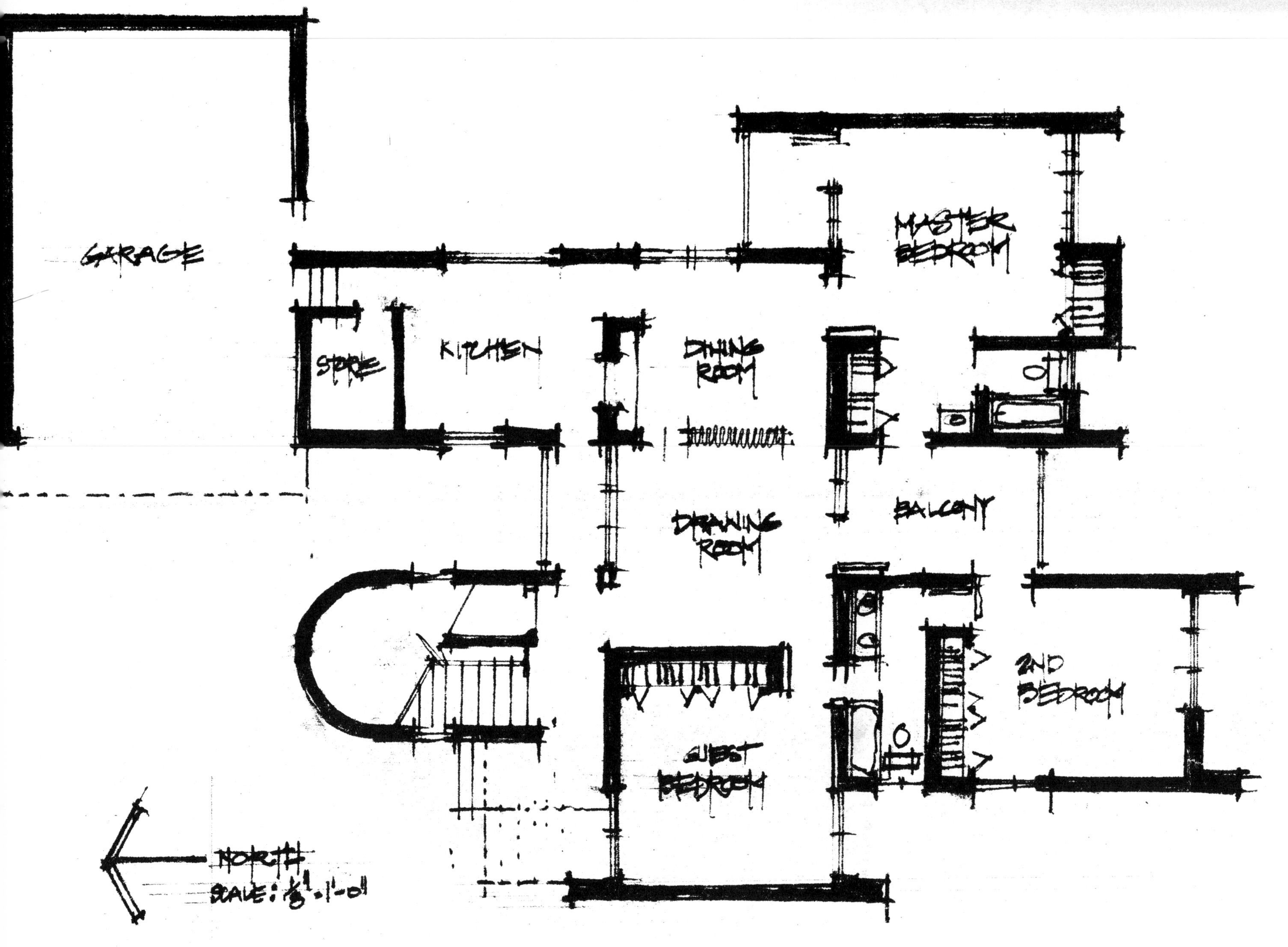
GARAGE
STORE
KITCHEN
DINING ROOM
MASTER BEDROOM
DRAWING ROOM
BALCONY
2ND BEDROOM
GUEST BEDROOM
NORTH
SCALE: 1/8" = 1'-0"

18

Spatial Dimension and Essence

Space is three-dimensional; yet we often use language to describe a space and expect that our description will be understood, but it rarely is. We also use two-dimensional maps and orthographic projections (plans, sections, elevations, etc.) to describe space. But they are insufficient to convey the three-dimensional quality of space. They only provide us with an intellectual understanding of space through logical reconstruction in the mind. But such understanding is somewhat removed from the sense of the spatial whole. Since perspective sketches are closer to the three-dimensional nature of space, they can bring out the feeling of depth or volume.

499
Floor plans are two-dimensional. They mostly provide us with an understanding of the organization of the various elements in them but convey very little of the spatial quality.

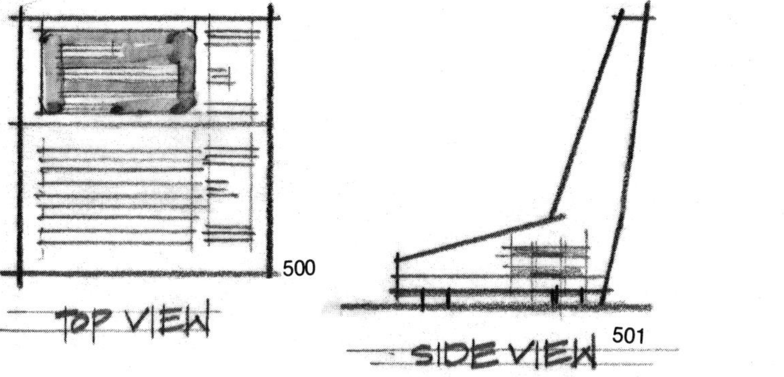

500–503
Two-dimensional orthographic projections (500–502) can give some understanding of the form of the object but the viewer has to reconstruct mentally such a form from these projections. A perspective sketch (503) can convey the form more quickly since it is closer to the three-dimensional reality.

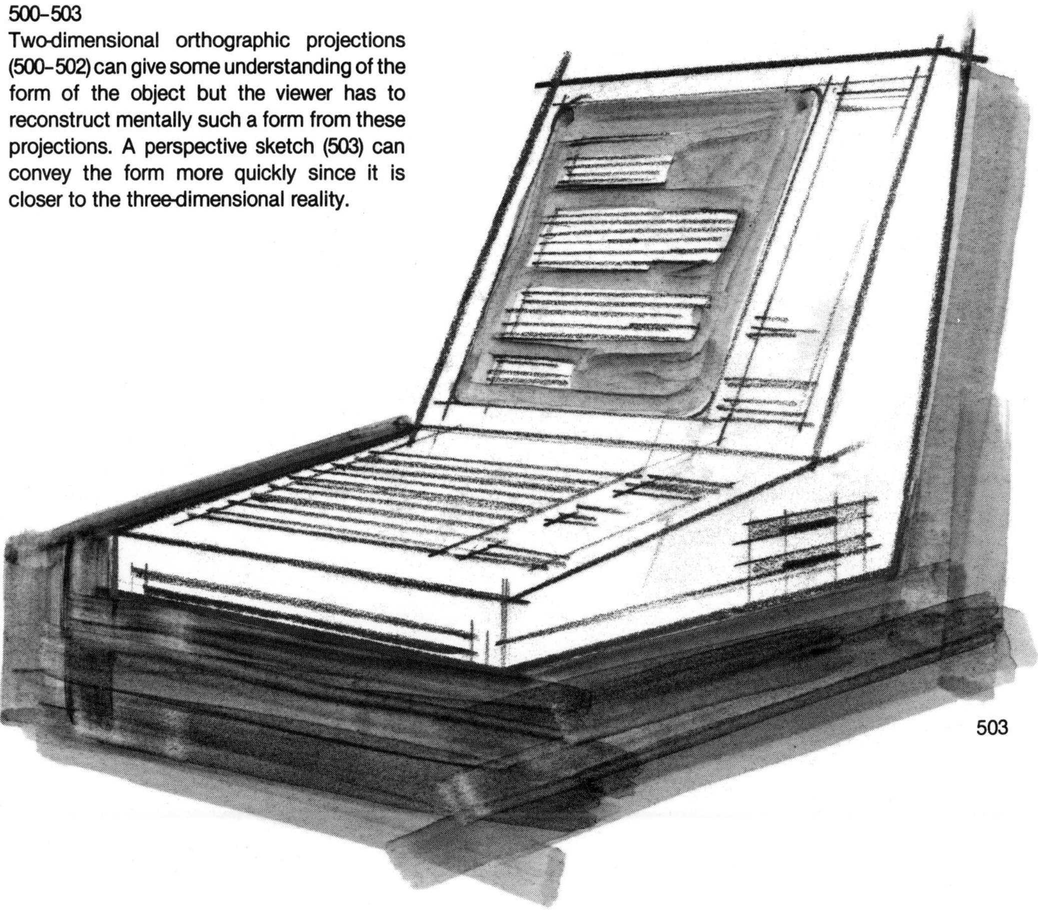

505

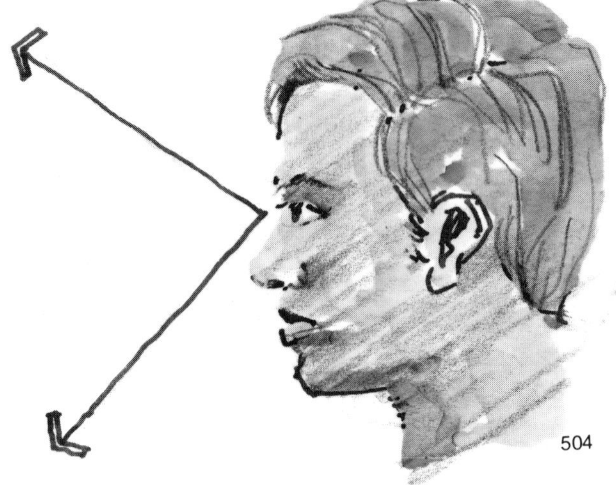

504

505–506
In an auditorium we mostly look at the stage (505) because that is how we are oriented. Seldom do we try to experience space by looking backward (506). A sensitive designer considers space from all directions.

504
Due to our physiological limitations we tend to ignore the space behind us.

PHYSIOLOGICAL LIMITATION

The location and orientation of the eyes with respect to the head is a physiological limitation that shapes the way we perceive a given environment. Because of this limitation, we tend to ignore the space behind us while our spatial experience seems to revolve around what appears in front of us. Thus, when we experience a space for the first time, our initial orientation in it greatly influences our perception of that space. To make our perception a complete one, we need to move around in it and look in different directions.

506

FOURTH DIMENSION

Space is actually four-dimensional with time being the fourth dimension. With the addition of the time dimension, space changes and becomes dynamic. Spaces, especially outdoor ones, change at various

507

times of the day, and considering seasonal differences, various days of the year bring about drastic changes with regard to the quality of space. When we perceive a space in three dimensions, our perception of it is a frozen one, and in this frozen form we store the experience of the space in our memory banks. In a sense, such a perception is a kind of simplification or abstraction since it is only a thin slice from the four-dimensional space-time continuum. For the purpose of studying design, we use plans, sections, elevations, etc., which are further abstractions of space. Such studies can get us bogged down too easily, and make us lose touch with the real nature of space.

GRAPHIC SIMULATION

Abstraction, especially through graphic simulation, is a convenient way to study design, but there should be various levels of abstraction for us to be

507–508
While a perspective sketch (507) freezes the four-dimensional space-time continuum into a three-dimensional abstraction, a section drawing (508) deletes another dimension, making it a two-dimensional abstraction.

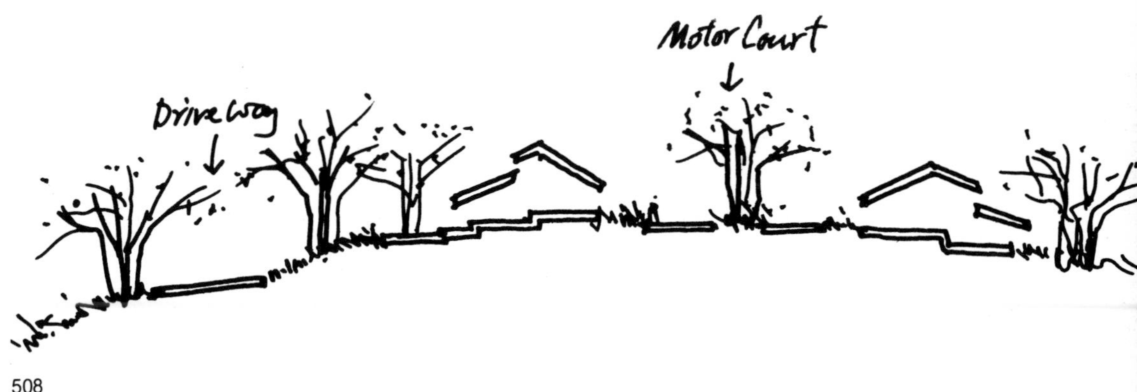

508

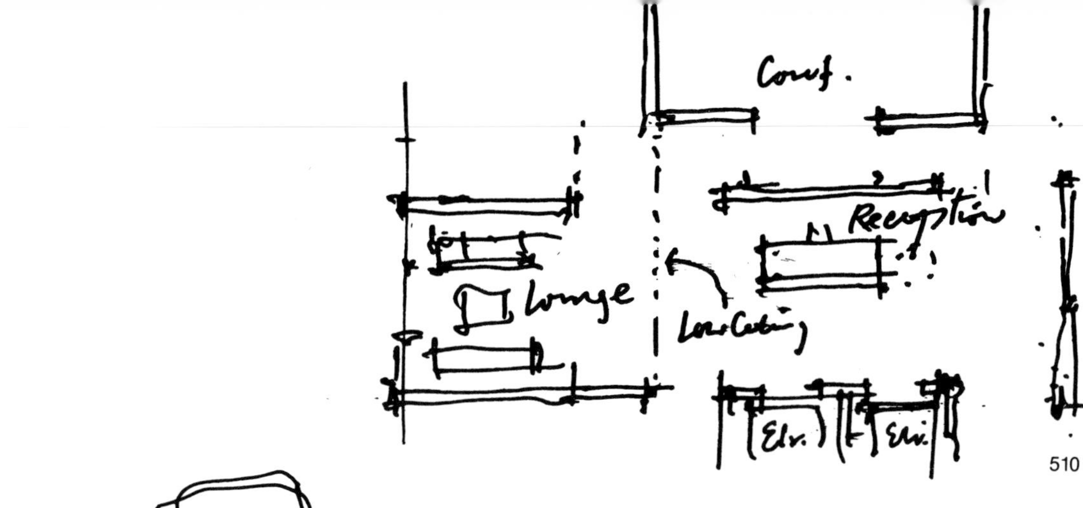

510

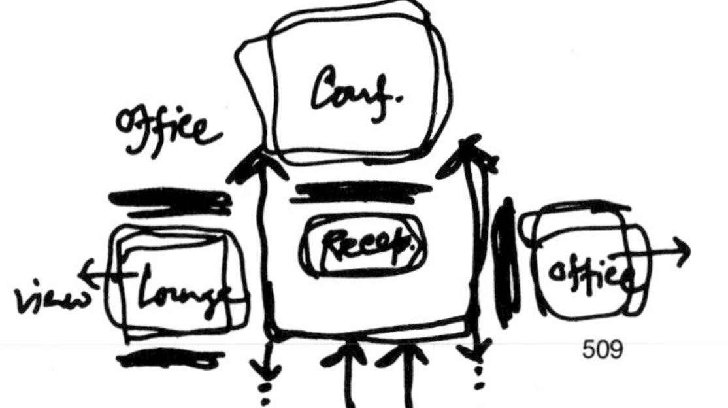

509

509–511
A conceptual diagram (509) synthesizes the program and site analysis. A plan (510) can be used in further development of the concept; three-dimensional sketching (511) is very helpful in visualizing the spatial consequences.

able to give appropriate considerations to all types of issues. Whereas one- or two-dimensional abstractions are very useful in studying logical consistencies and functional requirements or relationships, three-dimensional abstractions are indispensible in studying the volumentric relationship, spatial wholeness, and sense of unity. A series of perspective sketches can also capture the time dimension by depicting changes during various times of the day or various seasons of the year.

ESSENCE OF SPACE

Spaces are more than mere physical volumes. Aside from the dynamics of time, a space also has a perceptual dimension. This is the dimension of feeling. Together with all its volumetric dimensions, planes, details, texture, values, contrast, and

511

shadow patterns, it evokes a unified sense or feeling. Such feeling is the soul and character of that particular space. Every space has this regardless of whether it is pleasant, unpleasant, exciting, dull, or indifferent. So far as the aspect of feeling in design is concerned, this dimension is the most delicate and central one. I call it the "essence" of space.

FREEHAND SKETCHES

Graphic communication can and should be used to explore the essence of space, and to this end freehand perspective sketches are extremely useful. They need not be finished sketches. They are study sketches, but through suggestions of scale, certain details, spatial relationship, texture, values, contrast, and shadow patterns, they can display the very essence of the proposed space. This requires projecting oneself into the future, capturing the central theme or feeling of the space, and responding to one's intuitive world, dreams, and imagination. Three-dimensional studies, i.e., perspective

512
Freehand sketching can be quick and yet informative with regard to the overall design intent without involving extensive detailed information.

513

513–514
Quick freehand sketching can also be used to capture the character of a proposed environment.

514

sketches, fill in the gaps through leaps of insight and intuition, and thus formulate solutions having the desired essence or feeling. It is a process of discovery as well as an act of creation. In a sense, such graphic exploration itself is the act of designing, for this is where the critical connection is made between the logical and the intuitive, between the known and the unfamiliar, and between abstract and concrete thinking. Such is the nature of the creative act.

19

515

Sketching and Spatial Quality

Sometimes a frustrated student will come to me and say that he or she has tried out various techniques to make a perspective sketch of the design solution, but nothing seems to improve the sketch. Often, such a problem is not in the technicalities of sketching but in the very design of the space the student is proposing. It is the spatial quality of the design that makes the sketch look attractive regardless of how roughly or quickly the sketch is drawn.

Aside from the way a sketch is composed on a piece of paper, there are various other compositional issues associated with the spatial aspects of the design solution that are responsible for the merit of

516

515–516
Sketches can be drawn roughly and still be attractive if the spaces in them are interesting. Such rough sketches give clues as to the merits of the spaces.

517

517–518
Each of the elements depicted by dots (518) defines a plane or an edge that creates a spatial enclosure.

518

the design as well as the attractiveness of the sketch drawn of it. If these compositional issues are properly dealt with and resolved, the sketch of the solution generally becomes attractive, for the intuitive self senses the merit upon mere visual inspection. In the next few paragraphs, I will discuss these compositional issues of space, which are deeply linked with graphic problem solving.

SPATIAL ENCLOSURE

A frequent problem with design solutions is that the space is vague and not articulated. A space requires definition with respect to its volume regardless of its

519–520
The elements shown by dots (520) articulate various spaces. Note that the balcony helps to create a spatial enclosure for three different subordinate spaces: the space on it, the space in front of it, and the space under it.

519

size. Planes and edges make the *spatial enclosure.* They do not have to be solid walls or physical barriers. A row of trees, an earth berm, a partial fence, a retaining wall, a series of steps, a change in floor texture or value, a drop of the ceiling height—any of these can define a plane or edge, and thus can serve as a means to enclose a space. Space is a continuum, but spatial enclosures define subordinate spaces within this continuum, and thus they articulate and punctuate according to the functional constraints of individual spaces. Without such articulation a space becomes vague and tends to wander, lacking any containment. Any sketch of it also reflects such vagueness, thus making it unattractive.

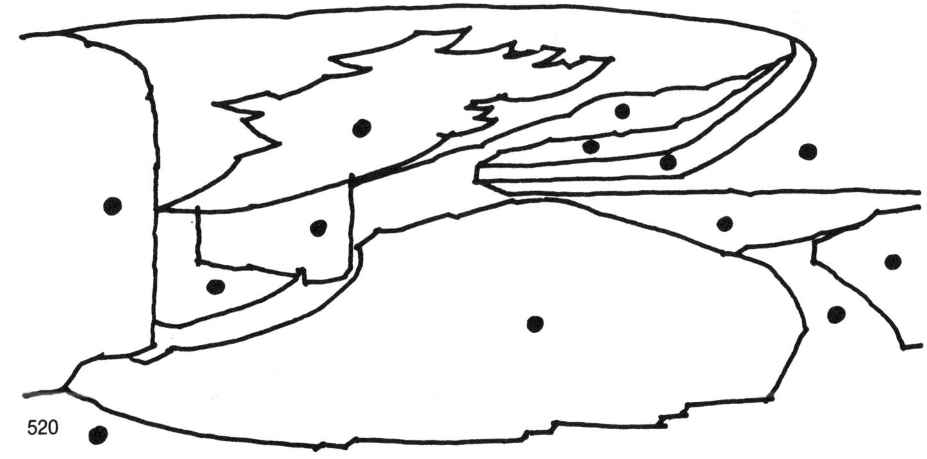
520

521–522
The volumetric relationship between the spaces A, B, C, D, and E is what creates interest in this sketch.

521

522

On the other hand, one can overdo the enclosing of space. One may literally put too many walls or planes, suffocating the space, thus destroying the flow of the spatial continuum. The key lies in achieving balance between providing enough spatial enclosure and still maintaining spatial continuity.

VOLUMETRIC RELATIONSHIP AND SEQUENCE

The volume of each space with regard to how it relates to adjoining spaces is critical in creating interest through variation and contrast. The relation-

523–524
The relationship among the narrow foreground (A-524), the wider middleground (B-524), and the vast space at the background (C-524) creates volumetric contrast. It is this spatial relationship that makes the design, and, consequently, its sketch, attractive.

523

ship of the foreground, middleground, and background in a sketch is essentially the result of such variation and contrast of the volumes of spaces.

Another important element in creating interest is the sequence of spaces in terms of their functions, volumes, and geometric forms. A well-thought out sequence of spaces in a given design leads the eyes through a series of interesting experiences while looking at the study sketch of the design solution.

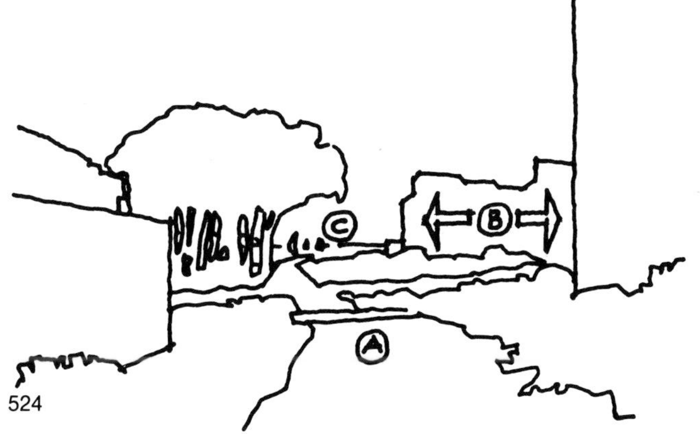

524

525
The recessed wall of the bathhouse as well as the overlapping wall at the left creates interest through the variation of planes.

526

526–527
The variation in planes and the contrast of solid and void spaces give a feeling of depth of space. They also create light and dark shadow patterns and emphasize the three-dimensionality.

VARIATION IN PLANES

Interest in a space as well as in a sketch drawn of it can be the result of achieving sufficient variation in planes. Positive and negative spaces can be created along a plane by projecting it out or recessing it. The contrast of positive and negative spaces provides for the interplay of light, giving a sense of unity, and is thus interesting to look at. Similar contrast can also be created through the solid and void relationship of a plane such as a facade with the fenestration in it.

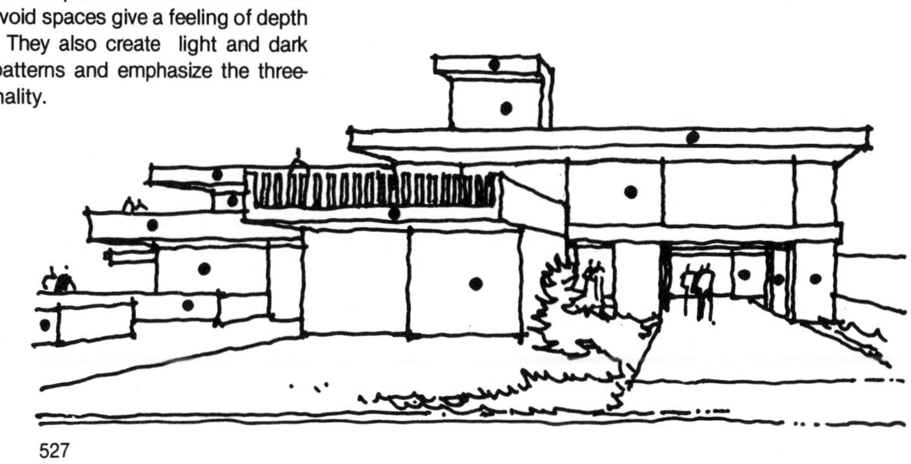

527

529

CHANGE OF LEVELS

Change of levels is also a kind of variation in planes, except limited to the ground plane in the vertical dimension. Such variations provide for different viewpoints by changing the eye level. This characteristic along with a feeling of depth in the vertical dimension makes the spatial experience an interesting one.

VARIATION IN TEXTURE, VALUES, AND SHADOW PATTERNS

Change of texture and values can emphasize changes of planes as well as variations in them. Pat-

528–530
Level changes are a variation in the third dimension of the horizontal plane and provide varied viewpoints (528). A person could stand at any of the spots shown as dots (530) and experience the space from various eye levels. Natural landform can provide various possibilities for creating attractive spaces through advantageous use of topographic changes and through the integration of buildings and objects with the landform (529).

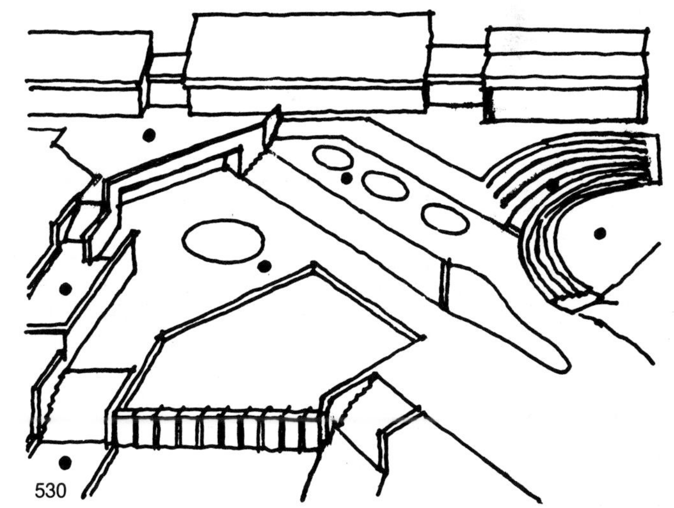

530

531

531–532
The trees at the foreground create a spatial window (A-532) while framing the distant view of the lake (B-532). The building on the left and the hillside on the right create a second spatial window in the middleground.

532

terns of modular materials such as bricks and concrete blocks not only provide distinct textures but also establish the scale. The shadow pattern can also emphasize changes of planes, variations in them, and the depth of space.

SPATIAL WINDOW AND VIEWPOINT

A spatial window is a space that connects a larger space allowing a view through the former to the latter. I call this the *spatial window* for it frames the view of a space while maintaining a spatial identity

533–534
The palm trees on the left and the temple on the right frame the view while one's attention is led to the distant horizon.

533

of its own. Since spatial windows frame views, they generate interest, curiosity, and a feeling of depth and spatial continuity. They establish a sense of unity between the parts (the spaces) and the whole (the spatial continuum).

The selection of the viewpoint for an attractive sketch requires the availability of those elements that make the spatial enclosure and spatial window. Thus, sketching forces us to give a series of considerations that are essential to the spatial quality of a given design solution.

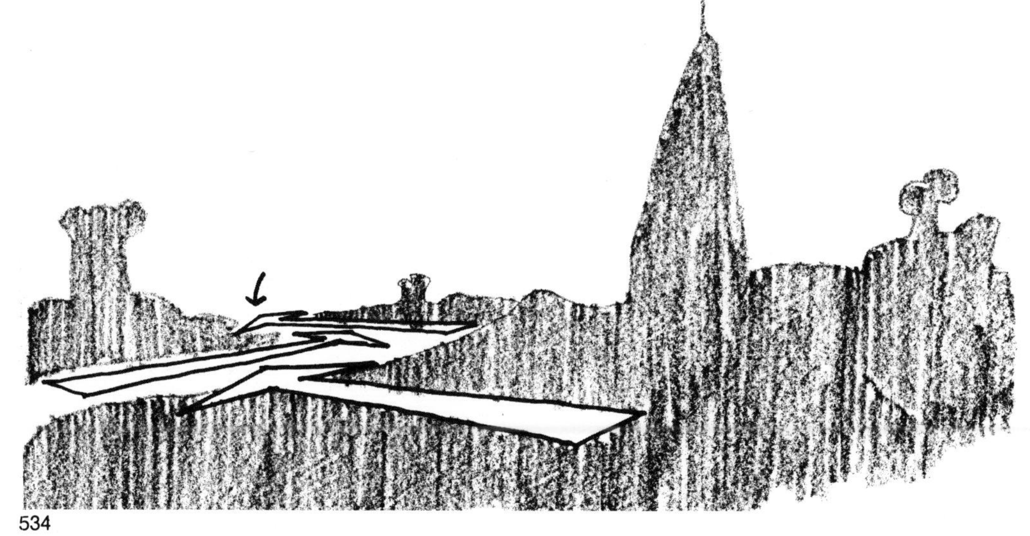
534

535

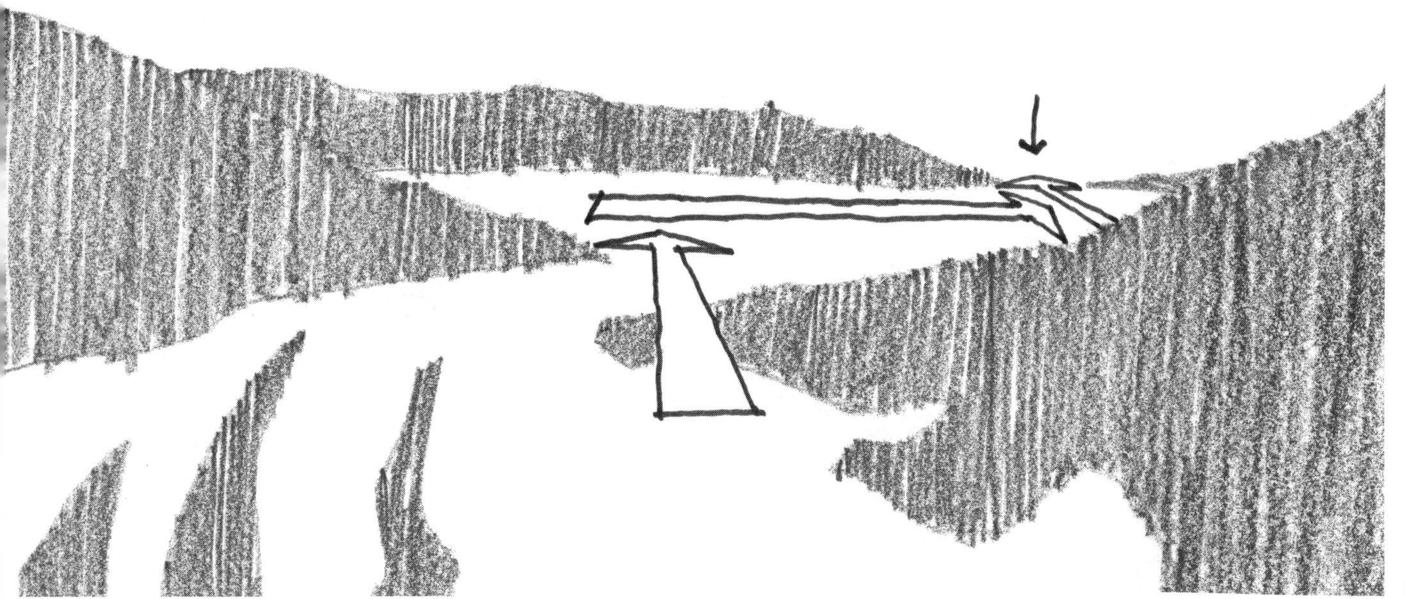

536

535–536
The sequence of how attention is led through is very important and gives both a feeling of the depth of the total space and a visual tour of subordinate spaces.

GATHERING EXPERIENCE

We have seen in the preceding paragraphs that the act of sketching is deeply linked to the substantive design of space. To evaluate the design through such sketching requires intense observation and experience on the compositional issues of space, which have just been discussed. One way to sharpen our observation skills and develop the experience is through sketching existing spaces,

537–538
Sketching an existing space can be useful for discovering the elements that contribute to its spatial quality.

537

Variation in rooflines

Variation in planes

Change of levels

The walls, columns, steps and shrubs are defining planes and edges, and thus giving a sense of spatial enclosure

538

539

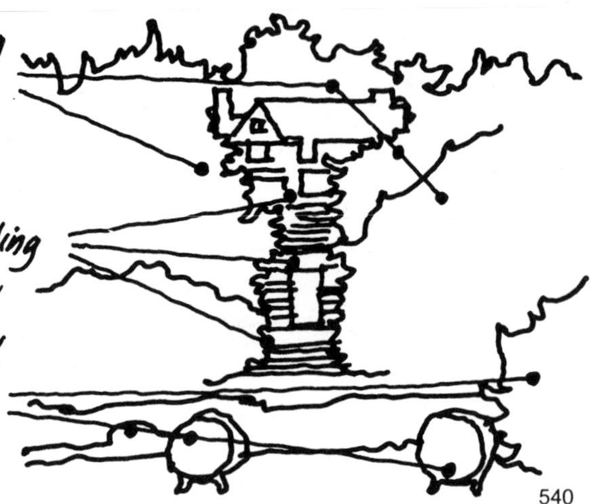

540

539–540
Since the act of sketching is inseparable from visual and spatial assessment, it helps develop insight for creative manipulation of space.

especially ones which are successful. I sketch whenever I find a space which is interesting, and this helps me discover the elements of design that make the space a successful one.

Part Eight

Epilogue

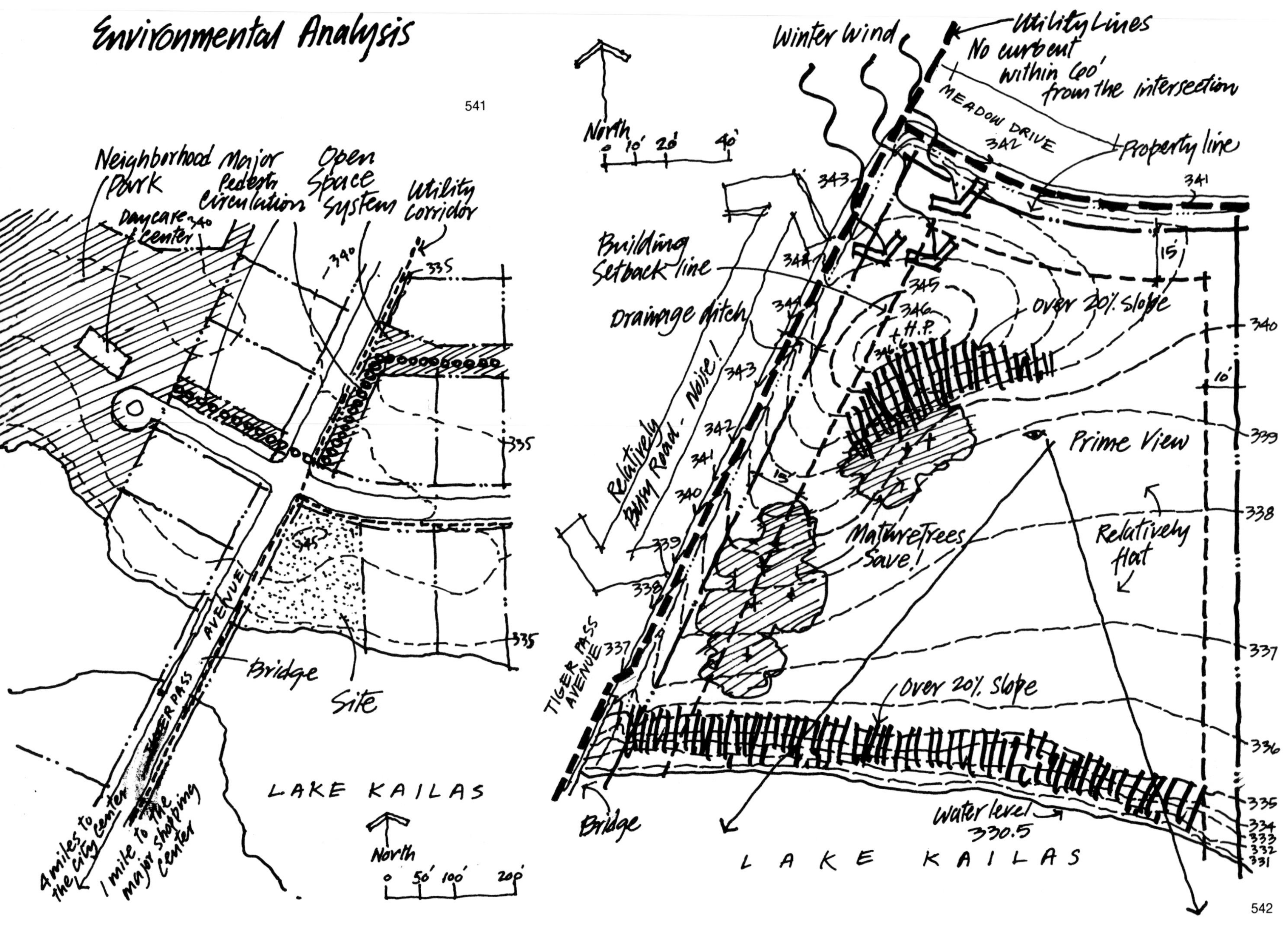
Environmental Analysis
Neighborhood Park
Daycare center
Major Pedestn Circulation
Open Space System
Utility corridor
Bridge
Site
LAKE KAILAS
North
0 50' 100' 200'
4 miles to the City Center
1 mile to the major shopping center
TIGER PASS AVENUE
North
0 10' 20' 40'
Winter Wind
Utility Lines
No curbcut within 60' from the intersection
MEADOW DRIVE
Property line
Building Setback line
Drainage ditch
Relatively Busy Road - Noise!
Over 20% Slope
H.P.
Prime View
Mature Trees Save!
Relatively flat
Over 20% Slope
Water level 330.5
Bridge
L A K E K A I L A S

20

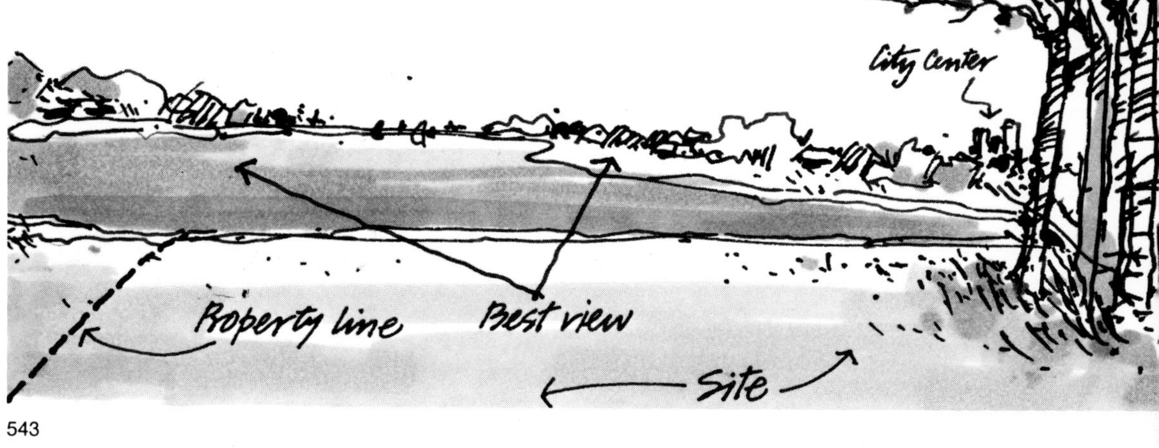

543

A Case Study

Thus far we have discussed various aspects of graphic communication as it relates to problem solving. These next few pages provide an example of graphic thinking and exploration as used in a design process. For our purpose, we have chosen the design of a residence as the problem. These drawings and sketches are only samples of various stages in the evolution of the design solution and do not pretend to be a complete account of a graphic exploration.

541–542
Depending on the nature of the problem, an environmental analysis can include studies of areas at various scale: the region, neighborhood, surrounding area (541), and the site itself (542).

543–544
Sketches of the surrounding area and the site give a better understanding of and feel for the context.

544

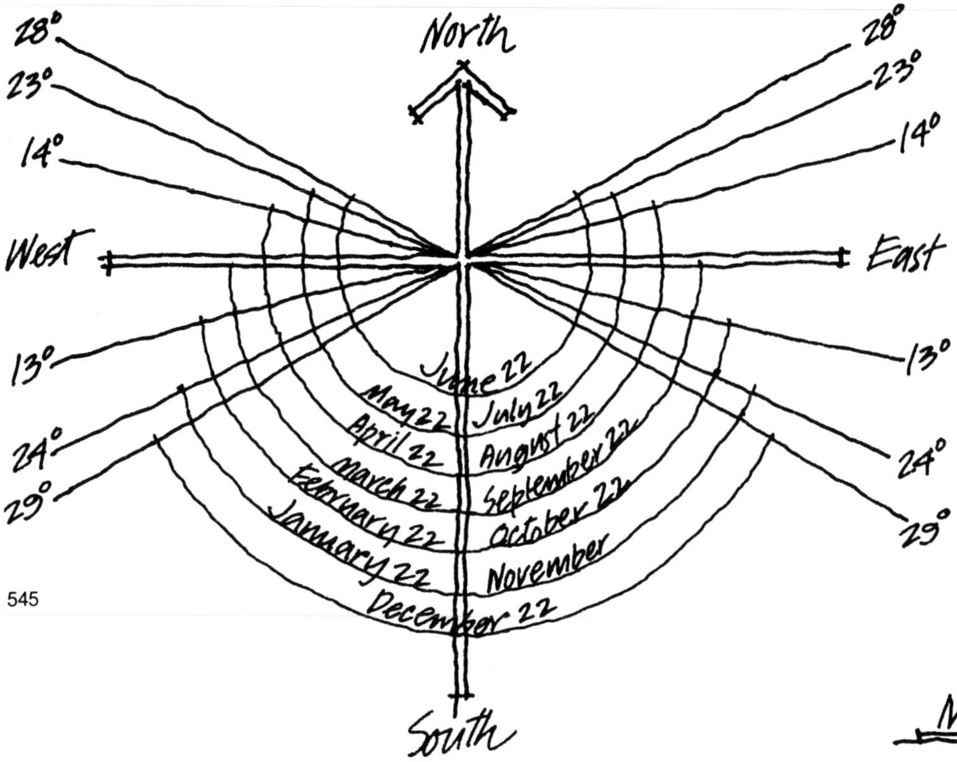

545

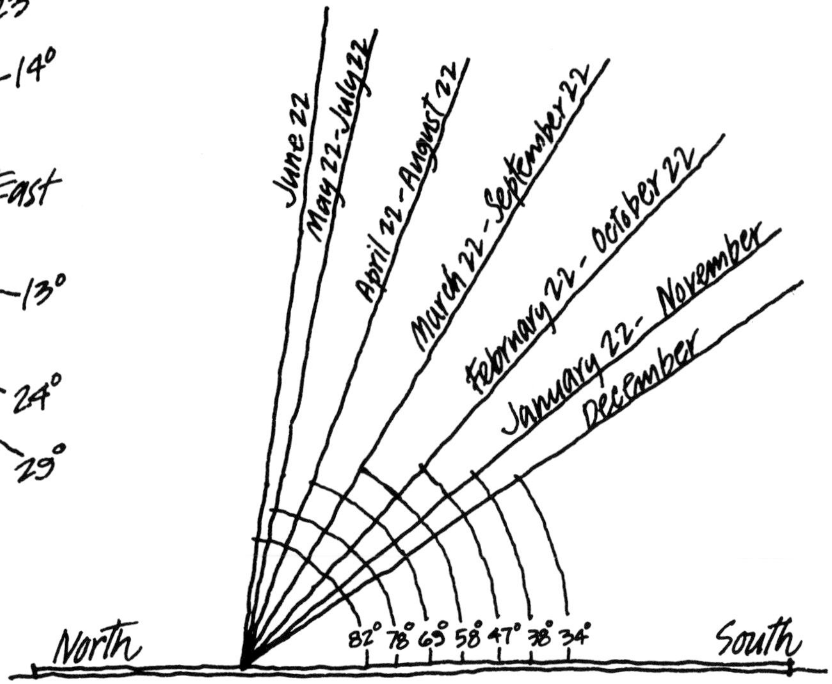

546

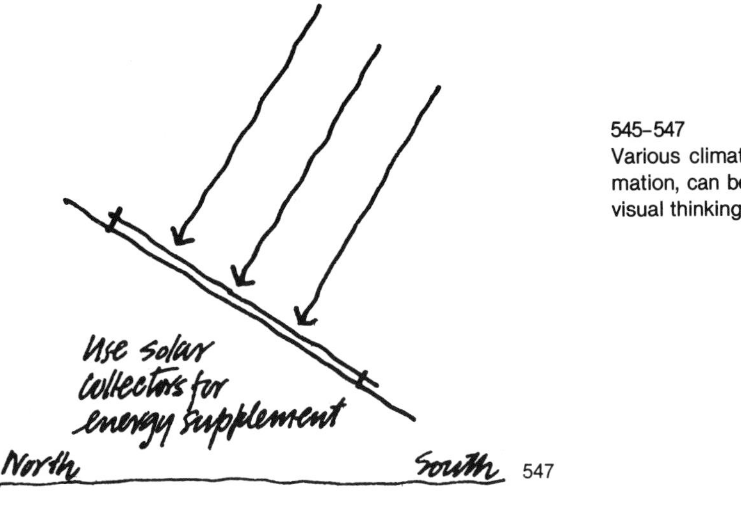

547

545–547
Various climatic data, including solar information, can be graphically translated to aid visual thinking about the problem.

548
Space requirements can be translated graphically in order to visualize the relative sizes.

549–553
Program goals with regard to functional relationships and proximity can be expressed graphically in a series of diagrams.

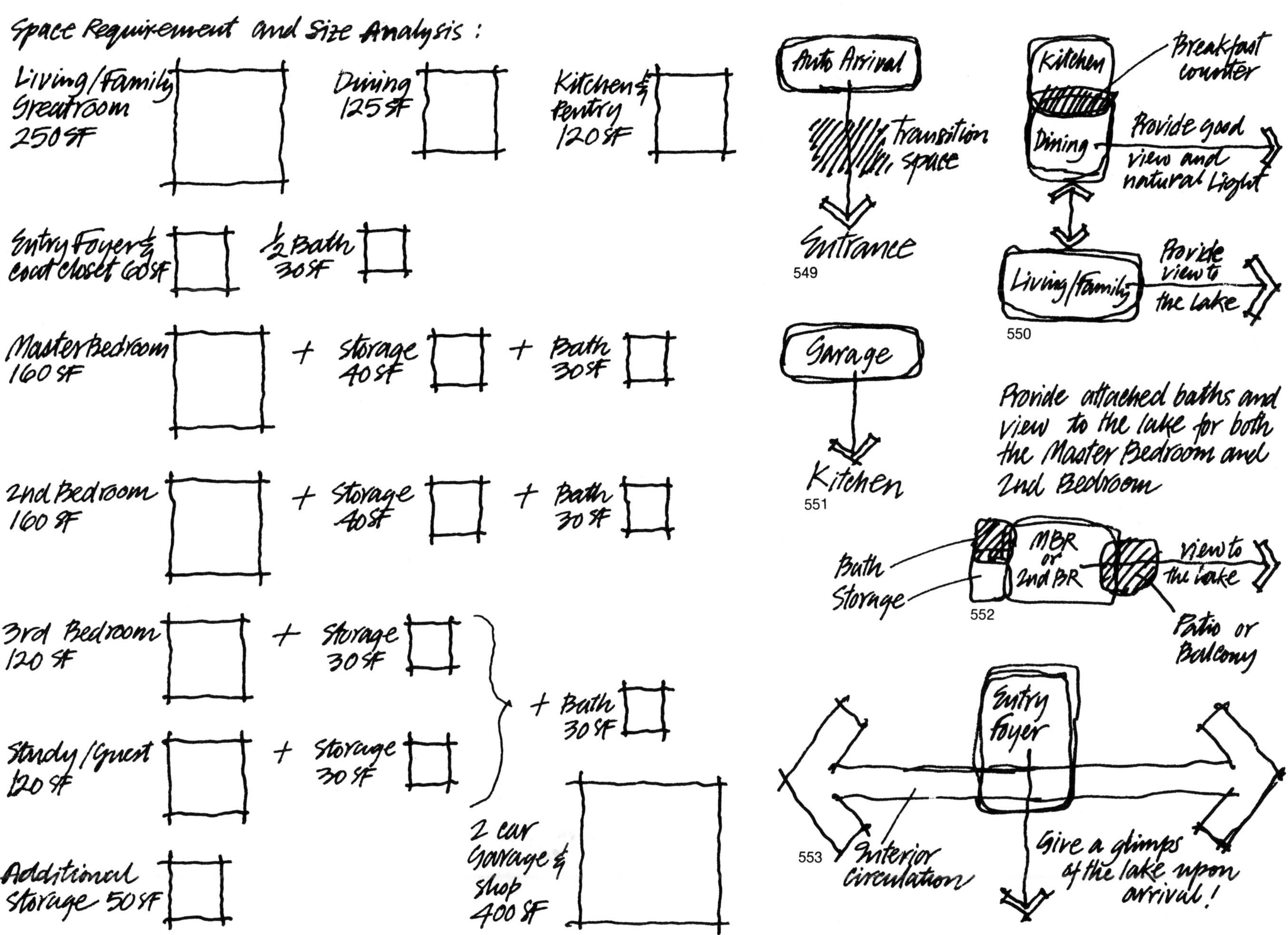

548
549
550
551
552
553

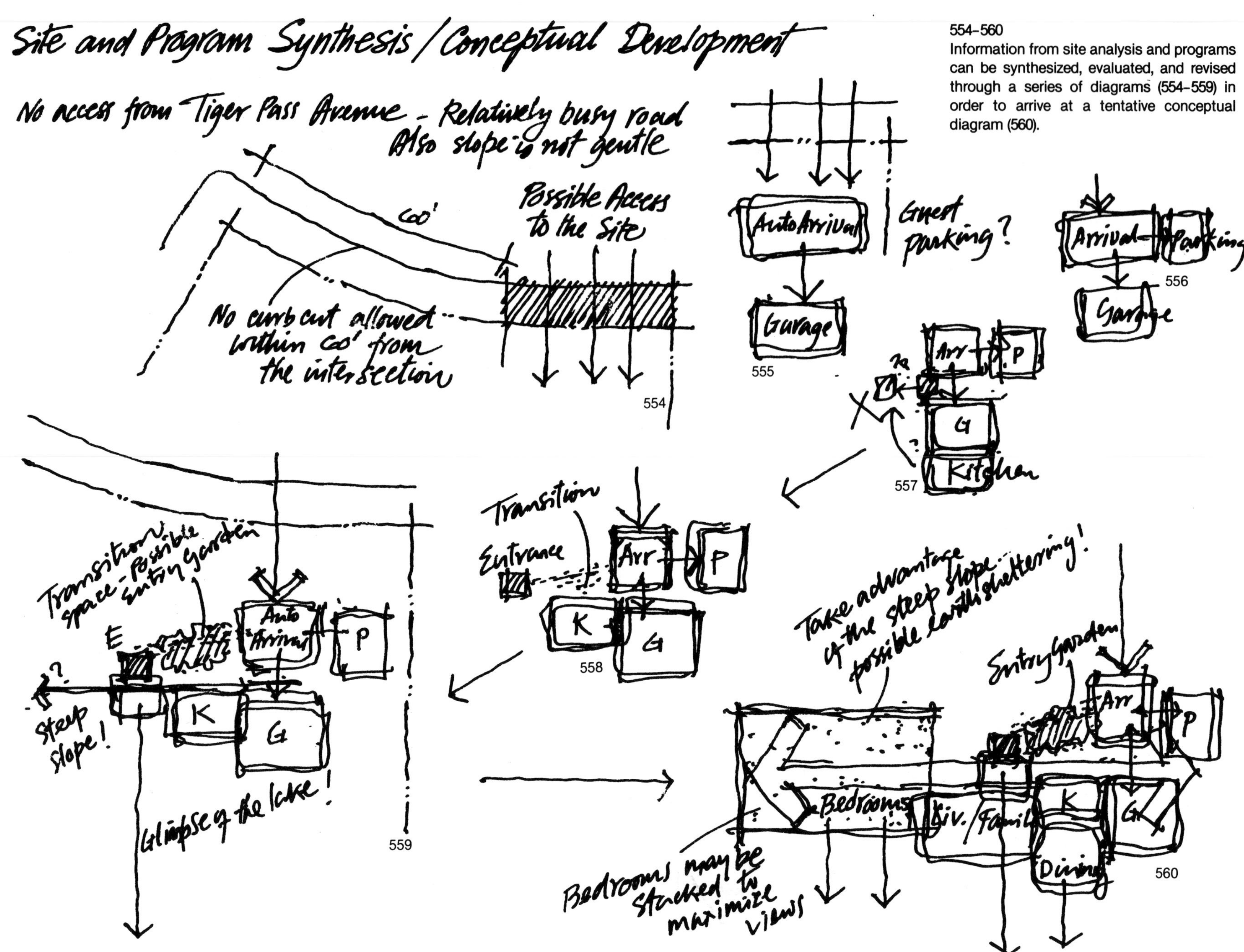

554–560
Information from site analysis and programs can be synthesized, evaluated, and revised through a series of diagrams (554–559) in order to arrive at a tentative conceptual diagram (560).

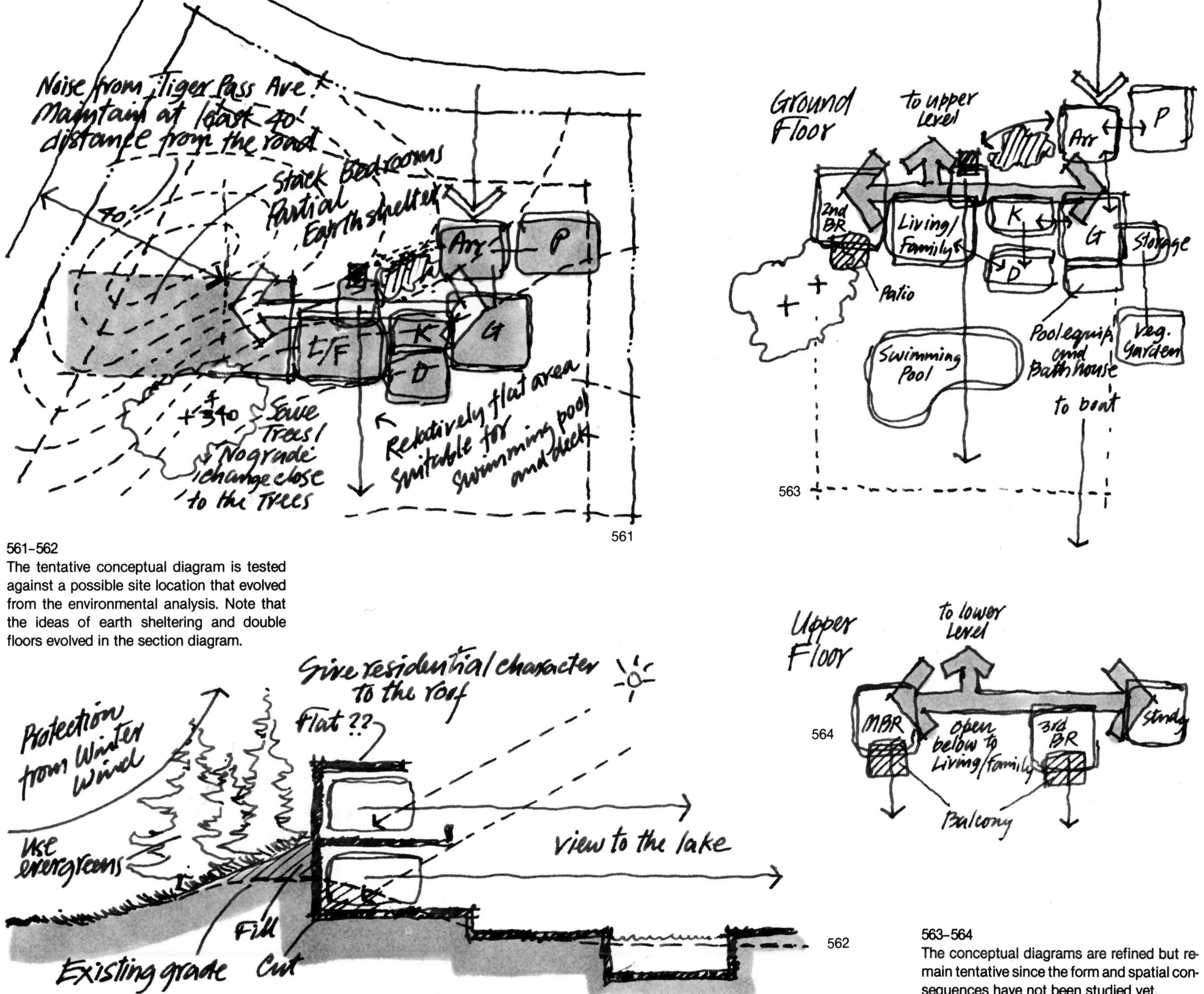

561–562
The tentative conceptual diagram is tested against a possible site location that evolved from the environmental analysis. Note that the ideas of earth sheltering and double floors evolved in the section diagram.

563–564
The conceptual diagrams are refined but remain tentative since the form and spatial consequences have not been studied yet.

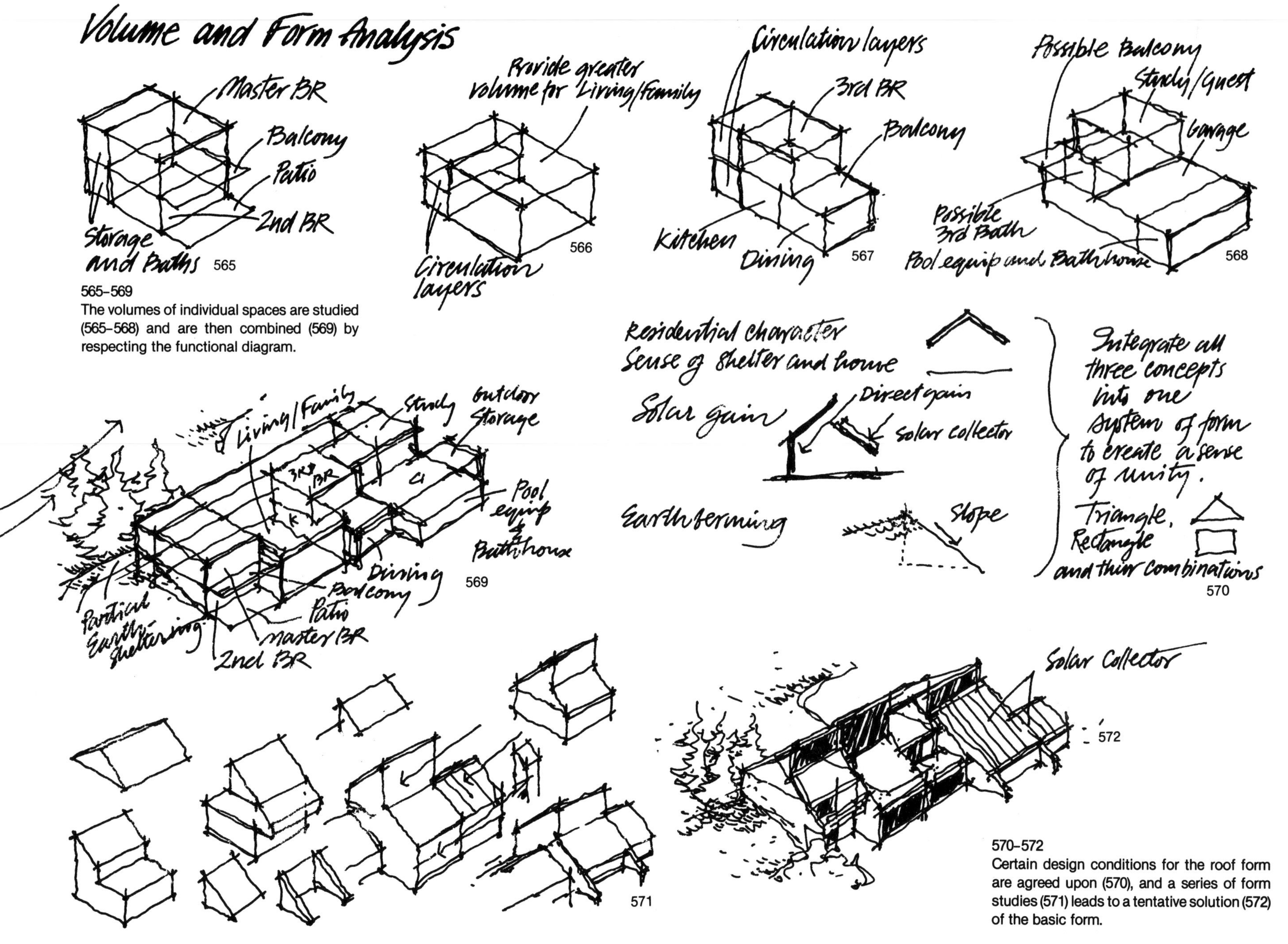

565–569
The volumes of individual spaces are studied (565–568) and are then combined (569) by respecting the functional diagram.

570–572
Certain design conditions for the roof form are agreed upon (570), and a series of form studies (571) leads to a tentative solution (572) of the basic form.

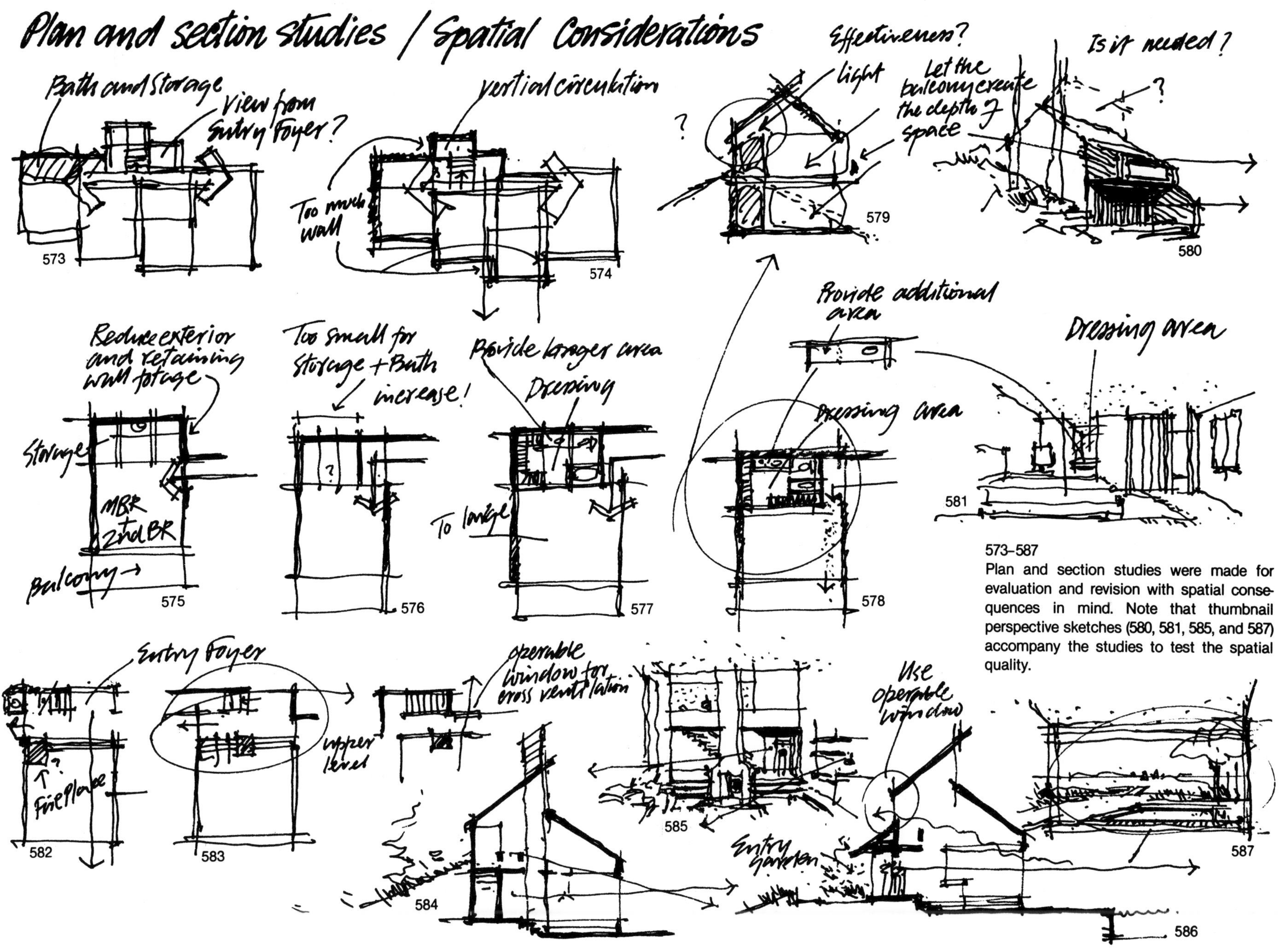

573–587
Plan and section studies were made for evaluation and revision with spatial consequences in mind. Note that thumbnail perspective sketches (580, 581, 585, and 587) accompany the studies to test the spatial quality.

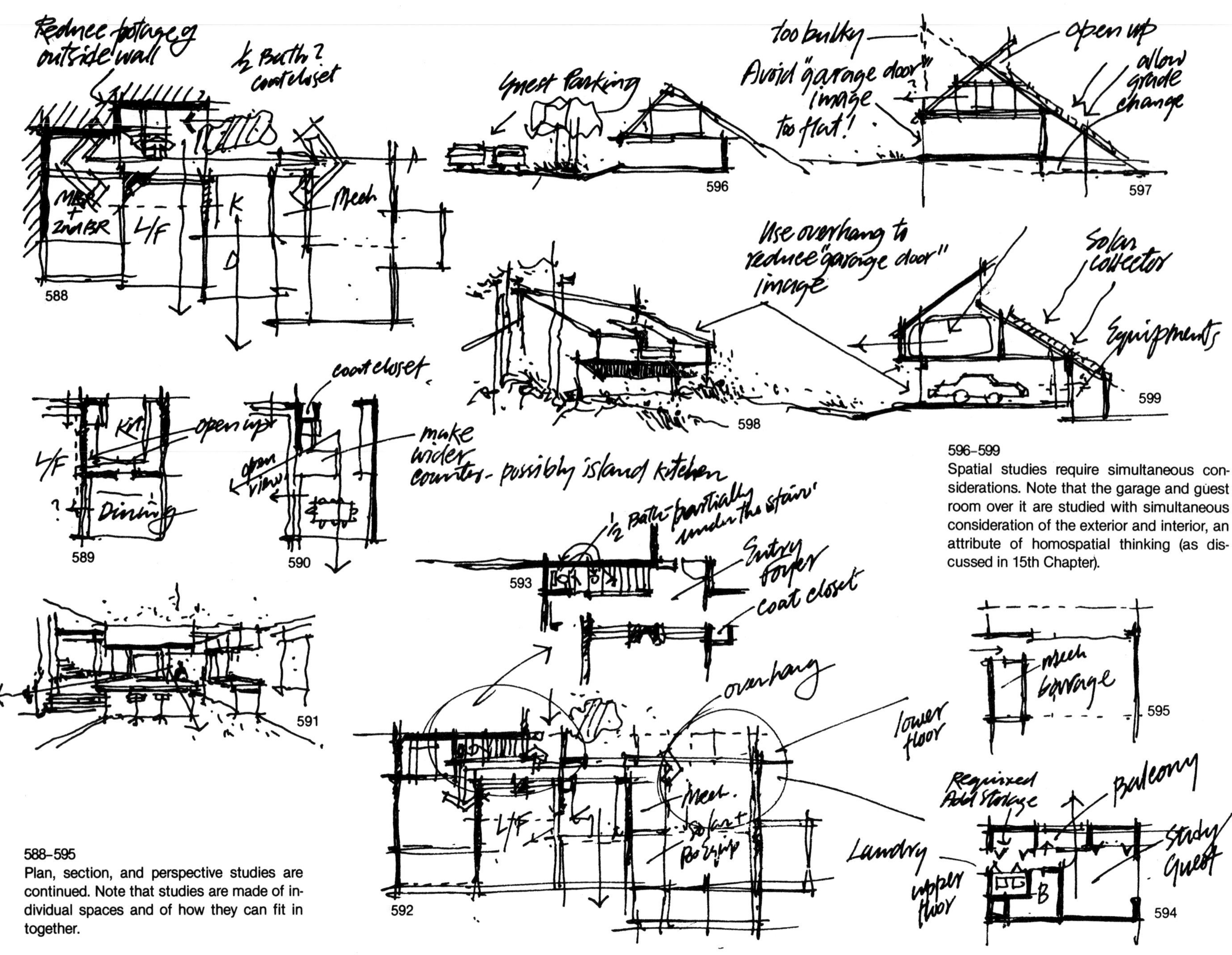

596–599
Spatial studies require simultaneous considerations. Note that the garage and guest room over it are studied with simultaneous consideration of the exterior and interior, an attribute of homospatial thinking (as discussed in 15th Chapter).

588–595
Plan, section, and perspective studies are continued. Note that studies are made of individual spaces and of how they can fit in together.

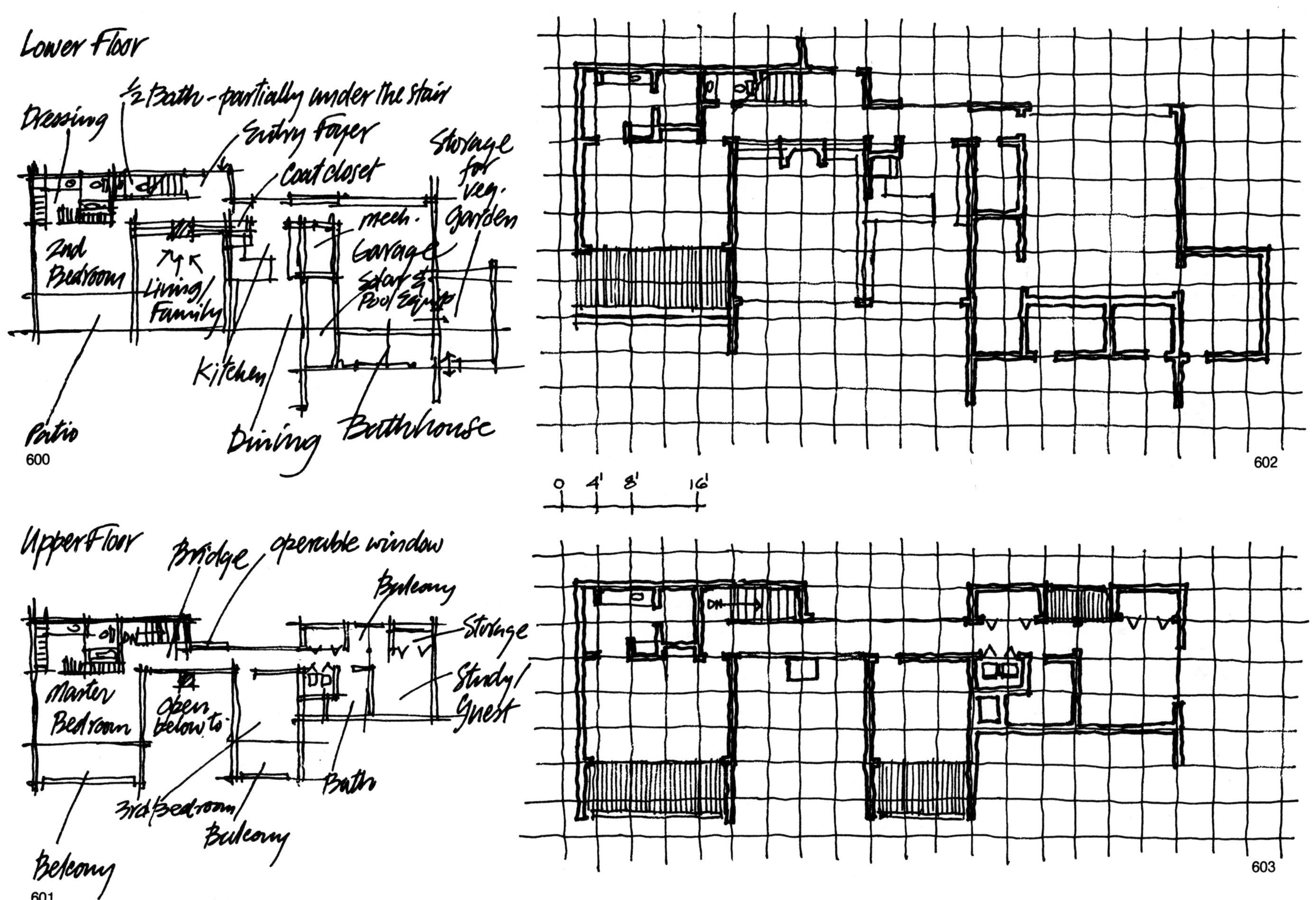

600–603
A tentative solution (600–601) is now refined with the help of a grid (602–603).

604
Several sections were superimposed to simultaneously study the roof form, floor levels, ceiling height, clearstory and solar collectors. Such simultaneous considerations can be attributed to Janusian thinking.

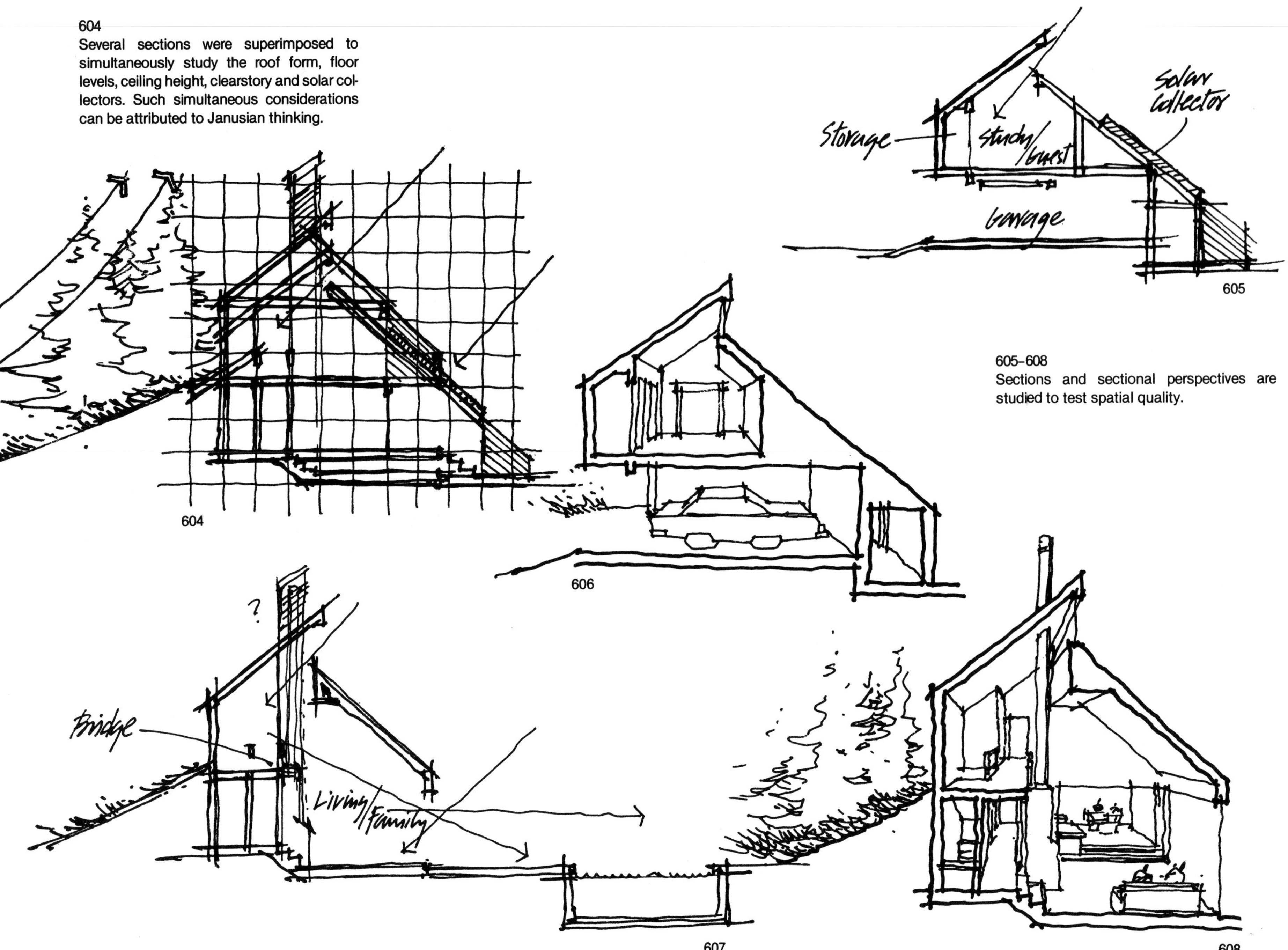

604

605

606

607

608

605–608
Sections and sectional perspectives are studied to test spatial quality.

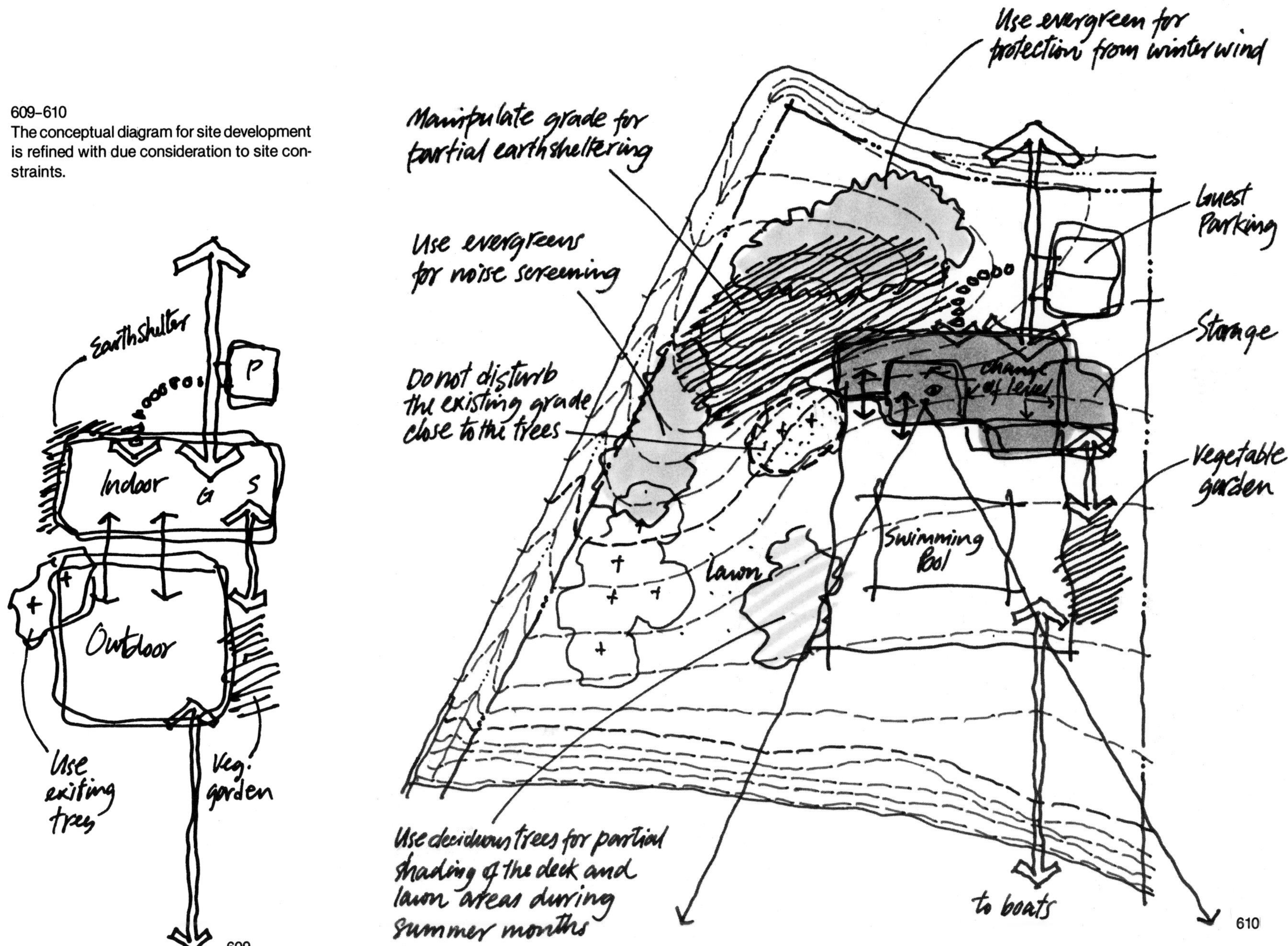

609–610
The conceptual diagram for site development is refined with due consideration to site constraints.

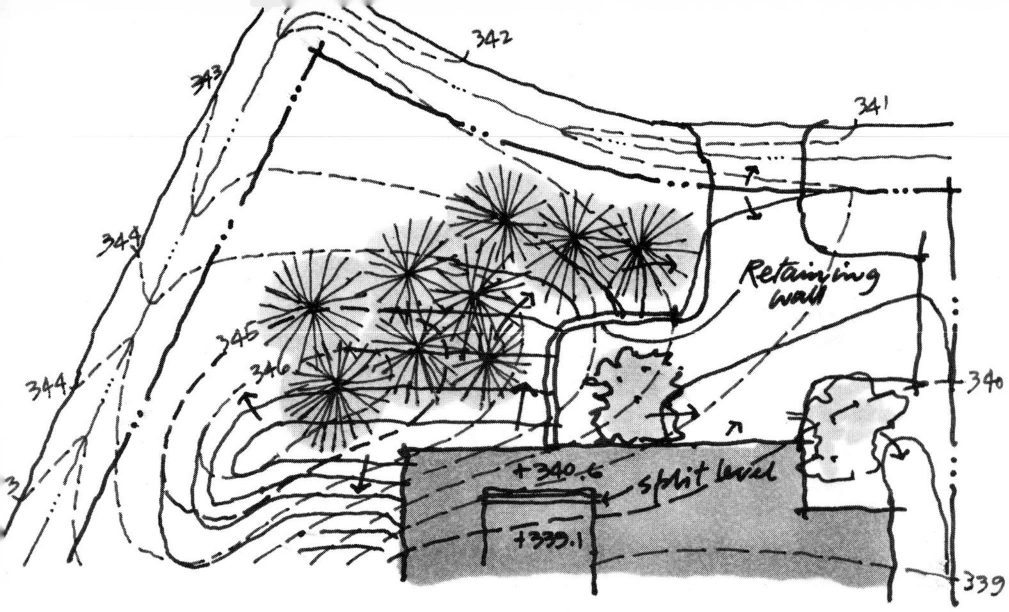

342

343

341

344

Retaining wall

345

346

344

+340.6

split level

340

+339.1

339

611

Entry garden

Use retaining wall for entry

reduce amount of fenestration

Guest parking

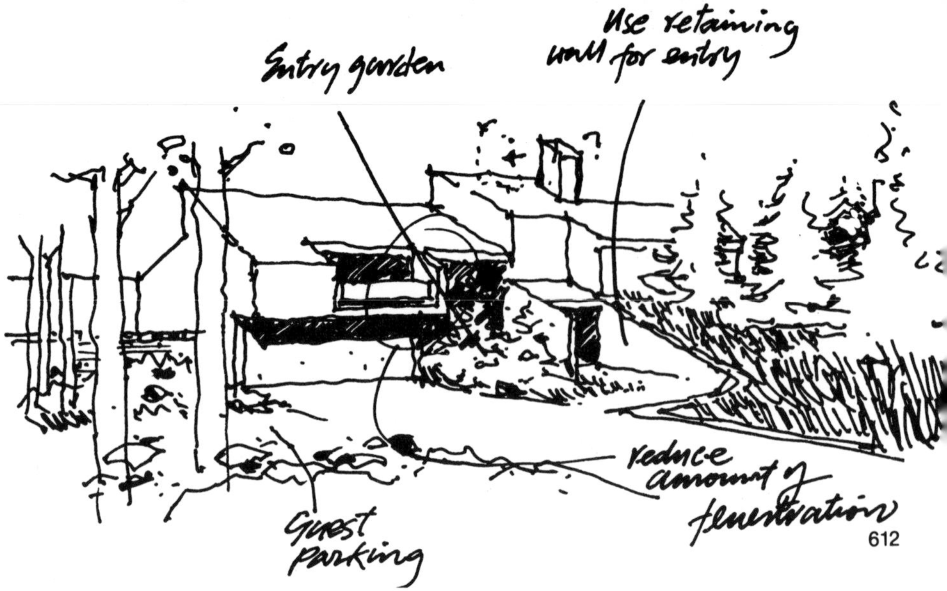

612

613

611–616
Additional refinements of the northern portion of the site were done with the help of plan (611) and perspective sketches (612–613). Likewise the southside is also studied for refinement through plan (614) and perspective sketches (615–616).

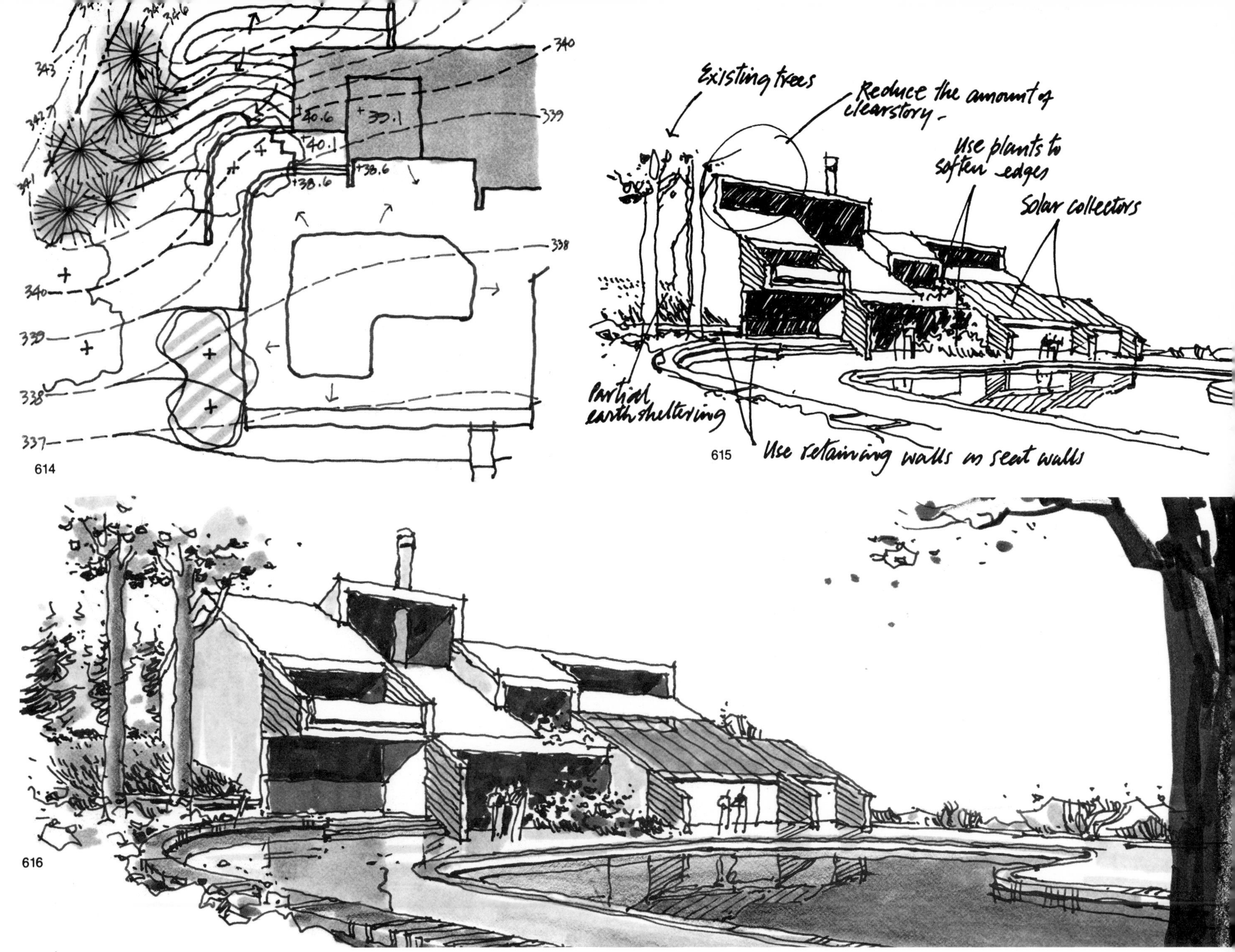

343
342.7
341
340
339
338
337
340.6
39.1
40.1
38.6
38.6
340
339
338
Existing trees
Reduce the amount of clearstory -
Use plants to soften edges
Solar collectors
Partial earth sheltering
Use retaining walls as seat walls

614

615

616

617–619
Site section is made to study the seat-wall and drainage (617). A further study of the seat-wall was made with the help of elevation (618) and section (619) studies.

617

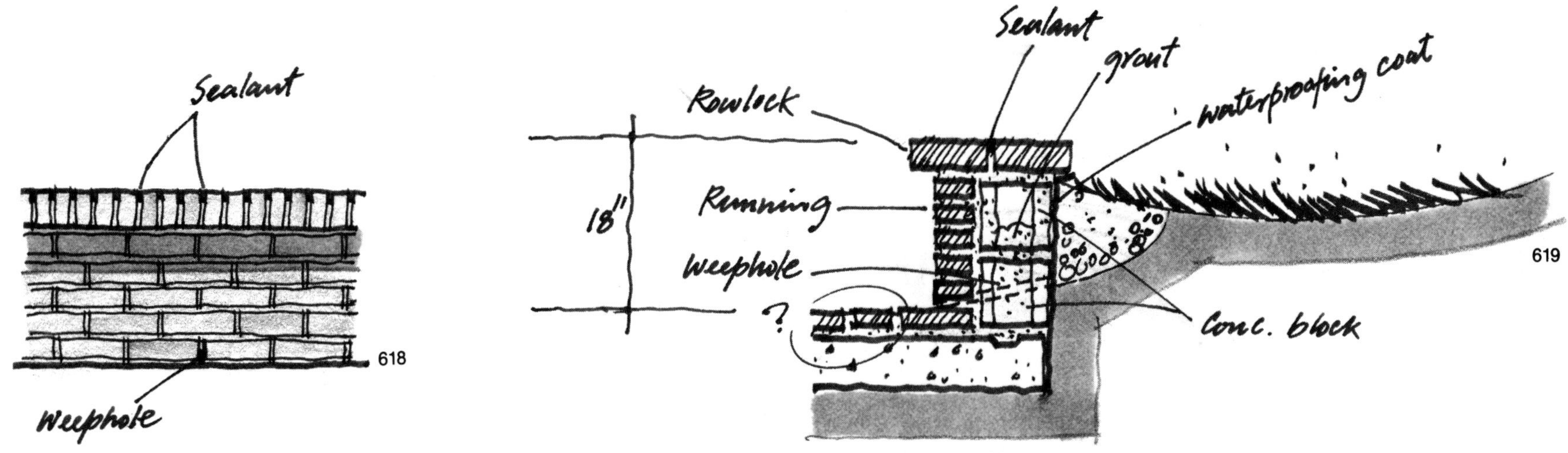

618

619

21

Concluding Remarks

Rudyard Kipling once said:

Oh East is East and West is West,
  and never the twain shall meet,
Till Earth and Sky stand presently
  at God's great Judgement Seat.

Having been exposed to both East and West, Kipling realized that the difference between them is not a superficial one. The difference is indeed fundamental and philosophical. It is a difference in the habit of thinking. Unless this fundamental difference is understood, the superficial differences appear overwhelming and can give a very disappointing impression as they did at the time Kipling made the above comment.

LOGICAL PRINCIPLES

Since the time of Aristotle, the Western world has been deeply influenced by the logical principles of Aristotelian philosophy. The law of identity states that *A is A;* for example, if we have identified something as a pen, it is a pen (and not something else). The law of contradiction states that *A is not non-A;* for example, if we have identified something as a pen, it cannot be at the same time a non-pen. The law of the excluded middle states that *A cannot be A and non-A,* and *neither A nor non-A* at the same time. These principles have been so well absorbed in the Western world that they are taken as self-evident. Any statement that makes a departure from these principles is thought to be nonsensical, contradictory, and fallacious. These logical principles also became the predominant driving force behind the analytic approach and scientific thinking.

Scientific thinking is anatomic; it looks at the world by parts and employs a process that is linear and logical. Aristotelian logical principles exclude simultaniety of concepts for it may make the argument "deleterious" and "contradictory." There is also an undercurrent of presumption behind the analytic investigation that the sum of the parts is equal to the whole. Deductive reasoning and empirical methods have become very much a part of the Western intellectual tradition.

PARADOXICAL LOGIC

On the other hand, paradoxical logic is predominant in Eastern thinking. Here the approach is intuitive and holistic. What is acceptable as a harmonious paradox in the East may very well be thought of as an unacceptable contradiction in the West. Both in Taoist and Indian thinking, the highest level of knowledge amounts to knowing that we do not know. The positive paradoxical formulation such as "it is and it is not" is predominant in Chinese philosophy while the negative paradoxical formulation such as "it is neither this nor that" is predominant in Indian philosophy. Yet both of these formulations would be considered contradictory in the West. In the East, the thinking habit is concrete (i.e., less abstract) seeking harmony, order and wholeness. It completes the pattern in absence of empirical data or evidence.

TWO EASTERN APPROACHES

In recent times, two of the Eastern philosophical approaches to life have received Western attention in the process of examining the nature of creative behavior. They are Zen Buddhism and yoga.

According to Zen, man is born in a state of self-fulfillment and thus in natural harmony with the universe. But because of too much striving and struggling, too much thinking and conflict, he is cut off from the bliss of harmony. To regain that harmony is to achieve the serenity of Zen, and to do this, one must return to one's real self almost without effort. A Zen way of life implies unfolding oneself through concentration, contemplation, and repetition so that one starts to *feel* rather than to think. The simplicity that somehow bypasses us in our attempts to accomplish this may one day very well present itself before us, and thus everything will be clear. Such an unburdensome contemplative life devoted to such a goal may appear to be too passive and accepting to the Western mind.

Zen emphasizes the experience of instant intuition and a spontaneity of reaction. The Zen approach to drawing is a kind of unfolding of oneself through the sense of seeing. It is a way of making direct contact with surrounding reality, unmasking its nature, and looking into its essence. It is, therefore, also getting in touch with one's real self through visual contemplation.

In Sanskrit, the word *yoga* means union. The aim of yoga is to establish union or oneness with the nonegocentric absolute through dissolution of personality. Various yogic techniques are employed to achieve this. Concentration, meditation, asanas or physical exercises, and pranayama or breath control are used to slowly draw one's mind inward to get in touch with or be one with the ultimate existence or consciousness, and thus be in heavenly bliss. Such a state releases tremendous creative and spiritual energies with greater intuitive insight and new vitality.

EAST-WEST DUALISM AND HEMISPHERIC ASYMMETRY

The two habits of thinking that separate the philosophies of East and West can be viewed as a kind of dualism for this planet. With few exceptions such as Heraclitus and Hegel in the West or Carvaka in the East, in general, the West is logical, analytical, and scientific, whereas the East is paradoxical, holistic, and intuitive. Interestingly enough, this dualism is analogous to the functional dualism of the hemispheres of the human brain. As we have discussed in earlier chapters, one hemisphere specializes in verbal, sequential, logical and analytic tasks, while the other handles nonverbal, spatial, intuitive, and holistic tasks.

We have also seen how recent findings indicate that specialized functions of each brain hemisphere are essential for balanced and creative thinking. For creative problem solving, we need both logical and intuitive formulations, both analytic and holistic approaches, and both abstract and concrete thinking. Similarly, the distinct habits of thinking that characterize East and West are also equally essential. Like the brain halves, each of these thinking modes contributes to balance, harmony, and creative decision making. Exchange of ideas, philosophies, and thoughts between East and West has already begun. Certain Western logical and analytic approaches have already permeated the East and similarly, some Eastern thoughts have found their appeal in the West. East is already meeting West and will continue to by the creation of a criss-cross of ideas on the surface of the globe. If Kipling were alive today, the world would have whispered to his ears:

Oh East is no longer East and West is no longer West,
and always the twain shall meet,
For Earth is a small planet, and for balance,
thoughts from both hemispheres must we greet.

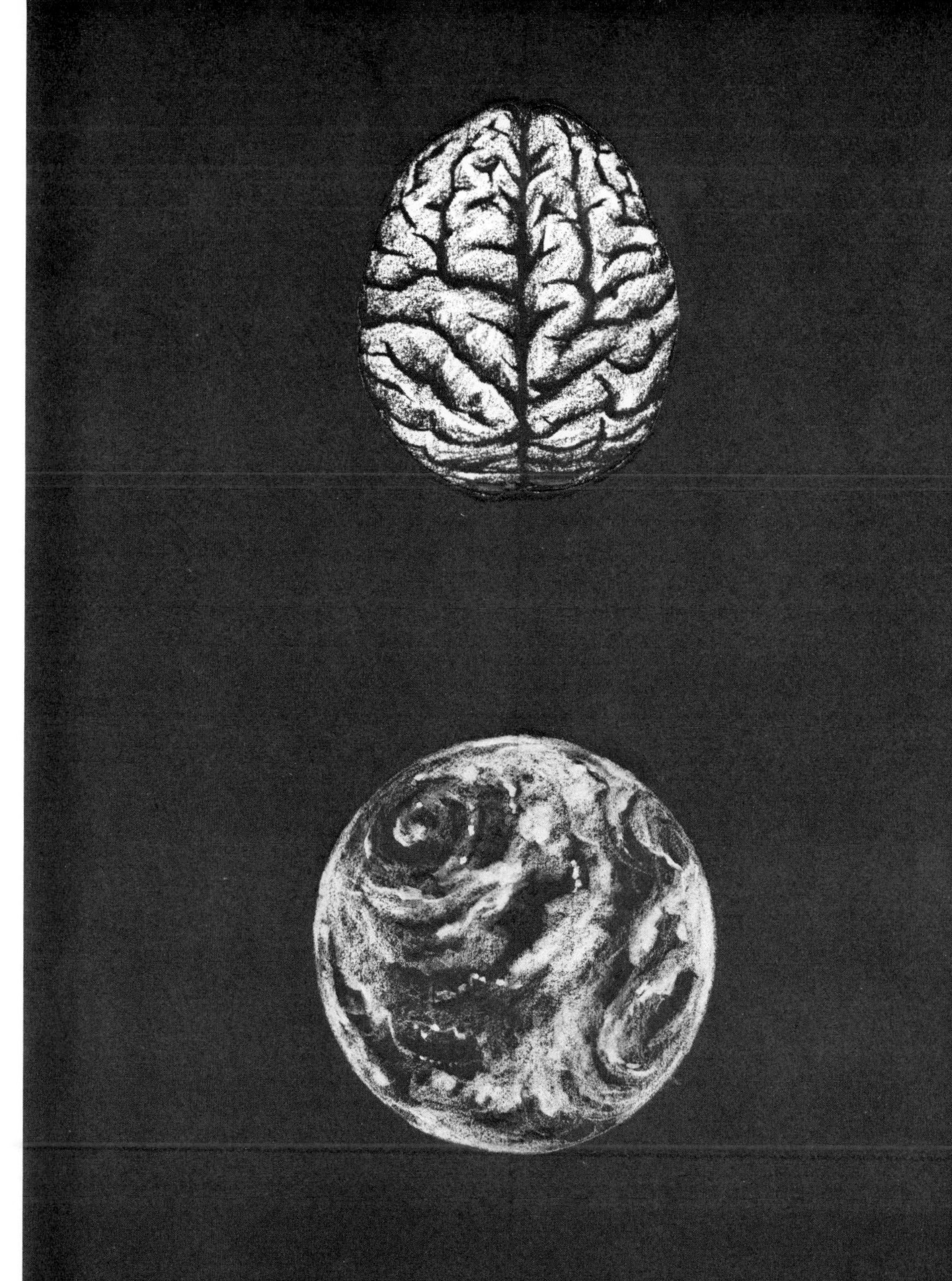

620
Like the brain halves, there exists East-West dualism in the habit of thinking.

Bibliography

Arnheim, Rudolf. *Visual Thinking.* Berkeley and Los Angeles: University of California Press, 1969.

Barr, Stephen. *Experiments in Topology.* New York: Thomas Y. Crowell Company, 1964.

Bernsen, Jens. *Design: The Problem Comes First.* Copenhagen: Danish Design Council, 1982.

Bevlin, Marjorie Elliott. *Design Through Discovery.* 3rd ed. New York: Holt, Rinehart and Winston, 1977.

Bogen, Joseph E. "Some Educational Aspects of Hemispheric Specialization." *UCLA Educator,* Spring 1975.

Bowman, William J. *Graphic Communication.* New York: John Wiley & Sons, 1968.

Capra, Fritjof. *The Tao of Physics: An Exploration of the Parallels Between Modern Physics and Eastern Mysticism.* Boulder: Shambhala, 1975.

Caudill, William W. *Architecture by Team: A New Concept for the Practice of Architecture.* New York: Van Nostrand Reinhold Company, 1971.

Collier, Graham. *Form, Space and Vision: Discovering Design Through Drawing.* 3rd ed. Englewood Cliffs: Prentice-Hall, 1972.

Doczi, Gygorgy. *The Power of Limits: Proportional Harmonies in Nature, Art and Architecture.* Boulder and London: Shambhala, 1981.

Edwards, Betty. *Drawing on the Right Side of the Brain: A Course in Enhancing Creativity and Artistic Confidence.* Los Angeles: J.P. Tarcher, Inc., 1979.

Einstein, Albert. *Relativity: The Special and the General Theory.* Translated by Robert W. Lawson. New York: Crown Publishers, 1961.

Franck, Frederick. *The Zen of Seeing: Seeing/Drawing as Meditation.* New York: Vintage Books, 1973.

Gazzaniga, Michael S., and LeDoux, Joseph E. *The Integrated Mind.* New York: Plenum Press, 1978.

Grillo, Paul Jacques. *Form, Function and Design.* New York: Dover Publications, Inc., 1960.

Gorb, Peter, ed. *Living by Design.* New York: Whitney Library of Design, 1978.

Hill, Edward. *The Language of Drawing.* Englewood Cliffs: Prentice-Hall, 1966.

Hutter, Heribert. *Drawing: History and Technique.* New York: McGraw-Hill Book Company, 1968.

Isaac, A.R.G. *Approach to Architectural Design.* Toronto: University of Toronto Press, 1971.

Koestler, Arthur. *The Act of Creation: A Study of the Conscious and Unconscious in Science and Art.* New York: Dell Publishing Co., 1964.

Le Corbusier [Charles Edouard Jeanneret-Gris]. *The Modulor: A Harmonious Measure to the Human Scale Universally Applicable to Architecture and Mechanics.* Cambridge: Harvard University Press, 1966.

Levy, Jerre. "Cerebral Asymmetry and the Psychology of Man." *The Brain and Psychology,* M.C. Wittrock, ed. New York: Academic Press, 1980.

Masini, Lara Vinca, ed. *Utopia e Crisi Dell 'Antinatura: Momenti Delle Intenzioni Architettoniche in Italia: Topologia e Morfogenesi.* Venezia: La Biennale di Vnezia, 1978.

Perkins, D.N. *The Mind's Best Work.* Cambridge: Harvard University Press, 1981.

Porter, Tom. *How Architects Visualize.* New York: Van Nostrand Reinhold Company, 1979.

Prentky, Robert A. *Creativity and Psychopathology: A Neurocognitive Perspective.* New York: Praeger Publishers, 1980.

Rayapati, J.P. Rao. *Early American Interest in Vedanta: Pre-Emersonian Interest in Vedic Literature and Vedantic Philosophy.* New York: Asia Publishing House, 1973.

Restak, Richard M. *The Brain: The Last Frontier.* Garden City: Doubleday & Company, 1979.

Riepe, Dale. *The Philosophy of India and Its Impact on American Thought.* Springfield: Charles C Thomas Publisher, 1970.

Rothbart, Harold A. *Cybernetic Creativity.* New York: Robert Speller & Sons, 1972.

Rothenberg, Albert. *The Emerging Goddess: The Creative Process in Art, Science, and Other Fields.* Chicago: The University of Chicago Press, 1979.

Safdie, Moshe. *Form and Purpose: Is the Emperor Naked?* Edited by John Kettle. Aspen: International Design Education Foundation, 1980.

Springer, Sally P., and Deutsch, Georg. *Left Brain, Right Brain.* San Francisco: W. H. Freeman and Company, 1981.

Steiner, Gary A., ed. *The Creative Organization.* Chicago: The University of Chicago Press, 1965.

Storr, Anthony. *The Dynamics of Creation.* New York: Atheneum, 1972.

Thiel, Philip. *Visual Awareness and Design: An Introductory Program in Conceptual Awareness, Perceptual Sensitivity, and Basic Design Skills.* Seattle: University of Washington Press, 1981.

Thomas, Lewis. *The Lives of a Cell: Notes of a Biology Watcher.* New York: The Viking Press, 1974.

Index